Eterne in Mutabilitie

Davis Philoon Harding

Eterne

in

Mutabilitie

The Unity of *The Faerie Queene*

Essays Published in Memory of
Davis Philoon Harding
1914-1970

Edited by
Kenneth John Atchity

ARCHON BOOKS
1972

© 1972
by The Shoe String Press, Inc.
Hamden, Connecticut
All rights reserved
International standard book number 0-208-01202-8
Library of Congress catalog card number 70-147174
Printed in the United States of America

FOR

May, Pamela,
Woody, and Susan;
and Davis

Contents

Eugene M. Waith

Davis Philoon Harding, 1914-1970

In the spring term of 1949 Davis Harding and I began a collaboration which lasted for several years. Although we had known each other since the end of the war, this collaboration was what drew us most closely together, and yet, in retrospect, it is surprising that it ever took place. We were not born to it nor was it thrust upon us. We achieved it in this way: for some years Professor Samuel Hemingway had taught a special Shakespeare course divided into four small discussion groups. When he was on leave that spring, Davis and I eagerly accepted the chance he offered us of teaching two groups each. Then for several years following Sam Hemingway's retirement, we offered the course on our own, each of us taking one division. The first year, since it seemed important to see that all the students we had inherited received similar instruction and did comparable amounts of work, we discussed each assignment in detail and even agreed on the topics for the students' papers. Later, though we were free to teach our divisions quite independently of each other, we continued what had proved to be a most congenial arrangement, and thus not only *achieved* collaboration but willed it. For both of us, I think—certainly for me—it was one of the most agreeable and fruitful of teaching experiences. Because Davis' office in Calhoun College was in a handsome

suite, equipped with a shower, we prefaced our weekly
deliberations with a game of squash and lunch in the college,
with the result that amiable discussions of the Shakespearian
corpus and corporeal struggle in the squash court are
inextricably yoked in my memory.

Although Davis was a remarkably learned and exacting
teacher, many of whose students distinguished themselves by
carrying out most ambitious projects, he was the very
opposite of a pedant. Sympathetic and flexible, he managed
to lure them into these tasks by arousing their intellectual
interest. His happy combination of rigor and flexibility
corresponded to certain other seeming discrepancies which
hinted at a paradox. Certainly his precision in matters of
scholarship was not suggested by his often disheveled
appearance or by his easy, informal manner; and one would
hardly have suspected from the warmth and gaiety of his
personality that so austere a figure as Milton was the object
of his lifelong admiration.

In his two scholarly works this untraditional professor
showed his keen sensitivity to tradition. *Milton and the
Renaissance Ovid* (1946), the outgrowth of his studies at the
University of Illinois Graduate School, was dedicated to
Harris F. Fletcher and Marvin T. Herrick and acknowledged
the help of T. W. Baldwin—three distinguished scholars who
were his mentors and contributed to the shaping of his
scholarly ideals. In writing about one kind of tradition he was
carrying on another. In *The Club of Hercules* (1962) he
turned to Milton's use of Homer and, even more, of Virgil,
explaining on the first page: "A tradition is a birthright,
renounced at the poet's imminent peril, enabling him to
profit from the experiments of others, to build upon their
strong foundations . . . he extends and enriches his meanings
by a strategy of deliberate allusiveness to the poetry of the
past." With great subtlety the nature of Milton's indebtedness
is revealed and the intended resonance of his allusions
recaptured. The title, alluding to the comment Virgil is said
to have made: "It is easier to steal the club from Hercules

than to take a line from Homer," reminds us of the difficulties Virgil or Milton faced in making the tradition work for them, though their brilliant success was sufficient to have justified the epigram made by T. S. Eliot in another connection: "Immature poets imitate; mature poets steal." The task of recognizing and appraising these thefts was also a risky one, and Davis' achievement in the two books showed the maturity of his scholarship and of his critical discernment.

Since Milton's education acquainted him with the traditions upon which he later drew, Davis was naturally attracted, like T. W. Baldwin before him, to the topic of English schooling. In a lecture, "Shakespeare the Elizabethan," given at the Yale Shakespeare Festival in 1954 he discussed with admirable sanity the relevance of this background to the response of Shakespeare's audience. Four years earlier, he had devoted an article to another historical problem relating to audience-response: "Elizabethan Betrothals and *Measure for Measure*," where he showed how inconsistent the Elizabethans were in their views of what was permitted to betrothed couples, and how this inconsistency might have affected their attitudes toward the odd behavior of Shakespeare's characters. His edition of the play for The Yale Shakespeare was published in the same year that he gave his lecture.

Gradually, it would seem, his concern with literary tradition led him backward in time from Milton to Shakespeare and then to sixteenth-century English literature, which he taught for many years to both undergraduate and graduate students. His success in interesting them in what many might initially have considered a rather formidable array of authors was only one more proof of his remarkable qualities as a pedagogue. Of their interest in a major poet, to whom Davis had increasingly turned, this volume of essays on *The Faerie Queene* is striking testimony. His commitment to the earlier years of the English Renaissance was deepened when he was asked to contribute to the Yale Edition of the *Complete*

Works of St. Thomas More. At the time of his premature death he was editing More's *Dialogue Concerning Heresies.* But the Renaissance, in which he was working and teaching in these years, had in reality been at the center of his vision all along, as the title of his first book showed. It seems fitting that this was so, for to most of us the Renaissance stands for the love of classical learning, the respect for tradition, and the commitment to individuality which were also Davis Harding's.

Eugene M. Waith

YALE UNIVERSITY

Introduction

My daughter Rosemary was born January 17, 1968. Two days later, beautifully and inexplicably, baby pink roses arrived from the Hardings. I had known Davis by then a few months only, yet well enough already to know that with him friendship and affection developed as suddenly as deeply, with no regard for careful time. He was my friend so soon after chance made him my teacher that I can't recall when our relationship was not personal. All who knew and loved Davis, I think, must share my wonder at the immediacy with which he opened himself to you—and found in you a place that could be taken by him alone. Although I knew Davis too briefly, because he was this kind of man I knew him well enough to hazard a biographical impression: that his greatest satisfaction was derived from his relations with others.

Among his effects which came to me most poignant was a group of undergraduate papers graded shortly before his death. What distinguished this set of essays from the hundreds Davis read throughout his career at Yale was the absence, from a good number of the papers, of any mark except the grade itself. Nothing could have said more surely than this silence that Davis was near the end. For nothing was more characteristic of him than his constant responsibility precisely in the matter, regarded as routine and ungratifying by too many teachers, of commenting on his students' work.

With Davis, of course, it went beyond any academically sanctioned or self-imposed sense of responsibility. The reading produced in him delight more often than despair. His students—sooner or later, but always—wrote their best for him, a response to his own response both to literature and to them. His sensitivity was neither purely emotional nor solely critical. It was, instead, a unique combination of the objectively aesthetic with the subjectively personal so that the two, so commonly disjunct, were yoked in a most happy manner which influenced all who inherited and came to treasure it as Davis' bequest. It was not then Davis' scholarship, nor his philology, which impressed us. Nothing so precise, but simply his humanistic perceptiveness. He perceived immediately the *heart* of the poem just as he did the heart—not the mind, not the emotions, only—of each student. It was his own *personal* involvement with literature which inspired the personal involvement on the part of his students, not at all methodically (Davis was nothing, if not unmethodical) but as if by osmosis. The process could not but continue; for Davis *recognized* your personal involvement with a poem, rejoiced in it (both privately and publicly), and thereby increased it. There was no petty jealousy in him, little reserve, less condescension. He understood at once, from his own engagement with the text at hand, your point of departure—what in this *work* excited *you*. He saw at a reading the very moment of your paper's conception, the mode of contact between the eternal art and the very temporal you.

No other words can speak more clearly of Davis Harding— not "as man and teacher," since such distinctions make no sense when applied to him, but as himself—than his own. This struck me as I read his voluminous and illuminating com- ments on student essays, graduate and undergraduate. Here Davis' personality speaks for itself and you can envision readily this paradoxical man who was direct without ever being mean, cantankerous while gentle, impatient yet not indifferent. There is another reason, more or less didactic, why I draw from the comments written by Davis in the last five years or so. Rarely is a teacher accorded tribute, or even recognition, for this infrequently satisfying, yet highly important, of his several labors. All teachers know how difficult it can be to tailor remarks to each personality and to each problem without being, on the one hand, irrelevant, and on the other, repetitive. Reading papers is an art which presumes a certain degree of inspiration but absolutely demands consistent cultivation. Davis read at one and the same time lovingly and effortlessly. Yet his remarks reveal the astonishing scope of a true humanist. He is a technician, for example, without being pedantic: "Steve, you too are ahead of your time in your cavalier disregard for apostrophes and semi-colons. You are too intelligent a guy to let such lapses mar your writing. The paper well illustrates both your virtues and defects. The virtues are predominant." His wit was dry and crisp at times: "You have a good thing going for you here. But it needs more work; then you would have a very fine essay. You need, however, to discover the small advantages of a good dictionary." But he can be less diffident: "I am not a pedant but, by golly, I am going to teach you how to use commas or die in the attempt. I can't see how you have demonstrated your case of Don Quixote's being a Christ-image. Do you wish to imply that Christ was deluded?"

Davis' concern with the use of language was unswerving and often revealed itself in unexpected ways: "A fine essay, Radey. You are rapidly coming into your own . . . I detest your use of the word 'physicality.' How did you come by it? Who has physicality? Joe Louis, Marciano, Cassius Clay, Big Yaz? If you went up to any one of them and said, 'Gee, I admire your physicality,' you would probably get punched in the nose." And his own concern Davis was quick to spot and encourage in others: "A brilliant essay, especially admirable for its candor. You are a philologist at heart, Jim. I recognize all the symptoms. Since I started out as a philologist myself."

Throughout the comments are examples of the way in which Davis disarmed the student, preparing him for criticism, by allowing glimpses into the purely personal—destroying, as he did so, the distance which so often separates student and teacher. Once he returned a stained essay with this explanation: "I am sorry to return this paper in a condition different from the shape it was submitted. My awkward daughter tripped over a glass of liquid on it, causing the pages to stick together, as if glued." He delicately fails to say whether Susan or Pamela was the culprit.

Relaxed yet accurate in his own writing, Davis was vigorous in his crusade against uptightness of any kind: "You are too self-conscious about your own writing—too much pomp and ceremony. You have a good mind. Relax and let it work for you." The refrain appears consistently, yet is couched always in personal terms: "A very good paper, Susanne. Honors. You seem to have a fine sensibility to . . . poetry. One small criticism: occasionally you have a tendency to become stilted in your writing—Can it. You write well enough as it is. Don't permit yourself the wicked luxury of self-consciousness." One could not be narcissistic in Davis' class for long before being invited into the pool: "O.K. Mike. But somewhere along the line the poem gets lost in the shuffle. As intelligent and perceptive as you are, how come? Besides, you are too nice a guy, too straightforward, to risk the horrors of pretentiousness." Talk about fattening up for the kill! The next paper from the same student produced this remark: "Good, Mike. You have a single, strong-hitting prose style, but temper it a little, so that you don't seem to be in the 'love-with-your-own-words' department. You can afford the luxury of moderation. I am not suggesting that you change your stance at the plate—you are, after all, you—but watch it, Buddy." Like a good coach—Davis' metaphors indicate his fondness for sports—he made his players proficient by making them themselves. Sometimes he employed rhetorical threats à la Lombardi: "If it's the last thing I do, it will be to get the pomposity and pretentiousness out of your writing. You do not demonstrate these qualities in the seminar. Why do you let them invade your writing? In other respects, I commend this essay. But your thinking is clouded by your rhetoric." The same fiery theme elsewhere develops gentler variations:

> Dick, this isn't very good and you know it yourself. It is stuffy, inadequate, and insensitive. Having said all these unkind words about this essay, let me reaffirm my faith in your abilities; you are not a stuffy, inadequate, insensitive sort of person. I would have given ten years of my life to have been able to write a poem like Spenser's Epithalamion. And what does it get from you? I want to see you next term, *on my own time*, and find out what's the matter. This is because I believe in you. "In lieu of many ornaments."

More than any other single statement, this expression of belief in the student characterizes Davis' written criticism.

He was of the old school, in this sense, that he believed that there is no such thing as a bad student. To Davis all was a matter of time and dedication: "Pete, I wish I had one more year to work you over. You read sensitively and intelligently, but you don't get across your ideas with sufficient clarity. Of course, this is a problem, in greater or less degree, which afflicts all of us, and I do not except your teachers. It is a hard thing to record thoughts on paper without blurring them. A very hard thing. But keep on trying, Pete. You have a good mind and a sense for self-discipline. Both qualities ought to take you a long way." First, the student was encouraged to know *himself*; then, to express himself *directly*: "This is a very good paper, although it could have been a better one. Shoot from the hip, old boy, and don't indulge yourself in the luxury of clichés. You write well enough as it is. You don't need them." So many luxuries did Davis oppose one would have thought he was Spartan. Instead he was Protean.

Although Davis was anything but detached, he *was* remarkably objective and, consequently, open-minded in every way. Somehow he managed to communicate his sense of objectivity toward all things and matters. On one paper he condemns the critical content out of hand, but commends the style: "Good as far as you go. But, as an old friend of mine used to tell me, you 'ain't went very far.' . . . As far as your writing is concerned, John, you are taking giant steps. Nothing should stop you now. You *know* when you are writing well and when you are writing badly. That makes all the difference in the world." Davis was one of the few men who was believed when he claimed to know you better than you did yourself: "You are better, in my opinion, than you are permitting yourself to be." We accepted what he said so confidently because he said it as a friend rather than as a judge: "Another very good paper . . . You may be dilatory, but you have an excellent potential, so why not work on the latter and down-grade the former? I have faith in you. Please try to justify it." Davis was always telling people that he thought they had talent. To say that he erred on the side of generosity is to be unduly cynical; for often his enthusiasm proved true beyond expectation. He asked students to know themselves first. Then he led them, by hook or crook, to surpass themselves. That they did so often was no surprise, but a constant source of pleasure, to Davis.

His students matured and developed because Davis believed in them, identified with them, and respected their accomplishments sincerely and expressly. In one comment we can reconstruct events by reading between the lines:

> Good girl. You have a tendency to let your paragraphs get too long on you with the result that you lose emphasis, but this is a telling comparison. And no more snide cracks about your Latinity. You are in the clear.
>
> Also the essay shows the degree to which Spenser cut his poetic teeth on Mantuan, who was invariably studied in Renaissance grammar school before Virgil's Eclogues.

For a poet of Spenser's genius, it was child's play to 'overgo' Mantuan. Not so Virgil. You have shown, in little, how easily Spenser could adapt Mantuan. Therefore this paper becomes more than just a gentle slapping on the wrist. You now qualify as an expert on Mantuan and Spenser—and there ain't too many of those around. I hope you don't mind. You can now go around cocktail parties and talk easily and glibly about the influence of Mantuan on Spenser—and everyone will recoil in terror. Kneel down, kneel down, and wonder.

Always with a subtlety which never approached deftness Davis managed to combine criticism with convincing encouragement: "Ingenious, Mark—perhaps a little over-wrought—but an Honors paper nonetheless. You really sock it to 'em. I doubt whether this sonnet has ever received a closer scrutiny. Condense, sharpen it up, and send off to Explicator. This little magazine will not accept essays of this length, but you can easily strip away the fat and retain the substance." It goes without saying that Davis' concern for his students went beyond their enrollment in his course: "Well, you're out of my clutches now. But this is a brilliant paper, and I hope you will keep on writing. You have a genuine talent. I am frequently wrong, but not in this area . . . Of course, it was only tangentially related to the material of the course, but that's O.K." There was an element of hope even in his despair; his valedictory address to one student reads: "I don't know, Mark. In my opinion, you have genuine ability, but you sometimes don't seem fully to realize it. You will in time. I *know* you will."

Davis was able so quickly to communicate with each student because he found in each something of himself; and each found himself somewhere in Davis. That is why he could get away with his gruff directness: "What is all this nonsense about a block against writing? Why don't you give yourself a decent chance? I believe in you. It is time you start believing in yourself. Homily for today." Or, "Unsatisfactory, Mike.

You can do much better than this, and I know it. And I hope
you do, too." Not that Davis was in any sense dogmatic,
searching for his idiosyncratic viewpoint in others. In one
comment he jokingly refers to his "thesis"—"that all great art
must be, to a certain extent, ambiguous. There are never any
easy answers." Thus Davis opposed glib responses to literature; when sincerity was in danger of becoming glib he
recoiled in terror. Once he cautioned an over-ambitious critic
of Aeschylus: "I agree with you that Agamemnon is one of
the finest tragedies ever written. But it's hard enough to
define tragedy without defining 'lyrical tragedy.' Perhaps you
ought to write a book on the subject. You can't dispose of
'lyrical tragedy' in a few paragraphs, as you well know. You
are, however, a very sensitive reader, and them are hard to
come by." Davis preferred take and give to give and take. He
is wholehearted in his recognition of sensitivities like his
own: "This is perhaps the most sensitive essay you have
written for me. Clearly, you were moved by the poem. I am,
too." It is this sincerity of response which he sought to
inculcate, nothing more complicated nor more specific:
"What impresses me about this paper is your obvious
enthusiasm for its subject matter, the poem itself. But you
must not be presumptuous—that is, give the impression that
the view of your listeners should, indeed, must, coincide with
your own."

Davis' open-mindedness and objectivity—toward himself,
his students, and the poetry which brought them together—
was all the more impressive because *all* of literature was his
province. The word specialization was abhorrent to him,
although he was called a Milton or Renaissance specialist. He
had the air and spoke with the authority of a man of letters
in the widest sense of the term. He was not awed automa-
tically by tradition: "An excellent paper, Tom. Don't ever let
your wit and humor fade out of anything you write. Bacon's
overpowering gravity, sobriety, and sharp intelligence is
almost an invitation to answer him in his own terms. I am
happy you do not see fit to do so. If Bacon were alive today,

it is inconceivable that, even in the hottest summer day, he would be caught walking down the street in shorts and a sport shirt. He just wasn't that kind of person." On the other hand, as his response to another paper on Bacon demonstrates, Davis had no truck with those who would dismiss tradition out of hand:

> Well, this is O.K., John, although I cannot bring myself to agree with all the conclusions you reach. And you ought not to denigrate one of the finest essayists of all time without giving him an occasional pat on the back—just for kicks, and in the interest of fair play. Although we may not like to hear home-truths, Bacon was pretty well conversant in the ways of that extraordinary phenomenon, the human animal, his strengths and weaknesses. It seems to be that a good deal of self-analysis finds its way into the Essays.

Bacon would have understood a man whose weaknesses were of his strengths.

When a student's disdain touched nearer home, Davis could be more truculent:

> You do Milton a grave disservice, and by so doing, after many centuries, constitute a minority of one. You must have read the essay with blinkers on, for in more than a few instances, you indicate that you do not know what Milton was saying. This is not like you. Neither is the writing, which is loose and flaccid. There are many typographical errors.
>
> Whether you liked the essay or not is of no moment. That is your business. But you have no right to treat England's second greatest writer in so cavalier a spirit. Any undergraduate who deals with Milton in this fashion is either arrogant or downright silly. Neither epithet properly applies to you—hence my surprise and dismay.

One can as soon unravel the elements of this comment—sarcasm, righteous indignation, insult, apology, comfort, consideration, condemnation, praise, gentleness, serious criticism—as say in simplistic terms what kind of man was Davis Harding. At this point more quotation is almost superfluous.

Yet there is something about that last batch of papers, some of which Davis must have read over the Christmas holidays while he was in the hospital with pneumonia, that continues to hold my attention. The few comments he did make on those papers seem special—this, no doubt, at least partly the product of my regretful imagination. The comments are so few that, in what they reveal of their author, they are as eloquent as all those explicable silences. Sometime after January 8, Davis wrote on one paper: "I would like to have a copy of this fine paper, if you have one. I have all your papers, and it goes almost without saying that you will be getting an 'Honors' in the course. I wish you the best of luck in all your future endeavors. DPH" Such farewells were made characteristically by Davis either in person or not at all—since he assumed that he would continue to see his formally departing students. And the initials—rarely used for this purpose. The sense of finality which their appearance here gives me I find again in his most extended comment:

> Excellent. But is God, in any sense, a tragic hero, or is this irony? Job's God is certainly not Milton's. On the other hand, if Job does not accuse God, he surely does complain, as you clearly indicate. He does not curse God and die. It *is* a fact of human life that the innocent frequently suffer and the wicked prosper. Sad, but true. How can we reconcile that fact with the theological notion of a benevolent, just, and all-powerful God. If you were to tell me that my ankles are swollen because I have sinned, I would throw an ash-tray at your head. Job, fortunately, didn't smoke. Fine essay, Steve.

Even later in January two students turned in their semester's-worth of essays with accompanying apologies. One displays a casualness inherited from Davis himself: "I'm awfully sorry that I am dumping these essays in your lap all at once like this, but between my banalities and the Yale infirmary and other odds and ends, things became rather disorganized." For Davis excuses need not be works of art in themselves to be accepted, weighed, and responded to with weathered suspicion. He took them at face value and nearly always with sympathy, whether warranted or not: "Since I have just emerged from the hospital after an attack of virus pneumonia, I can sympathize with your situation." Taking advantage of Davis' kindness was taking advantage of yourself; thus it happened infrequently—at least only when necessary. You paid the consequences to yourself, not to him.

It is because Davis Harding was so special a man that this book has been made in his memory and honor. More honor than memory since, without being melodramatic, Davis still lives, effectively; his students that were are now themselves teachers and cannot teach without being conscious of his quiet influence. All of us feel we owe a personal debt to him of which this is at least a token of our earnest. A token only because his influence not only continues but grows continually. To employ one of those impossible distinctions, we remember him as a friend but honor him as a teacher of teachers. He did not have to state his philosophy of teaching for it to be fixed in the minds of his students. He communicated a concept of teaching which *depends* upon personal involvement in almost every direction imaginable. What all students have proclaimed and teachers have secretly known for ages, Davis actually practiced: that the best, indeed, the only, teacher is yourself. What, then, is the function of the professional teacher? In Davis' way of looking at things, teaching and learning have to do alike with the expansion of the self. Consequently it is his *self*, not ideas, material, or data, which the sane professional teacher must impart to his students. He guides; he does not lead. He inspires, whether by affirmation or aggravation; he does not demand. This is no new *method*; it is a simple matter of human communication. Simple, but rarely accessible, practiced only with the greatest of difficulty or dedication. Davis was a great teacher because he had a way of discovering— often, I suspect, instilling—self-confidence in each individual student. He was midwife not of ideas but of men and women, of personalities. We did and still learn from him.

Few poems are more difficult to confront holistically in an academic curriculum than is *The Faerie Queene*. Yet in the space of a semester Davis was able to bring the individuals in his Spenser classes to an involvement with this very peculiar epic which was at one and the same time comprehensive, penetrating, and personal. His favorite technique for achieving this difficult alliance of the reactionary Renaissance poet and the 20th century Yale student was to throw down, without prejudice in one direction or the other, the time-honored challenge of whether or not *The Faerie Queene* is unified. As Allen Tate would put it, the question is impossible, but necessary. It was maddening but it produced some rather sensible and sane results. That the results of Davis' determination that we share his love for Spenser were successfully forthcoming was due very largely to his customarily straightforward reticence concerning his own view of the matter. In Davis, reticence of this kind was acceptable precisely because it was forthright, not coy nor hypocritical. He did not mean to lead us into a trap and then spring it by countering with his own opinion. He quite willingly entered with us. His mind was truly open, a difficult pose for *anyone* to maintain artificially in a time the ills of which Davis would have traced, I feel sure, directly to the fact that far too many minds are "made up."

The complementary proof of Davis' uniqueness as a teacher, then, is the work of his students as it has been revised for this book. Here is appropriate testimony in every sense of the term. For the ten essays included here

demonstrate very clearly the critical value of a personal
response to the poem. As approaches to the same problem
they indicate the inexhaustibility which characterizes those
works of literature that have come to be regarded as
permanent inhabitants of our shelves, if not of our minds and
hearts. Judith Cramer compares *The Faerie Queene* to
Beethoven's last piano sonata, opus 111, as it is discussed by
the narrator in Thomas Mann's *Doctor Faustus*. Susan Fox
(in the essay from which the title of this collection is
borrowed, as Davis himself had planned)—speaks of the poem
as an increasingly desperate moral odyssey. In the depths of
its heart we discover the poet, Spenser, himself. Janet Gezari
discusses the tension between a structural progress toward
perfection and mutability, seeing creative love in the center
of the epic's mode of existence. In his brief but incisive essay,
"Form or Process?", Gerald Grow likens *The Faerie Queene*
to things as various as a tree, a DNA molecule, and a Krazy
Kat comic strip. Jean Humez approaches the problem of the
poem's peculiar kind of unity in terms of the medieval
illuminated manuscript.

John Stillinger, of the *Journal of English and Germanic
Philology*, gracefully allowed us to preempt Paula Johnson's
"Literary Perception and *The Faerie Queene*." Mrs. Johnson,
in a work whose significance ranges far beyond Spenser's
poem, treats of the progressive and retrospective aspects of
form before studying the matters of closure, balance,
coherence, and the "fruitful resolution of tensions." Susanne
Murphy suggests a parallel between this poem and Petrarch's
Secretum Meum, finding in the embryonic conception of
both works love as the union of opposite principles. John
O'Conner defends, quite convincingly, the character of
Arthur as both the link between the virtues projected in the
letter to Raleigh as the structural coefficients of the epic and,
consequently, the basis of the poem's ultimate unity.
Comparing the fate of "critics in Faerie" to that of
"Napoleon in Russia," Richard Pindell with careful temerity
finds the poem's unity in its mutable nature, specifically

interpreting Spenser's view of the continual creation of man as the poem presents it thematically. Finally Sherry Reames finds the unity of *The Faerie Queene* neither in Arthur nor in the proposed feast of Gloriana but in the ever-changing relationship among its books.

As striking as the variety of approaches and viewpoints found in the ten essays is the consensus which arises from the variety. All see the unity of the poem as having to do, in one way or another, with progress, process, change. (No one was affected by the knowledge that this book would be called *Eterne in Mutabilitie*, since no one knew that before they had written their first drafts.) As Davis would have had it himself, we have here both individualism in criticism and general agreement. One's sense of the extraordinary beauty of Spenser's vision is not deadened by a sameness of approach. On the contrary, it is enhanced and confirmed by the fact that so many minds beginning at as many points come together in an aesthetic appreciation of *The Faerie Queene* which can be called, quite properly, objective.

Acknowledgements for a book of this kind are somewhat of a puzzling nature. It is not really my place to be grateful to those who have contributed to the making of this book; nonetheless, I am. The rapidity with which the ten essayists turned good intentions into good works must be attributed to Davis; it was, after all, evoked by and directed to him. All of us feel some small consolation for being able to express our feelings toward him concretely. Moreover I am personally grateful to those who helped me in the preparation in various ways—Eugene Waith, Paula Johnson, Susan Fox, Martin Price. I also appreciate the encouragement of A. B. Giamatti, Thomas Greene, Harry Berger, Jr., and Richard Sylvester. My colleagues at Occidental have been a source of sudden assistance in matters small and large. And I am especially grateful to Robert Ryf through whose offices a grant was made available for the completion of our book. Finally I must recognize Marilyn Robertson and Barbara Heinzen for clerical service above and beyond the call of duty. It goes without saying, almost, that May Harding has a central role in this remembrance of Davis.

Citations from the text of *The Faerie Queene* refer to the Oxford edition of J. C. Smith, 2 vols. (1909/1961/1964), and are given in this form: II.6.8.1-2 = Book II, Canto 6, Stanza 8, Verses 1-2.

K. J. A.

OCCIDENTAL COLLEGE

Judith Cramer

Motif and Vicissitude in
The Faerie Queene

*Much else happens before the end. But when it ends and
while it ends, something comes, after so much rage, persistence, obstinacy, extravagance: something entirely unexpected and touching in its mildness and goodness. With the
motif passed through many vicissitudes, which takes leave
and so doing becomes itself entirely leave-taking, a parting
wave and call. . . . so that it no longer scans "heav-en's
blue," "mead-owland," but "O-thou heaven's blue," "Green-
est meadowland," "Fare-thee well for aye," and this added C
sharp is the most moving, consolatory, pathetically reconciling thing in the world. It is like having one's hair or cheek
stroked, lovingly, understandingly, like a deep and silent
farewell look. It blesses the object, the frightfully harried
formulation, with overpowering humanity, lies in parting so
gently on the hearer's heart in eternal farewell that the eyes
run over. "Now for-get the pain," it says. "Great was-God in
us." " 'Twas all-but a dream," "Friendly-be to me." Then it
breaks off.*[1]

In this passage from Mann's *Doctor Faustus*, the narrator
describes what he hears in the second movement of
Beethoven's last piano sonata, *Opus 111*, as it is being played

by Kretschmar, the piano teacher. Kretschmar is playing the piece, interpreting it as he goes along, to illustrate his lecture on why Beethoven did not go on to write a third movement, following the convention of the sonata form. In the lecture Kretschmar tells his audience that Beethoven had answered this question, put to him by critics who had attacked his piece, by saying simply that he had not had time to write a third movement and instead had extended the second movement to bring the sonata to a close. In this remark Kretschmar hears more than the composer's contempt for his critics. He hears Beethoven's awareness of approaching death. It was the consciousness of death, Kretschmar explains, that lifted Beethoven's late works out of the realm of the traditional into the "other—worldly or abstract." In the Sonata in C minor, conditioned by death, Beethoven's art had "overgrown itself," entering in the impressive second movement "into the mythical, the collectively great and supernatural."[2] To ask for more, after such an ending, Kretschmar concludes, is simply to admit that one had not really listened to the work: the Sonata in C minor spoke for itself—it was whole, it was sustained, and it was final.

Kretschmar's analysis of Beethoven offers a striking and, I think, a suggestive parallel for the student of Spenser. The problem presented by *The Faerie Queene* is similar to that presented by the C minor Sonata, not only because Spenser's work ends, like Beethoven's, at its formal mid-point, but also because it does so by rising into the "mythical" and the "supernatural." According to Spenser's letter to Raleigh, which he published with the first three books of *The Faerie Queene* in 1590, the poem was to consist of twelve books, each of whose heroes would represent one of the twelve private moral virtues according to Aristotle. In the twelfth book, the poem was to end with a vision of Gloriana's feast, the origin of the quests undertaken by the twelve representative knights. When Spenser died in 1598 he had completed six books of *The Faerie Queene*, Books IV-VI having been published in 1596. In addition, he had written two cantos and a prayer, which appeared in the 1609 edition of his poem under the editor's title "Two Cantos of Mutabilitie: Which, both for Forme and Matter, appeare to be parcell of some following Booke of the *Faerie Queene*, Under the Legend of Constancie," and which were numbered by the editor as cantos 6, 7, and 8, respectively.

Because there is no other external evidence, most readers have taken the editor's word for this last part of Spenser's poem, viewing it as the center of an unwritten book. Together with the letter, the Mutabilitie Cantos and the prayer define the critic's problem in deciding whether *The Faerie Queene* is an incomplete work or a whole. The letter, I think, does not present as much of a problem as critics suppose because Spenser did not republish it in 1596, a fact which suggests that he no longer considered it an adequate description of his work. Besides, even when he did publish it, in 1590, it was not a precise account of what he had already written in the first three books.[3] For these reasons, it seems safe, if not to ignore the letter completely, at least to treat it with only as much respect as the poet did, refusing to let it dominate our idea of his work. Putting the letter aside for the time being then, let us turn first to the prayer:

> When I bethink me on that speech whyleare,
> Of *Mutability*, and well it way:
> Me seems, that though she all unworthy were
> Of the Heav'ens Rule; yet very sooth to say,
> In all things else she beares the greatest sway.
> Which makes me loath this state of life so tickle,
> And loue of things so vaine to cast away;
> Whose flowring pride, so fading and so fickle,
> Short *Time* shall soon cut down with his consuming sickle.
>
> Then gin I think on that which Nature sayd,
> Of that same time when no more *Change* shall be,
> But stedfast rest of all things firmely stayd

Vpon that pillours of Eternity,
That is contrayr to *Mutabilitie*:
For, all that moueth, doth in *Change* delight:
But thence-forth all shall rest eternally
With Him that is the God of Sabbaoth hight:
O that great Sabbaoth God, graunt me that Sabbaoths
sight.

[VII.8.1-2]

Whatever else one may want to say about these lines, and I
will return to them later, it seems impossible not to hear in
them the "consolatory," "reconciling" leave-taking that
Kretschmar hears in Beethoven's added C sharp. Like
Beethoven, Spenser "blesses the object," his own "formulation" in the Mutabilitie Cantos, and ends with "a deep and
silent farewell look." As an ending nothing could be more
final. As John Arthos says, "in its expression of religion this
is as profound as any poetry in English, and however
extended *The Faerie Queene* should be it could not have
carried a meaning to go beyond this."[4]

The meaning of the prayer, then, seems clear; but does it
relate to the meaning of the rest of *The Faerie Queene*? In
other words, is this ending, moving though it is, an arbitrary
one, or is it, like Beethoven's in the C minor Sonata, a
culmination of everything that has gone before? In answering
this question, the critic must decide whether the two
Mutabilitie Cantos on which Spenser comments in the prayer
may be read as an epilogue to the whole poem; or whether, as
C. S. Lewis maintains, they must be regarded strictly as a
fragment of a new book. According to Lewis,

> In the poem as a whole our understanding is limited by
> the absence of the allegorical centre, the union of Arthur
> and Gloriana. In the Mutabilitie cantos the opposite
> difficulty occurs—we have there the core of a book
> without the fringe. . . . But we lose much by not seeing
> the theme of change and permanence played out on the

lower levels of chivalrous adventure. It is obvious, of
course, that the adventures would have illustrated the
theme of constancy and inconstancy, and that the
mighty opposites would have appeared in the form of
Mutabilitie and the Gods only at the central allegorical
gable of the book—which is the bit we have. It is obvious
too, that the Titaness, despite her beauty, is an evil
force. . . . She is, in fact, Corruption, and since corruption, "subjecting the creature to vanity," came in
with the Fall, Spenser practically identifies his Titaness
with sin, or makes her the force behind the sin of
Adam.[5]

This reading seems to me much too narrow. Mutabilitie's
beauty, for one thing, is not an illusion. In the confrontation
with Jove, the Titaness is described as

Beeing of stature tall as any there
Of all the Gods, and beautifull of face,
As any of the Goddesses in place.

[VII.6.28.3-5]

By this beauty the King of the Gods is literally disarmed
("Such sway doth beauty euen in Heauen beare
[VII.6.31.4] ") and, what is more significant, the poet is too.
Before Spenser allows his Titaness to be judged by Nature, he
"abate[s] the sternesse of my stile [VII.6.37.3] " to sing a
pastoral song about Arlo Hill, on which the final judgment
will take place. In this episode, the story of Faunus, what we
have is a comic version of the Fall, and it ought to warn us
that Mutabilitie will not be judged too harshly.
   In the judgment of Nature, if Spenser identifies Mutabilitie
with the sin of Adam, as Lewis asserts, he interprets that sin
as *felix culpa*. By Nature's assessment,

. . . . . . all things stedfastnes doe hate
And changed be: yet being rightly wayd
They are not changed from their first estate;

But by their change their being doe dilate:
And turning to themselues at length againe,
Doe worke their owne perfection so by fate.
                                              [VII.7.58.2-7]

With this statement, which Mutabilitie's parade of elements,
seasons, months, and the rest serves to illustrate rather than
refute, showing as it does the orderliness of earthly changes,
Spenser insists on the fundamental goodness inherent in the
mutable world. Things are not really "changed from their
first estate," despite the Fall, because they inevitably seek
that good estate again. Like Arlo Hill, which in spite of the
wolves and thieves left by Diana's curse still has "faire
forrests" and "the richest champian [VII.6.54.6-8] "; and like
Molanna, who despite being "whelm'd with stones" still
combines with her beloved Fanchin "in one faire riuer spred
[VII.6.53.4-9] ," the mutable world perpetually renews itself,
working out the perfection that "was implicit from the
beginning."[6] As William Nelson puts it, "the perpetual
whirling of the wheel in time expresses the nature of the
wheel."[6]
    There can be no doubt that this theme is not, as Lewis
implies, articulated for the first time in the Mutabilitie
Cantos. Every reader must be reminded at this point in the
poem of the constantly renewing forms in the Garden of
Adonis and of Adonis himself, whom Spenser describes in
words very much like those of Nature quoted above:

        . . . . for he may not
        For euer die, and euer buried bee
        In balefull night, where all things are forgot;
        All be he subiect to mortalitie,
        Yet is eterne in mutabilitie,
        And by succession made perpetuall.
                                              [III.6.47.1-6]

And there are other specific instances in which this theme appears. Graham Hough points out that "in the proem to Book V the poet himself speaks of change in the planets and the spheres, in exactly the same terms as Mutabilitie does. The communist giant and Artegall argue on the same theme in V.2. . . "[7] But even more important than such specific instances, I think, is Spenser's exploitation of the theme of change and permanence—in all the books of *The Faerie Queene*—through the central motif of the quest. From the first vision of Red Crosse and Una on the plain to the last sight of Calidore pursuing the Blatant Beast, the quest motif dominates the poem. In this way, the theme of change and permanence *is* "played out on the lower levels of chivalrous adventure" before it is recapitulated so magnificently on the higher levels of cosmic adventure in the Mutabilitie Cantos and the final prayer.

If we look at *The Faerie Queene* in terms of this motif, "the motif passed through many vicissitudes," to borrow Kretschmar's phrase, I think we can see a general movement in the first six books which parallels the movement of the Mutabilitie Cantos and the prayer. I am going to look at Spenser's idea of the quest in terms of the whole poem, concentrating more specifically only on Book VI where, as Kretschmar says, "something comes, after so much rage, persistence, obstinacy, extravagance" (especially in Book V); "something entirely unexpected and touching in its mildness and goodness." It is at this point, in the Arcadian world of Book VI, that Spenser's central motif "takes leave," as Beethoven's does just before the impressive ending of the C minor Sonata. Perhaps, when Spenser wrote Book VI, which critics agree is one of the last-composed parts of *The Faerie Queene*, he knew his work had overgrown itself, like Beethoven's, and was complete. Since it appears that the Mutabilitie Cantos and the prayer, which take *The Faerie Queene* into the "other-wordly," "the collectively great and

supernatural," were composed late, it is tempting to speculate that he did know this.[8] But in any case, as Kretschmar
says, "much else happens before the end." To understand
The Faerie Queene as a whole, we must look at Spenser's use
of the quest motif in the six books, where "it goes through a
hundred vicissitudes, a hundred worlds of rhythmic contrasts,
[and] at length outgrows itself."[9]

By definition the quest implies movement toward some
end. Although the end or goal of the quest may not be
clearly articulated at its beginning, nevertheless the movement that it implies is not arbitrary, simply because there is
some direction of the will involved in it. The quest also
implies obstacles to be overcome, if only obstacles of time
and travel, since it would not be undertaken at all if the goal
were already attained or attainable by other means. Together,
this directed movement and the "vicissitudes" through which
it must be made form the context in which the solitary
individual of *The Faerie Queene* comes to life. As Arthos
remarks,

> all is part of one conception, the isolation of humans
> moving forward in an unfamiliar world, but moving
> forward urged from within with the desire for glory and
> love. Those that are moving towards glory may know
> where they are going, although the roads they follow
> they come across by chance, and the journey is not
> measured by miles or days; those moving after love
> wander blindly, but not less faithfully.[10]

The words "desire" and "faith" in Arthos' comment are
particularly important because they immediately suggest the
informing spirit of the poetry of the quest: desire is the
motive of the journey and faith is the means by which the
journey can be sustained. Glory and love, toward which
Arthos asserts these figures move, may be defined at this
point simply as the fulfillment of desire and faith. Broadly
taken they constitute that condition in the quester by which
his quest is known to be completed. I am using these words

broadly here because, as we shall see, they can only be defined more specifically by the poem itself, as it grows out of and around the central motif of the single figure in quest. The figure whose life is conceived in terms of a quest is represented not only by all the major figures of *The Faerie Queene*, the titular heroes and heroine of its books, but by many of the minor figures as well. Prince Arthur himself, who though not the hero of any of the books is the hero Spenser names for the poem in the letter to Raleigh, is also portrayed in terms of the quest. The letter says "Arthur saw in a dream or vision the Faery Queene, with whose excellent beauty ravished, he awaking resolved to seeke her out in Faerye land." A more elaborate description of the motivating impulse of his quest is given by Arthur in Book I, when he relates to Una how he thought the Faerie Queene made love to him while he slept, and how disappointed he was to find her gone when he awoke:

> But whether dreames delude, or true it were,
> Was neuer hart so rauisht with delight,
> Ne liuing man like words did euer heare,
> As she to me deliuered all that night;
> And at her parting said, She Queene of Faeries hight.
>
> When I awoke, and found her place deuoyd,
> And nought but pressed gras, where she had lyen,
> I sorrowed all so much, as earst I ioyd,
> And washed all her place with watry eyen.
> From that day forth I lou'd that face diuine;
> From that day forth I cast in carefull mind,
> To seeke her out with labour, and long tyne,
> And neuer vow to rest, till her I find,
> Nine monethes I seeke in vaine yet ni'll that vow vnbind.
> [I.9.14.5-9.16]

What is not portrayed in the poem, however, although it is described in the letter, is Spenser's intention "in the person

of Prince Arthure [to] set forth magnificence in particular,
which vertue for that (according to Aristotle and the rest) is
it the perfection of all the rest, and conteineth in it them
all. . . . "

Yet, if *The Faerie Queene* does not portray "magnificence
in particular" in the person of Arthur, it does portray
magnificence in general; that is, magnificence in the sense of
the possibilities for spiritual greatness inherent in the
individual human being—in his desire to fulfill these possibilities, and in his faith that he can. By the end of the poem we
see that "magnificence" is indeed a good term for that virtue,
or power, which "conteineth in it them all": the power of
the human imagination to conceive (and the power of the
human soul to fulfill) all its possibilities. As we read *The
Faerie Queene*, we grow with the poet to understand, to
cherish and revere this all-comprehending power, which he
saw in the poem's first vision, "with whose excellent beauty
ravished, he awaking resolved to seek it out." In this sense
The Faerie Queene is the quest of the single individual
Edmund Spenser: dreamer, seer, and poet—who being armed
with its magic, and thoroughly instructed in its art, went into
the imagination to seek and fulfill the glory of its vision. In
the Proem to Book VI Spenser makes this aspect of the quest
explicit:

> The waies, through which my weary steps I guyde,
>   In this delightfull land of Faery,
>   Are so exceeding spacious and wyde,
>   And sprinckled with such sweet variety,
>   Of all that pleasant is to eare or eye,
>   That I nigh rauisht with rare thoughts delight,
>   My tedious trauell doe forget thereby;
>   And when I gin to feele decay of might,
> It strength to me supplies, and chears my dulled spright.
>
> Such secret comfort, and such heauenly pleasures,
>   Ye sacred imps, that on *Parnasso* dwell,

And there the keeping haue of learning threasures,
Which doe all wordly riches farre excell,
Into the mindes of mortall men doe well,
And goodly fury into them infuse;
Guyde ye my footing, and conduct me well
In these strange waies, where neuer foote did vse,
Ne none can find, but who was taught them by the
Muse.

[VI proem.1-2]

I have been using the word "figure" to describe the various
inhabitants of Spenser's poetic world because the single
figure in quest that is the motif of *The Faerie Queene* is not a
character in the dramatic sense of the word. Even Britomart,
who is doubtless the most fully realized of the titular knights,
is not a character comparable, say, to Milton's Satan or any
of Chaucer's pilgrims. As Hough says, "whatever she represents allegorically, she is also a girl in love, and is capable of
jealousy, suspicion and anguish. But even she remains to
some degree typical and impersonal; the principal knights
Artegall, Scudamour and Guyon still more so."[11] The figures
that surround these questing heroes are still less personalized,
some of them, like Disdain and Scorn in Book VI, being
simply allegorical representations not of people at all, but of
states of mind. Many reasons have been given for Spenser's
habit of representing human experience in this pictorial
rather than dramatic way, and most of them have centered
around questions of poetic technique—the formal demands of
allegory and romance. Lewis, it seems to me, has put his
finger on the origin of Spenser's pictorial method when he
attributes it not to any formal requirements, but to the
poet's own sense of psychic experience:

For all these [figures] are translations into the visible of
feelings else blind and inarticulate; and they are translations made with singular accuracy, with singularly little
loss. The secret of this accuracy . . . is partly to be

sought in his humble fidelity to popular symbols which
he found ready made to his hand; but much more in his
profound sympathy with that which makes the symbols,
with the fundamental tendencies of human imagination
as such.[12]

The inhabitants of Faery all represent the various potential-
ities for mental, emotional, and spiritual experience inherent
in the individual human being. As such they are not so much
aspects of man's character as embodiments of the sense of
possibility Spenser has about man's character when he looks
at it in the light of man's imagination.

But *The Faerie Queene* is not merely a tapestry-like display
of all the things a human being might be, of all the ways he
might live. The relationship between the figures of the poem
is not the mutually exclusive one between life-alternatives,
but the relationship of moral interdependence. Spenser's
figures qualify, they deepen and expand each others' meanings as their interactions are presented to us from a clearly
defined moral perspective. This moral perspective is the
viewpoint of the poet as author of what Arthos calls *"le
roman educatif,"* and it is obviously from this point of view
that Spenser was looking at his poem when he declared its
purpose "in the person of Prince Arthure [to] set forth
magnificence in particular."[13] According to this viewpoint
the stories in *The Faerie Queene* serve as exempla of right
action that must be taught to a prince or gentleman (Spenser,
of course, was writing for a princess and a gentlewoman).
Consequently there are specific moral principles which
govern the interactions of the poem's figures, principles
which are stated openly in the titles of the books; and if the
didactic poet does not always point them out directly, he at
least does so indirectly. We notice as we read, for example,
that figures who embody spiritual possibilities that ought to
be rejected are usually notable for their ugliness, an ugliness
which if not at first apparent, is revealed later on. The
stripping of Duessa at Orgoglio's Castle in Book I [I.8.46-48]

is an especially graphic instance of Spenser's method here. From the point of view of the poem's most inclusive meaning, however, what Harry Berger, Jr., calls its "vision," these specific principles must be considered as they are integrated into the larger, and finally deeper moral world of *The Faerie Queene*. As Berger says:

> The term vision means, after all, more than something seen: it is also something given to the seer. Didactic utterances, personified abstractions represent moments of conscious focus on the larger vision; that which permits of so discursive a presentation is perhaps only a small part of the vision.[14]

The moral world of the poem's vision is one in which no single ethical principle is an adequate expression of "the fundamental tendencies of human imagination as such." The inadequacy of such principles is conveyed to us through Spenser's use of the motif of the quest. The quest implied a sense of incompleteness on the part of the quester; hence his necessity, his desire to undertake the journey. But the quest is not a simple matter: it does not end with the overcoming of obstacles or the defeat of antagonists. The restlessness which pervades *The Faerie Queene* is symptomatic of Spenser's sense of the quest as a perpetual motion of the human imagination. His figures are constantly in search, and the desire that they represent is not easily satisifed. It is significant that the victories which the poem's figures achieve are only partial: Red Crosse slays the dragon, but is not finally married to Una; Guyon destroys the Bower of Bliss, but not Acrasia; Britomart rescues Amoret, but does not destroy Busirane (or marry Artegall); Artegall rescues Irena, but does not restore order fully in the state; Calidore rescues Pastorella, but does not kill the Blatant Beast. No one of Spenser's heroes comes to perfection, for there is always another evil to be destroyed, another foe to be vanquished. This is fitting because the foes who attack the heroes of *The*

Faerie Queene are as much a part of the human imagination as the heroes themselves. As Arthos remarks, "for Spenser, the greatest evils are of one's own creation, and most often the dangers of the forest are only likenesses to the darkness of the soul, at once hindering the aspirations of his heroes and providing the means by which they achieve their realization."[15] Not only are the poem's major figures incomplete in themselves, however, they are also incomplete together. That is, Red Crosse and Una, for example, represent part of the story but not all of it; the *imitatio Christi* which is the pervasive metaphor of the quest in Book I adequately describes one direction of the striving imagination, but not all the possibilities for movement which the imagination includes. It is for this reason that the figures of *The Faerie Queene* must be viewed together as they lend wider and deeper meaning to the poet's central motif.

What emerges when all these figures are viewed together, and evaluated according to the poem's moral viewpoint, is a sense of man's life as struggle—not as a struggle against, but a struggle *for*. Spenser's moral world is essentially a comic one where the forces of evil, though they may never be completely conquered on earth, at least can be controlled. What man struggles for, what he is directed toward, is not something unknown; for just as possibilities that ought to be rejected are revealed as ugly, so possibilities that are to be valued are seen as beautiful. Nothing is unknown or arbitrary. The sense of incompleteness which motivates the quest is not a free-floating anxiety, but a profound nostalgia for fulfillment of what the imagination instinctively senses as a real possibility. I use the word nostalgia here because "throughout *The Faerie Queene* the unending struggles and incomplete victories of the champions of virtue are set against Eden and the Age of Gold."[16] The myths of Eden and the Age of Gold are the Christian and pagan versions of the fundamental belief in the good nature of man's first estate. It is this belief which, cast in rather somber moral tones at the beginning of the poem in Book I, is finally brought to its most convincing and lovely expression in Book VI.

The movement of the imagination which Book VI culmin-
ates is a movement inward into the very sources of human
life. *The Faerie Queene* begins with the allegory of what
Lewis calls "sanctification—the restoring of the soul to her
lost paradisal nature by holiness."[17] The emphasis at the
poem's beginning is on faith: the soul's belief in the truth and
strength of its aspirations. It is faith, and faith alone, that can
sustain the quest. In Book I of *The Faerie Queene* faith is
explored in Christian terms and the quest is presented as
imitatio Christi. Desire here is metaphysical—the soul's
yearning for reunion with God. By the time we come to
Book VI, however, the poet's imagination has moved from
metaphysical desire to what might be called natural desire. As
the poem develops the references to Eden and the Age of
Gold become longer and more numerous. If Spenser had
continued in the austere mood of Book I, we might expect
these references to be an expression only of his painful sense
of disparity between the way things are and the way they
ought to be. And we might expect further that the poem
would progress, in the manner of Dante's *Commedia* for
example, to a vision of the eternal by which the earthly and
the mutable is judged and found wanting. But this does not
happen in *The Faerie Queene*. Instead, Spenser progresses
inward into man's imagination—from its first outward manifestations in longing for the eternal, to its inner, fundamental
sense of the possibilities inherent in the mutable. In Book VI,
"like those wonder-working heroines in Shakespeare,
Pastorella and all her world are put quite simply before us for
our acceptance."[18] And we are meant to accept this world,
as we are meant to accept the justice of Elizabeth in the
Proem to Book V, as evidence of the potential for good on
earth.

The pastoral world of Book VI is a world, very much like
Eden and the Age of Gold, which symbolizes the good nature
of man's first estate. It is in this world that the vicious do not
need to be destroyed but only instructed. Many of the figures
in Book VI who represent spiritual possiblities that are meant
to be rejected (Crudor, Turpine, Scorn, Disdaine, and the

cannibals, for example) are given reprieves just before they
are about to be destroyed by the champions of virtue. These
reprieves indicate the main mood of Book VI, a mood of rest
and redemption: the vicious figures may be redeemed, and
the virtuous figures may rest. Calidore is allowed to give up
his quest when he enters Pastorella's world. "Ne certes mote
he greatly blamed be/From so high step to stoupe vnto so
low [VI.10.3.1-2]," says the poet, for here the poet himself
parallels Calidore's action. In the vision on Mount Acidale
Spenser projects himself into the pastoral world he has
created, exchanging the "trumpets sterne" of the poetry to
the quest for his original "Oaten reeds [I.proem.1.4]":

> That iolly shepheard, which there piped, was
> Poore *Colin Clout* (who knowes not *Colin Clout?*)
> He pypt apace, whilest they him daunst about.
> Pype iolly shepheard, pype thou now apace
> Vnto thy loue, that made thee low to lout:
> Thy loue is present there with thee in place,
> Thy loue is there aduaunst to be another Grace.
>   [VI.10.16.3-9]

In Pastorella's world the quest is not the primary motif for
experience because desire is satisfied in love and faith
fulfilled in the glory of existence. It is this world, after all,
which is what the struggle is *for*, and it is this world, now
lost, that occasions the imagination's nostalgia and desire.
But Pastorella's world is not the world of *The Faerie Queene*.
The world of the poetry of the quest is a postlapsarian one in
which the loss of Eden and the Age of Gold is a loss not yet
restored. Consequently the brigands come and both Calidore
and the poet must unhitch their weary barques again
[VI.12.1]. Pastorella's world, the world of the Graces who
"on men all gracious gifts bestow/Which decke the body or
adorne the mynde [VI.10.23.1-2]," is man's *inspiration*. And
the glimpse of it the poet gives us is not only a look into
man's first estate, but also an insight into man's primary

desire. It is hither those "fundamental tendencies" of the imagination tend, whatever the symbols or the principles man may evoke in an effort to name his desire and describe his faith. And it is beautiful, like everything else that is beautiful in *The Faerie Queene*, because it is good. At the end of Book VI, we understand the feeling of love and reverence for life which the vision of Arcadian society brings forth in the poet: indeed "it is most straunge and wonderfull to fynd/So milde humanity, and perfect gentle mynd [VI.5.29.8-9]."

When we look at the Mutabilitie Cantos and the prayer in the light of Spenser's interpretation of the quest, I think we can see that they do recapitulate his theme. In this last part of *The Faerie Queene*, the poet's mind moves into a vision of the "mythical" and the "collectively great" that parallels his vision of the earth in the six books. Here the subject of the six books is integrated into the larger context of the whole created universe:

> And men themselues doe change continually,
> From youth to eld, from wealth to pouerty,
> From good to bad, from bad to worst of all.
> Ne doe their bodies only flit and fly:
> But eeke their minds (which they immortall call)
> Still change and vary thoughts, as new occasions fall.
>   [VII.7.19.4-9]

From this perspective the restlessness of the human imagination, symbolized in the perpetual questing of Spenser's heroes, and in his own questing as poet, is seen as part of the restlessness of the entire cosmos. And just as Spenser follows the movement to its source in (human) nature in Book VI, so here he follows it to its source in Nature: "still moouing yet vnmoued from her sted [VII.7.13.2]." In Nature's judgment Spenser's discovery of the fundamental goodness of the human imagination is restated "so that it no longer scans 'heav-en's blue,' 'meadowland,' but 'O-thou heaven's blue,' 'Green-est meadowland,' 'Fare-thee well for aye.'" Once again the poet takes leave; like the Graces on Mount Acidale, Nature vanishes with the "whole assembly quite dismist [VII.7.59.8]."

The poem is over, the quest complete. Like the Creator, the poet has wrought the work of his imagination and found it good. In his last Sabbath words Spenser stands before us in the attitude of prayer, incarnating before our eyes the solitary figure of the quest. The poet looks upward at the end of *The Faerie Queene*, as he did at its beginning in Book I, in a profound expression of faith and desire—now grown into glory and love. " 'Now for-get the pain,' it says. 'Great was-God in us.' 'Twas all-but a dream,' 'Friendly-be to me.' " The prayer bears witness to the end of his quest: it is a testament to the truth of the human imagination. For "dreams too are bestowed by God: life, soul, and imagination are gifts. Men are spurred to action by their dreams, moved to attain the object beyond their reach. But the very action and movement is itself a perfection. The dream seeks the reality, and the idea seeks the flesh, for love is a double desiring."[19] Like Beethoven's last sonata, Spenser's poem is all of a piece—it is a whole, it is sustained, and it is final. As Kretschmar had said, we had only need "to hear the piece to answer the question ourselves. A third movement? A new approach? A return after this parting—impossible! It had happened that the [work] had come, in the second enormous movement, to an end, an end without any return."[20]

TEMPLE UNIVERSITY

1. Thomas Mann, *Doctor Faustus: The Life of the German Composer Adrian Leverkuhn, as told to a Friend*, trans. H. T. Low-Porter (New York, 1965), p. 55.

2. Mann, p. 53.

3. Most obviously the letter does not correspond to Book II. In the letter Spenser describes how, on the second day of Gloriana's feast "ther came in a

Palmer bearing an Infant with bloddy hands, whose Parents he complained to
haue bene slayn by an Enchaunteresse called Acrasia: and therefore craued of the
Faery Queene, to appoint him some knight, to performe that aduenture, which
being assigned to Sir Guyon, he presently went forth with that same Palmer:
which is the beginning of the second booke and the whole subject thereof." In the
poem itself, however, Guyon and the Palmer find the bloody babe and hear the
story of Acrasia from Amavia [II.1.34-56].

4. John Arthos, *On the Poetry of Spenser and the Form of Romances* (London,
1951), p. 198.

5. C. S. Lewis, *The Allegory of Love: A Study in Medieval Tradition* (New
York, 1958), pp. 353-354.

6. William Nelson, *The Poetry of Edmund Spenser: A Study* (New York, 1963),
pp. 300, 310.

7. Graham Hough, *A Preface to the Faerie Queene* (New York, 1963), p. 215.

8. See Josephine Waters Bennett, *The Evolution of "The Faerie Queene"* (New
York, 1960), p. 206f.

9. Mann, p. 52.

10. Arthos, p. 91.

11. Hough, p. 93.

12. Lewis, pp. 312-313.

13. Arthos, p. 42.

14. Harry Berger, Jr., *The Allegorical Temper: Vision and Reality in Book II of
Spenser's Faerie Queene* (New Haven, 1957), pp. 188-189.

15. Arthos, p. 79.

16. Nelson, p. 311.

17. Lewis, p. 224.

18. Arthos, p. 135.

19. Berger, p. 171.

20. Mann, p. 55.

Susan C. Fox

Eterne in Mutabilitie

Spenser's Darkening Vision

Obviously Spenser never completed his plan for *The Faerie Queene*. Just as obviously what he did complete has enough unity of action and significance to be read as a whole—or nearly a whole—poem. We may deduce from this fortunate coincidence either that Spenser's plan itself was loose or superficial or otherwise unimportant, or that by the miracle of poetic genius which conceived the plan, a part of it could be nearly as splendid as the whole. Since I am a devout believer in miracles, at least poetic ones, I prefer the second deduction. I believe that the design of *The Faerie Queene* is much of its greatness, and that the nature of that design explains Spenser's inability to complete it.

What we have of *The Faerie Queene* stands as a great work of art because its unity is governed not only by this partially realized design, but also by the fully realized imaginative universe in which it operates, what C. S. Lewis calls its milieu:

> "Faerie land" itself provides the unity—a unity not of plot but of *milieu*. . . . Few poems have a greater harmony of atmosphere. The multiplicity of the stories, far from impairing the unity, supports it; for just that multiplicity, that packed fullness of "vehement adven-

tures," is the quality of Faerie Land; as tragedy is the quality of Hardy's Wessex.[1]

For Graham Hough, this unity of atmosphere is the poem's only unity:

> *The Faerie Queene* is composed of many relatively small parts, each commanding our appreciation by itself and all harmonious with each other; and this is its structural principle. Its essence is immanent in these multitudinous local effects, not in an over-riding plan which could be abstracted and schematically displayed.[2]

Hough defends the cantos we have as a whole poem, though he is always aware that it might have been an entirely different poem had Spenser lived to double the number of its cantos. His defense yields a unified reading of the extant cantos which ably represents the fullness of vision we may find in them:

> It begins with the book of Holiness, because for Spenser this is the necessary ground of all human development. A Catholic poet might have put it at the end; Spenser's placing it as he does corresponds to the Protestant theology of prevenient grace—without it all other activity is worthless. Next comes Temperance, as the first condition of any possible human integrity. . . . These books are self-contained, complete within themselves; they have perhaps greater density and complexity of organization than all the others; yet they are in a sense preliminary to Spenser's main preoccupations.
>
> Then we have Books III and IV, called the legends of Chastity and Friendship, but really to be taken together as the poem's great central area, concerned with Love. . . . The celebration of love, the distinction of its different tempers and varieties, the portrayal of the conditions which foster it, and of its enemies in the heart and in the outer world—it is this that forms the main substance of *The Faerie Queene*. . . .

Since man is a political animal the force of concord must be prolonged into the social and political sphere. This is the function of the book of Justice. . . . By now the main lines of Spenser's view of life are laid down. There remains the final enhancement of a spontaneous natural grace. This is celebrated in the book of Courtesy. It is a natural flowering that crowns the whole with loveliness. But the scene of the poem is the world, and no achievement of virtue or beauty in the world is lasting. Everything is subject to change, and this seems at first subversive of all happiness and all good. By submitting to the judgement of nature it is just possible to see this change as life-giving and re-creative. But man can never fully see it so; the weight of mutability presses too heavily upon him. It is only by projecting his mind outside the created world, by seeing it for a moment in its eternal setting, that a resting-place can be found. This takes a step beyond the ideal naturalism that is the normal temper of Spenser's mind.[3]

It is quite possible, as Hough demonstrates, to read *The Faerie Queene* as a whole poem, to half-pretend (and Hough is always aware of the pretense) that it exists as it was always intended. The only concrete obstacle to such agreeable fancies is Spenser's letter to Raleigh, that mind-teasing document which attempts to explain the plan, the projected structure of *The Faerie Queene*. "The generall end" of the poem, according to the letter, "is to fashion a gentleman or noble person in vertuous and gentle discipline." To dramatize the didactic vision, the author proposes to figure forth the twelve virtues attributable to such a man in the persons of twelve separate knights. The unifying factor of their adventures is to be the annual feast of the Queen of Faery, at which each knight has been assigned a quest. Except that several details in the letter clash with parts of the poem already finished when Spenser wrote the letter, the explanation seems straightforward and general enough to be accepted as an indication of what the poet expected to become of his poem. The discrepancies—notably the origin of Guyon's quest (Did the Palmer find Ruddymane and beg justice for him of Gloriana, as in the letter, or did Guyon himself find the child and assume the quest, as indicated in the poem?)— may be laid to the poet's reconsideration as he outlined his intentions.

According to the letter, then, Hough is wrong to say that *The Faerie Queene* has no over-riding plan. He defends himself on the grounds that the letter was probably a second thought, a necessary and perhaps temporary prop brought in to support the structureless initial vision of the poem. Discounting the letter as a hasty expediency, he suggests that the real formal principle of the work "would be something inherent in the original vision, that had never reached the level of conscious formal exposition at all."[4] C. S. Lewis, on the other hand, though it was he who so eloquently developed the idea of "harmony of atmosphere" or of milieu in the first place, is too much aware of an over-riding plan in *The Faerie Queene* to accept the cantos we have as a complete poem. He turns for evidence of design not to the ambiguous letter, but to the poem itself, and to the vital questions it leaves unanswered. We cannot know from the cantos we have, he argues, who their hero really is, or how he fulfills his quest, or how the quests of the lesser heroes relate to his:

> Spenser must have intended a final book on Arthur and Gloriana which would have stood to the whole poem as [the] central or focal cantos stand to their several books. If we had it we should know what the city of Cleopolis and its tower Panthea really are; we should have the key to the tantalizing history of Elfe and Fay; and we should be much less troubled than we are now by the recollection of Queene Elizabeth throughout the poem. As things are, however, Arthur is inexplicable. . . . The poem is not finished. It is a poem of a kind

that loses more than most by being unfinished. Its
centre, the seat of its highest life, is missing.[5]

We must, of course, both appreciate with Hough the great
poem we have and mourn with Lewis the greater poem we
have lost. But we must come eventually to decide between
the approaches of these two critics. Hough recognizes that
the poem is incomplete but protests that "how much its
incompleteness matters will depend on what kind of design
we expect it to have."[6] Since he expects only the loose
design of a vision which subsumes its structure in its own
luxuriant growth, he is not frustrated by the incompleteness.
Lewis, on the other hand, projects from the nature of
existing cantos a controlled design which, however simple, is
so dominant a force in the poem that the vision cannot be
realized unless it is complete. Hough seems to be arguing
from the milieu of the poem, from its richness of significance
and its variety of poetic forms. Lewis is guided by its internal
structures and by the allegory those structures support. I
find, as indicated earlier, that I must agree with Lewis in his
conception of a deliberately exercised and profoundly
influential structural idea in *The Faerie Queene*. Yet at the
risk of sounding hopelessly equivocal, I must add that in the
poem's milieu I find suggestions that what we have of *The
Faerie Queene* is all that we could ever have had. Spenser's
poetic universe seems to me to darken during the course of
the extant books, as his sense of its beauty and its potential
perfection yields to a bleaker sense of its evils and corrupt-
ibility. This darkening vision must ultimately conflict with
the ideal of a perfectible hero which is the basic structural
principle of the poem. That conflict is realized, I believe, in
the Mutabilitie Cantos, which neither the dark nor the ideal
vision survives.

    To understand that conflict, let us examine first its more
concrete element. The general structure of *The Faerie
Queene* is, as the letter to Raleigh explains and the poem
itself demonstrates, allegorical. Each book is endowed with a

hero whose exploits perfect him in a particular virtue—that he may finally overcome the corresponding vice. Within this very general structure design each book follows a slightly more specific pattern. In order to fulfill his quest, each knight must pass through what Lewis calls the "allegorical centre"[7] of his book. That center at once symbolizes the action of the book and, dramatically, allows it to proceed: the House of Holinesse, the House of Alma, the Temple of Venus, the Church of Isis (or the Castle of Mercilla), and Mount Acidale all strengthen the knights that they may fulfill their quests. The trial on Arlo Hill, if we can imagine it at all in the context of a whole book, is conceivably a vision of the Knight of Constancy, and thus presumably strengthens him as the vision on Acidale enlightens Calidore. The Garden of Adonis alone, the allegorical center of Book III, is unvisited by its knight in the course of its book. Britomart was born of Adonis as all mortals are, and she, in her acceptance of the quest of true love, proves that she knows from whence she has come. She cannot return to Adonis, for return is death. Instead, in one of the most curious turns of the poem, Britomart visits the allegorical center of her lover's book. Lapse of judgment has enthralled Artegall to Radigund, and only Britomart can save him. But her love is distorted by jealousy; her judgment has also lapsed. She passes the night in the Church of Isis, where her judgment is restored; having assumed the very quality of justice her lover had let slip from him, she is permitted to save him. So perfectly matched are these two lovers, that one may be substituted for the other in the allegorical structure of the poem without disturbing its delicate decorum. If this switching of roles, this purifying of the wrong knight, is an example of Spenser's absent-mindedness, his is the most fortunate absent-mindedness conceivable.

The substitution of Britomart for Artegall in the allegorical core of Book V demonstrates, I believe, the superb and highly conscious artistry through which all the quests of *The Faerie Queene* are structured and interrelated. The quests of holiness and temperance are unique in their poetic and allegorical compression, and, as Hough argues, preliminary to the perfection of the virtuous man. Yet echoes of them inform all the following books of the poem, and the heroes themselves appear occasionally to complicate the action and to demonstrate that no achievement in his life is lasting, that mortal holiness is in danger of sin (Britomart must save Red Crosse from Malecasta's knights.) and mortal temperance may still be tempted into excess (Artegall must subdue Guyon's rage over Braggadochio in V.3). Other quests of virtue are so delicately interwoven that we may scarcely isolate them. Chastity, Friendship, Justice, Courtesy, and Constancy are interdependent. The Red Crosse Knight and Guyon join hands; Guyon and Britomart joust: it is easy to see the quest handed on, relay fashion, in the first three books. By Book IV, relay has become grand right-and-left. It remains so until the action is again simplified at the beginning of Book VI, when Artegall resumes the relay by passing most of the burden of the plot on to Calidore. Justice bows out of the quest for the Blatant Beast; he is immune to the monster [VI.1.9] and, since it is not his problem, uninterested in pursuing it. Courtesy seems to stand alone, isolated from all the other virtues of the poem. If we look closely, though, we see that instead it comprises them: Calidore sentences Briana and Crudor judiciously enough to make Artegall proud (the two knights have just parted); he learns humility, temperance, love, and friendship among the shepherds, and afterwards he enchains the beastliness which endangers all these qualities.

So the individual quests are woven together. Elements appear and reappear in the pattern. The smallest details are repeated over and over: magic swords, garlands, gnats, dwarves, tapestries, salves, books, foundlings, women pursued turn up again and again throughout the poem, each time in a new context with a new significance. More important elements of the poem are also repeated. Archimago fashions a false Una, a witch, a snowy Florimell. The Hermit who saves

Serena and Timias was once a valiant knight like the Red
Crosse, and now he enjoys the solitary life the Red Crosse
had been promised; Britomart's quest is for her beloved
(reuniting Amoret and Scudamour is merely an important
diversion), whose face she has beheld in a magic glass, just as
Arthur's quest is for his Gloriana, whom he beheld in a
charmed dream.
     Both mortals who have entered Faery Land in pursuit of
perfect love, the Briton Prince and the Briton Maid, are
revealing counterparts. It is as if Britomart's quest is a
microcosm of Arthur's. Neither quest can be accomplished in
a single book, though the Knight of Chastity does have a
whole book to herself in which to conquer her chief enemy,
love-doubt. Neither quest is, in fact, accomplished in all the
books we have, though Britomart's nearly is, and Spenser's
concentrated attention on her gives us a good idea of its
meaning and ultimate fulfillment. That sense of Britomart's
quest may be our clearest definition of Arthur's, which is
discernible in the extant books only by analogy: as Britomart
moves closer to lasting union with Artegall by a series of
saving and renovating acts, so, we may conjecture, Arthur
moves towards Gloriana as his adventures rescue others and
educate him.
     As Britomart's quest spans three books, in which she is
constantly called upon to aid helpless innocents, Arthur's
quest extends through the whole of *The Faerie Queene*. In
each book save the third (Britomart is so much like him that
she can apparently handle her own book without his help; he
must come to the aid of the questing knight.) he frees Red
Crosse from Orgoglio and saves Guyon from the Paynim; he
stops the battle Britomart has been unable to stop in Book
IV; he saves Artegall in the Souldan's castle; and though he is
never called upon to rescue Calidore, he does do a great deal
of his fighting for him. Furthermore, as he comes into
contact with each questing knight, Arthur seems to absorb
some of that knight's virtuous quality: he receives a Bible
from Red Crosse; he enters the House of Alma with Guyon,

and spends his time learning about himself; in Britomart's book his pursuit of Florimell intensifies his ardor for Gloriana, for whom he nearly mistakes her, praying that she be his Gloriana, for that Gloriana be as fair as she [III.4.54.6-8]; he ends strife in the book of Friendship; he learns mercy with Artegall in Book V and exercises it in Book VI, calling off the "saluage mann's" attack at Turpine's castle even as the chastened Artegall called Talus off in V.11; in the last book he rescues Serena much as Calidore rescued Priscilla, he conquers Turpine and overcomes Disdaine.

Yet Arthur, who is so integral to every other quest in *The Faerie Queene*, never seems to get any closer to fulfilling his own quest than he is at the start of the poem. Furthermore, though all the other quests except Britomart's are indeed fulfilled, none of the other questing knights is granted lasting union with his beloved. Red Crosse must leave Una and Guyon Medina (presumably she is his betrothed). Artegall and Britomart have not married. Triamond has his Canacee, to be sure, but he is no knight of Gloriana—and I hardly believe he can be the hero of Book IV. For some strange reason Amoret and Scudamour have missed each other again in IV.9—and because of Arthur's oversight—or Spenser's—in permitting this, we never do find them happily married; Calidore leaves Pastorella to go out after the Beast and he does not return to her in the poem as it now stands. All the important lovers are left separated when Book VI ends. Surely Spenser intended to reunite them, perhaps in that same Book XII where Arthur was presumably to meet his Gloriana. Even if we can, with Hough, pass lightly over the miscarriage of Arthur's quest in the work *The Faerie Queene* is now, how can we overlook the dangling states of all the other love affairs in the poem? They are allegorical disaster, as the poem now stands. Even Books I, II, and VI, which seem like self-sufficient units, are not allegorically whole in themselves. Since allegory. dictates the structure of *The Faerie Queene* in the first place, allegorical disaster is also structural disaster. Not only is the climax towards which the

whole poem is built missing, but the supports upon which the
structure is to have rested—and seems, as far as it goes, to be
resting—are not themselves complete. It is probably in its
very incompleteness that the over-riding plan of the poem is
most evident. Though I do believe there is such a design, I concede to
Hough that it is simple and very fluid. The elementary plan
of embodying individual moral virtues in individual knights is
so flexible, as Spenser employs it, that it permits great
freedom. The undissipated compression of Book I seems
hardly of the same art with the shifting configurations of IV;
the difference is like that between a procession and a
square-dance. The implementation of the plan in a series of
discrete incidents appears even less a product of conscious
design than the plan itself: saving knights and thieving villains
appear suddenly as the poet needs them; quests are forgotten
and new quests pursued as the occasion dictates. The poem,
as Spenser himself described it, is full of "accidents," of
episodes which, though they reinforce our apprehension of
the central action of each book, are actually digressions from
that action and bear little or no structural relation to it.
Flexibility does not, however, imply want of controlling
design. As each mood shifts and each incident gives way to
the next, something new and vital has been added to our
comprehension of holiness, of chastity, of magnificence. The
action of *The Faerie Queene* is an accruing action; nothing is
lost in its cantos. Elements spiral through our consciousness,
altered each time they appear to us but always recognizable
in their new contexts, always enhanced in significance by
their old. Spenser manipulates these elements with perfect
deftness and tact, juxtaposing them with the sureness of
timing of Shakespeare or Webster.

To this extent the poem's milieu enhances its structure.
Yet the very flexibility of that structure renders it vulnerable
to the milieu, which changes as the poet's vision or
temperament changes. We may see the tension between
structure and milieu in the difference between the three

books of the 1590 publication and the three of 1596. It is
almost as if Spenser lost or abandoned the vigorous compression of Books I-III, and kept experimenting in the later books
to recapture or replace it. In the later publication he altered
the end of Book III, casting out several of his most luxuriant
stanzas for several of his most pedestrian in order to build a
strange new sort of book for his fourth virtue, friendship. As
if to say that friendship is but an extension, a different
version of the love between man and woman, Spenser makes
Book IV almost totally an extension of Book III. My feeling
for a long time was that this peculiar book with no defined
hero, little new action (except the parable which governs its
tone, but not its plot), and a disconcertingly intricate pattern
of events is merely an addendum to Book III—that Spenser
might just as easily have packed its highlights into the earlier
book and forgotten the rest. Even its allegorical center is but
a memory, a left-over experience which antedates even the
Legend of Chastity. Little is resolved in the book; the task of
reconciling Florimell and Marinell, Britomart and Artegall, is
passed on to Book V. I recognize now—though I have
occasional feelings that I am only making excuses—that Book
IV is very cleverly devised as an extension of Book III, that
each element of the seemingly aimless involutions of the
action can be justified structurally and allegorically, that
there is often a delightful and relaxing comedy in the antics
of friends, false friends, and foes. Even the disconcerting
herolessness of the book can be explained away: perhaps the
Legend of Friendship ought to have no single hero. Friends
like Britomart and Scudamour ought ideally to be equal.
What remains to my mind a significant failure of Book IV is
that the beautifully functioning system of accruing action of
the earlier books seems to get tired out in this first book of
the poem's second installment. The endless spiraling of poetic
elements, the carefully contrived repetition of effects, is no
longer paying off. The stories are just plain dull and, though
there are certain moments (the true meeting of Artegall and
Britomart, Scudamour's tale, Belphoebe's rebuff of Timias)

which are definitely high Spenser, the poetry itself is bland and often flaccid.

If the convoluted action becomes tired in Book IV, it is downright mechanical in Book V. The iron man is not the only robot in the book. Spenser himself seems rigid and unapproachable. The action proceeds with the mindless bludgeoning of Talus: all the battles seem the same, and it matters little whether Artegall, Britomart, or Arthur is doing the sanctioned fighting. The language is numbing in its relentless sameness; there are few memorable passages of poetry. The Castle of Mercilla, which might be construed as the allegorical center of the book (though I think the Church of Isis can better bear the burden), is a jarring failure poetically and allegorically; it is a rash and unsatisfying statement, and it sounds hasty and insincere. I should like to defend Book V, for it has some graces, but in the context of the rest of *The Faerie Queene* it is clearly a disappointment. The technique which elsewhere flowered so bountifully looks parched and scrawny in Book V.

The flowers abound again in Book VI. Without abandoning his technique of accruing action, Spenser revives it and cultivates it and rejoices in its new vitality. The Legend of Courtesy is a return to the very well-spring of poetry, where Spenser seems to attain a personal and poetic apotheosis. Poetry and virtue are twin gifts of the Graces. All the quests of men, all their battles, and all their instruction cannot evoke them. A man may wander long among men performing feats of strength and deeds of justice, but only in a sublime moment of calm and longing may he be granted a portion of those gifts. Spenser fought with Red Crosse and resisted with Guyon, searched with Britomart and judged with Artegall— and still his poetry, and with it his moral trustworthiness, faltered. A gentle, unexpected, most beautiful and most gracious inspiration rescued both.

If *The Faerie Queene* had ended with the vision on Acidale—and somehow that could be made to include both union with Pastorella and destruction of the Blatant Beast—it would be merely a splendid *Bildungsroman* with a Protean hero. The incident ends with Colin's breaking his pipe, with the anticipation of a new poetic voice after a pastoral education. But in Book VI that new poetic voice never sounds; Colin speaks no more after the descent from Acidale, and Calidore is no poet. After Acidale come loss and anguish. Though there is, inevitably, restoration (Pastorella to Calidore, to her parents), it can never erase the memory of slaughter and despair. The book ends on the ominous note that, though Calidore could restrain the beast of uncivility, he could not vanquish him utterly. The beast is free once more; it "raungeth through the world againe,/And rageth sore in each degree and state;/Ne any is, that may him now restraine..." [VI.12.40.1-2].

Books IV and V suffer a declining poetic vigor and invention, and the sixth book, which restores Spenser's art, ends in an outburst of bitterness and fear. This change in the milieu of *The Faerie Queene* reflects the poet's darkening vision, his new preoccupation with the force which the Blatant Beast, without directly embodying, certainly suggests: the uncontrollable destructive force which conforms to no witnessed laws and responds to no human defiance, the force of death and decay which threatens every human joy, the force of mutability. There are allusions to this cruel force everywhere in the poem, but in the first published books, mutability is accepted in all its dread power as part of the order of things, and no outcry is raised against it. Arthur, speaking of his vulnerability to love, admonishes calmly that

> Nothing is sure, that growes on earthly ground:
> And who most trustes in arme of fleshly might,
> And boasts, in beauties chaine not to be bound,
> Doth soonest fall in disauentrous fight,
> And yeeldes his caytiue neck to victours most despight.
> [I.9.11.5-9]

Despayre's whole argument is based on mutability: things can only get worse, so let us give in to the death which is inevitable anyway, and thus thwart the process of decay. But Una answers that heavenly Grace alone can thwart mutability, that we must trust in it and go on; and her knight does trust and go on. Spenser summarizes his attitude:

> What man is he, that boasts of fleshly might,
> And vaine assurance of mortality,
> Which all so soone, as it doth come to fight,
> Against spirituall foes, yeelds by and by,
> Or from the field most cowardly doth fly?
> Ne let the man ascribe it to his skill,
> That thorough grace hath gained victory.
> If any strength we haue, it is to ill,
> But all the good is Gods, both power and eke will.
>
> [I.10.1]

Fidelia demonstrates the awesome power of faith to counteract mutability; she can kill and raise again to life, she can stay the sun or turn it backwards, she can stop armies and part ocean waters [I.10.29-30]. Acrasia, who turns men into beasts, has a force opposite to Fidelia's. Though Acrasia seems to counter decay in her bower of eternal spring, the counter is merely a ploy, a semblance of redemption which occupies her courtiers as they hasten unwittingly to final corruption. Mutability in the Bower of Bliss is thus, ironically, a vindication of right order and not a corruption of it. Even the House of Alma is destined for decay. Built of the "slime" which formed both Adam and the Tower of Babel, this structure of flesh must pass into dust: "But O great pitty, that no lenger time/So goodly workemanship may not endure:/Soone it must turne to earth: no earthly thing is sure [II.9.21.7-9]." But heavenly things are sure and, if the flesh perishes, the soul endures.

In the allegorical center of Book III we find Spenser's great
consolation for mutability. "Substance," drawn from chaos,
nurtured in the Garden of Adonis, invested in flesh by
Genius, and sent out into our world of mortal life, can never
die; only the form of that substance is subject to mutability:

> That substance is eterne, and bideth so,
> Ne when the life decayes, and forme does fade,
> Doth it consume, and into nothing go,
> But chaunged is, and often altred to and fro.
>   [III.6.37.6-9]

Substance returns to Adonis when form dies, and is planted
deep into the soil of chaos to grow a thousand years.

> The substance is not chaunged, no altered,
>   But th' only forme and outward fashion;
>   For euery substance is conditioned
>   To change her hew, and sundry formes to don,
>   Meet for her temper and complexion:
>   For formes are variable and decay,
>   By course of kind, and by occasion;
>   And that faire flowre of beautie fades away,
> As doth the lilly fresh before the sunny ray.
>   [III.6.38]

The destruction of form by Mutabilitie's henchman Time is
anguish even to the gods, and melancholy inhabits the
garden. But as the destruction is natural and impermanent, so
is the melancholy. Joy is the prevailing mood of the garden,
full, rich, uninhibited joy. Like Adonis, who must live to
father all life, all mortal beings are "eterne in mutabilitie
[III.6.47.5]." Only the imitations of life, the evil semblants
of reality, vanish utterly and never return to the nursery of
Adonis; the Bower of Bliss is totally destroyed, and the
House of Busirane is extinguished with its curtain of flame.
   So in the first installment of his poem Spenser seems
troubled by the prospect of loss and decay, but well able to

absorb that prospect in a confident, hale, and hopeful conception of the cyclical nature of life. By the time the last three books of *The Faerie Queene* were published six years later, his confidence was shaken and his dread increased. The poet, older and now disappointed in his political and social ambitions, seems unable to maintain his poised view of the cycles of nature. Again and again he speaks of the cruel and inevitable force of decay, and he cannot keep bitterness out of his tone when he does. He finds he must defend himself for his paean to love [IV.prologue.1]. He must defend also his archaic language and his poetic source in vague antiquity. In this defense, he for the first time explicitly applies the concept of mutability to poetic art. Chaucer, the "well of English undefyled," is "On Fames eternall beadroll worthy to be fyled,"

> But wicked Time that all good thoughts doth waste,
>   And workes of noblest wits to nought out weare,
>   That famous moniment hath quite defaste,
>   And robd the world of threasure endlesse deare,
>   The which mote haue enriched all vs heare.
> O cursed Eld the cankerworme of writs,
>   How may these rimes, so rude as doth appeare,
>   Hope to endure, with sorkes of heauenly wits
> Are quite deuoured, and brought to nought by little bits?
>
> [IV.2.33.1-9]

Language, too, decays, and even poetry is subject to mutability. Spenser, attempting to keep alive the thoughts and rhymes defaced by time, seeks to form a chain like the chain of life Agape devises for her sons: the length of Chaucer's thread is to be added to Spenser's, and that of Spenser's to succeeding authors':

> Ne dare I like, but through infusion sweete
> Of thine owne spirit, which doth in me surviue,

I follow here the footing of thy feete,
That with thy meaning so I may the rather meete.

[IV.2.34.6-9]

But if poetry ought to be preserved, Spenser is no longer
certain that life itself should be. He questions Agape's
prolonging the life of her "Telemond." Sounding suspiciously
like Despayre, he complains,

O Why doe wretched men so much desire
    To draw their dayes vnto the vtmost date,
    And doe not rather wish them soone expire,
    Knowing the miserie of their estate,
    And thousand perills which them still awate,
    Tossing them like a boate amid the mayne,
    That euery houre they knocke at deathes gate?
    And he that happie seemes and least in payne,
Yet is as nigh his end, as he that most doth playne.

[IV.3.1]

Spenser has no Una to remind him of Grace and of the return
to Adonis. He is all too much aware that once, in "the
infancie/Of time [IV.8.30.1-2]," all was harmony and joy;
but now beauty is perverted and innocence decayed
[IV.8.32-33]. Spenser's yearning for the early time, for a
time undefiled by mutability, permeates the second section
of his poem. It even accounts in parts for his antique verse:

So oft as I with state of present time,
    The image of the antique world compare,
    When as mans age was in his freshest prime,
    And the first blossome of fair vertue bare,
    Such oddes I finde twixt those, and these which are,
    As that, through long continuance of his course,
    Me seemes the world is runne quite out of square
    From the first point of his appointed sourse,
And being once amisse growes daily wourse and wourse.

> Let none then blame me, if in discipline
> Of vertue and of ciuill vses lore,
> I do not form them to the common line
> Of present dayes, which are corrupted sore,
> But to the antique vse, which was of yore,
> When good was onely for it selfe desyred,
> And all men sought their owne, and none no more;
> When Iustice was not for most meed outhyred,
> But simple Truth did rayne, and was of all admyred.
>   [V.prologue.1.3]

The heavens have "wandred much" from their first, their ordained positions [V.prologue.5-7]. Their deviation reflects man's deviation from initial purity. The Ptolemaic world was collapsing and Spenser knew nothing of Copernicus. For him, in the Prologue to Book V and elsewhere, the only explanation for this terrifying deviation from law was a counter-law of chaos and ruin. To a great extent, the last three books of the poem are an attempt to find order even in that chaos, to reconcile himself and his faith to decay.

We have already seen that Spenser considered love the primary human weapon against mutability. True lovers are crowned with "immortal blis [IV.prologue.2.8]." In this life and in the Garden of Adonis they are "eterne in mutabilitie." Artegall represents a second force against corruption, justice "that doth right define [V.7.1.3]." He repeats the lesson of Adonis:

> What though the sea with waues continuall
> Doe eate the earth, it is no more at all:
> Ne is the earth the lesse, or loseth ought,
> For whatsoeuer from one place doth fall,
> Is with the tide vnto an other brought:
> For there is nothing lost, that may be found, if sought.

> Likewise the earth is not augmented more,
> By all that dying into it doe fade.

> For of the earth they formed were of yore,
> How euer gay their blossome or their blade
> Doe flourish now, they into dust shall vade.
> What wrong then it is, if that when they die,
> They turne to that, whereof they first were made?
> All in the powre of their great Maker lie:
> All creatures must obey the voice of the most hie.
>   [V.2.39.4–40.9]

It is by just vision and just action that man may restrain the forces of mutability within himself. True lovers make laws for themselves, and do not exceed them. Just men guard that those who are not bound by laws of love conform still to social laws. That justice has the power to compel obedience is attested by the trial of Mutabilitie, who must submit to the judiciary decree of Nature.

But human justice cannot always prevail. As Artegall affirms, the final power over man resides in God. When human laws fail, divine Grace intercedes. Thus Calidore, whose quest and whose love are thwarted by his own lack of vision, is permitted to witness for a moment the dance of the Graces of Acidale. Infused with the virtue and knowledge they command, he wins Pastorella and subdues the Blatant Beast.

Even divine Grace is a fleeting thing. Subject not to mutability but to divine will, it is nevertheless an evanescent force in man's life. Inspired by it, Calidore captures the Beast—but Calidore himself is subject to mutability, and when he dies the Beast ranges free again.

The monster threatens, the stars run wild, innocence and beauty decay, justice decrees unheard—life itself seems a trial to Spenser in these late books. His consolation is a vision of the pure time, the fairy time when mutability did not sway. His consolation is his own defiance of mutability, his own grasping of the poetic life-line reaching backward through Chaucer and the Italians, and forward, perhaps, into succeeding ages of decadence and ruin. The Beast is free and the poet's verses are derided, but he clutches the line.

Like Hough, I seem to be describing the six books of *The Faerie Queene* as a kind of shaky totality, a moral odyssey with a beginning, a middle, and an abrupt but still viable end. Unlike Hough, I cannot fit the Mutabilitie Cantos comfortably into any such totality. They do not seem to me "a step beyond the ideal naturalism that is the normal temper of Spenser's mind,"[8] a "resting-place" in the "eternal setting" of the created world.[9] They seem instead a kind of doubling back, a passionately restless attempt to deal finally and conclusively with the issue which gathers dread for Spenser throughout the second publication, the corruption which is the ultimate enemy of the poem's ultimate good, human perfectibility. The Cantos have to my ear a desperate and very personal quality, not only in the starting rawness of the final two stanzas, but in the grand pageantry as well: it is as if Spenser deliberately calls up all the luxuriant formality of his language and vision in one last attempt to defeat loss and change, as if he would imprison Mutabilitie in the elaborate conventions of poetry itself, and render her powerless there. The decree of Nature is less important to his victory than the judgment of posterity, which considers not the philosophical arguments of the contenders, but their sheer strength: is the poetry proof against the corruptions of time? If it is, then Mutabilitie is defeated the only way mortal beings can defeat her. And it is. But the struggle cost Spenser the plan of his poem.

It is clear at the end of Book VI that *The Faerie Queene* must change if it is to go on. The Legend of Courtesy is a poetic clarification; poetry itself becomes a virtue in its cantos. The pastoral rebirth it describes implies a new poetic voice to come. The Mutabilitie Cantos are the song which that voice sings. Yet instead of giving the poem new direction, new impetus, the Cantos bring it to a passionate but strangely paralyzed end. The poet is exhausted; he longs, not for strength and courage, but for rest and peace of the end of time. He cannot, like his own Knight of Holiness, survive despair. He will no longer battle the evils of this life, but begs entry into the New Jerusalem to escape them.

The Mutabilitie Cantos thus mark the end of Spenser's struggle in his poetry with dread and despair. They seem to provide an answer to his own search for permanence, but it is not a viable answer. Mutabilitie may not rule eternity, but she is the mistress of our realm of time. As the final two stanzas indicate, this is no answer to satisfy the searching soul. It provides no resolution—only deadlock. The great plan of *The Faerie Queene* was left unfinished not because of Spenser's death (He died three full years after the publication of Books IV-VI.), but because of a poetic juggernaut.

The Faerie Queene started out an exploration of the virtues men may attain. Within the confines of its design, the poetry turned subtly into a deeply personal account of one man's coming to terms with death and decay. The structure held to the initial plan, but the milieu darkened gradually until it cut off that plan. Arthur's place in the center of the poem was slowly taken over by Spenser himself. Arthur, a mortal whose vision led him into a world of glass, was ostensibly to have been granted union with his ideal world. Spenser, too, sought union with an ideal—but for him, union could be achieved only in the act of writing poetry. Spenser was subject, as Arthur as a literary creation with a magical healing balm was not, to death and to decay of faculties and aspirations. There could be no literal permanence for him; he could defy loss and change only in the endurance of his art, of the truth and beauty it embodies. His quest, then, was to maintain the honesty of his poetic vision, to propagate truth as he saw it in order that that truth, at least, might survive. When he could no longer reconcile his ideal of human perfection with that truth, he abandoned Arthur's quest in the name of his own. In a very real sense, Spenser himself is the Knight of Constancy.

NEW YORK UNIVERSITY

1. C. S. Lewis, *English Literature in the Sixteenth Century* (Oxford, 1954), p. 380.

2. Graham Hough, *A Preface to The Faerie Queene* (New York, 1963), pp. 93-94.

3. *Ibid.*, pp. 234-235.

4. *Ibid.*, p. 91.

5. C. S. Lewis, *The Allegory of Love* (New York, 1958), pp. 336-337.

6. Hough, p. 83.

7. Lewis, p. 336.

8. Hough, p. 235.

9. *Ibid.*, p. 235.

Janet Gezari

Borne to Live and Die

Although it may be that Spenser, had he lived longer, would have added to *The Faerie Queene*, the poem which he accomplished is hardly unfinished. Like Mozart's brilliant *Mass in C Minor*, *The Faerie Queene* remains a torso. But both works are whole, although Mozart did not fulfill the requirements his form demanded and Spenser did not complete the task which he set for himself in the letter to Raleigh. It is futile to speculate about what critics would have done had there been no letter, but it is certain that the letter has raised more questions than it answers. A. C. Hamilton's assertion that Spenser "labours to reveal his meaning, not to conceal it"[1] ignores the difference between an ambitious idea and a poetic creation as well as the circumstances of the letter's composition. As Josephine Waters Bennett points out, the letter written in 1590 can hardly be a preliminary sketch of what the poet was planning in 1580. "On the contrary, it is much more probably a piece of apologetics, an attempt to rationalize what was being published and to sketch a plan which, in 1590, seemed to the poet a possible one for the completion of a poem which he had long ago begun, perhaps with very different plans in mind."[2]

We can consider the letter to Raleigh in relation to *The Faerie Queene* only after we have put it in its proper place beside rather than before or behind the poem. Critics have too often treated the letter as a guide to the poem and been dismayed when it led them into the Wood of Error. The letter's two proposals for providing the poem with a narrative unity are an instance of the gap which separates the putative plan from the poem we have. The first, the twelve-day annual feast at Cleopolis which would tie together the quests of the twelve knights, does not find expression in the poem at all. Spenser explains in the letter that he has reserved the introduction of the Faerie Queene and her court for Book XII. The second, Arthur's quest for Gloriana and his role as Magnificence, which embraces the twelve special virtues of the twelve knights, is only imperfectly adumbrated in the poem. Allegorically the letter would indicate that Glory sends out each virtue to be perfected and awaits its return at which time Magnificence and Glory are united.[3]

If we agree with C. S. Lewis that Arthur "explained and united with Gloriana" is the poem's "centre, the seat of its highest life,"[4] we will be disappointed in the poem we have and likely to agree with Lewis that *The Faerie Queene* is a "fragment, hastily sent to press."[5] But the evidence of the poem calls for a different verdict. Arthur's quest for Gloriana, initiated by the dream which Spenser borrowed from Chaucer's tale of Sir Tophas, never becomes more than a device for doing homage to Arthur as the national hero of Britain and therefore the appropriate mate for the Queene of Faery. When we bid him farewell in Book VI Spenser has to remind us that he is "still/On his first quest, in which did him betide/A great aduenture [VI.8.30.7-9]," for he is no nearer the Faerie Queene than he was when we met him in Book I. The poem never makes clear what keeps him from finding Gloriana (since he is already in the Land of Faery) or what several tasks he must complete before he is fully worthy of her. Arthur's regular appearances in times of stress suggest that he is primarily a device to keep the other knights in action rather than a significant character in his own right. Harry Berger sees him as "everyman struggling with sin,"[6] but his antagonists are never as threatening as those of Red

Crosse, and his temptations are not even as convincing as
those of Guyon. Arthur's pursuit of Florimell "in hope to
win thereby/Most goodly meede, the fairest Dame aliue
[III.1.18.7-8]," is problematical. We are later told that

> Oft did he wish, that Lady faire mote bee
> His Faery Queene, for whom he did complaine:
> Or that his Faery Queene were such, as shee:
> And ever hastie Night he blamed bitterlie.
>
> [III.4.54.6-9]

Because Night prevents Arthur from catching up with
Florimell, we never know whether a real woman might claim
the love he has vowed to the woman of his dream. If
Florimell is a temptation, Arthur never has the opportunity
to confront it.

Spenser's intention may have been to allow Arthur to share
in each knight's adventure and so confirm his status as
Magnificence. But Arthur, like the virtue he embodies,
remains a vague idea in the poem. His failure to develop into
its hero contributes to a lack of narrative unity of the sort
that is supplied by Britomart's quest for Artegall in Books
III, IV, and V. We can only conclude that the poet who built
The Faerie Queene did not want to conform to the plans
which the architect of the letter to Raleigh drew for him, or
found it impossible to do so. The letter describes a poem
which we do not have and might not have had, after all, even
if Spenser had lived longer and continued *The Faerie Queene*.

The unity of the poem we have is not narrative but
imaginative. It is the poet's vision which realizes completion
in the course of six books and the Mutabilitie Cantos. This
vision is what Northrop Frye calls the poet's dream of the
"strenuous effort, physical, mental, and moral, of waking up
to one's true humanity."[7] True humanity, in its richest sense,
is the poem's subject and the particular concern of those
books which deal with the virtues of Love and Courtesy. In
order to understand the nature of this humanity and how it

manifests itself, we must explore the world of Spenser's poem.

The world of *The Faerie Queene* includes both Britain and Faery, and the relationship between them is a subtle one. Of the five characters who give their names to the poem's books, Britomart is the only British knight who has been brought up in Britain and the only knight without an assigned quest. She has a very personal mission, and she neither belongs to an organization of knights nor owes allegiance to a ruler. She must find Artegall, marry him, and raise the progeny whose greatest flower will be Elizabeth. Guyon and Calidore are the only knights who are Faeries by birth, but both Red Crosse and Artegall were stolen by Faeries when they were babies. If Faery is, as Berger claims, the world in which Everyman finds his dream,[8] it is difficult to explain the holy hermit's feelings about its inhabitants:

> . . . a Faerie thee vnweeting reft,
> There as thou slepst in tender swadling band,
> And her base Elfin brood there for thee left.
> Such men do Chaungelings call, so chaungd by Faeries theft.
>
> [I.10.65.6-9]

Spenser is, of course, drawing on the folk lore about faeries, but there is a sense in which he seems to agree with the holy man's idea that a knight's real work must be accomplished in the real world, which is Britain. Allegorically, this is particularly applicable to the work of Red Crosse, which is nothing less than the redemption of the fallen world.

If Britain and Faery are different worlds, the one is "mirrored" in the other: "And thou, O fairest Princesse vnder sky," as Spenser addresses Elizabeth,

> In this faire mirrhour maist behold thy face,
> And thine owne realmes in lond of Faery
> And in this antique Image thy great auncestry.
>
> [II.proem.4.6-9]

But although Gloriana functions in the poem as an image of Elizabeth and hence her kingdom is in one way an image of England, Faery has an important role of its own. First, Spenser's assertion that "none, that breatheth liuing aire, does know,/Where is that happy land of Faery [II.proem.1.6-7]" clearly implies that men once did know its whereabouts. Faery is no "painted forgery" but "matter of iust memory [II.proem.1.4-5]." Second, Spenser's enumeration of the various discoveries which have been made in his time serves not only to compliment Elizabeth but also to suggest that men may indeed find Faery sometime in the future. But Faery, unlike Peru and Virginia, can only be found by following "certaine signes" set within Spenser's poem; and the poet states that the man who cannot find Faery must "yield his sence to be too blunt and bace [II.proem.4.2-4]." If we substitute "sensibility" for "sence" we will be closer to Spenser's original meaning. For it is the fallen sensibilities of his age which the poet bemoans. They are manifested in those who "in their frosen hearts" cannot "feele kindly flame [IV.proem.2.2]," for men who "first were framed/Of earthly mould, and form'd of flesh and bone,/Are now transformed into hardest stone [V.proem.2.3-5]." Truth and Justice have given way to deception and ambition. Courtesy has degenerated into "fayned showes. . . ,/Which carry colours faire, that feeble eies misdeeme [VI.proem.4.8-9]."

Spenser's vision of a better world existing both in the past and the future has precedent in classical and Christian thought. The temporal world of the poem extends back to Eden and the Golden Age and Spenser's knights are closer to an uncorrupted era than the men of his own time. Artegall was raised by Astraea, who dwelt on earth during the Golden Age and left when the "world from his perfection fell [V.1.5.6]." It is significant that Virgil's prophecy that she would return and bring the Golden Age again was later interpreted as a prophecy of the Christian redemption through the coming of Mary and Christ. The fact that

Artegall has lived in the world before its corruption and the possibility that the other knights have done so also gives them a special claim to the virtues they embody:

> For that which men then did vertue call,
> Is now cald vice; and that which vice is hight,
> Is now hight vertue, and so vs'd of all:
> Right now is wrong, and wrong that was is right,
> As all things else in time are chaunged quight.
> Ne wonder; for the heauens revolution
> Is wandred farre from where it first was pight,
> And so doe make contrarie constitution
> Of all this lower world, toward his dissolution.
>
> [V.proem.4.1-9]

Spenser's profound dissatisfaction with a world which "growes daily wourse and wourse [V.proem.1.9] " is very much like that of Thenot in the February eclogue of *The Shepheardes Calendar*:

> Must not the world wend in his commun course
> From good to badd, and from badde to worse,
> From worse vnto that is worst of all,
> And then return to his former fall?
>
> [II-14]

Yet Spenser's dissatisfaction with the world is never unmitigated. Just as Thenot's bitterness in the February eclogue is balanced by Cuddie's youthful good humor, Spenser's pessimism in *The Faerie Queene* finds a balance in the Mutabilitie Cantos. They proclaim the "Sabbaoth sight" as the poet surveys the world he has created and declares it good.

Several critics have noted the meaningful arrangement of the six books of *The Faerie Queene*. Although Spenser announces his intention in the letter to Raleigh to deal only with the image of a knight perfected in the private moral virtues, exactly half the poem is concerned with public moral virtues. In addition the virtues stand in a mirror relation to each other: Courtesy, Justice, and Friendship can be seen as the manifestations in society of Holiness, Temperance, and Chastity (true and honorable love) in individuals. More importantly, since Love is the root of all virtue [IV.proem.2.6], and Courtesy involves all the virtues (knowing its part "vnto euery person [IV.10.51.4]"), it is appropriate that the portion of the poem which deals with the private virtues should culminate in Book III and that the poem as a whole should close with Book VI. It is significant that the virtues of Holiness, Temperance, and Justice do not stand alone in the poem. Red Crosse requires the presence of Una, Guyon relies on the Palmer, and Artegall depends heavily on Talus and, to some degree, on Britomart. Only Love and Courtesy can stand alone, and the fact that they are virtues of sensibility makes them central to Spenser's vision of a redeemed humanity.

The mode of Book III is significantly different from that of the first two books of *The Faerie Queene*, for Book III is less an allegory of love than an elaborate exploration of the psychology of love. Its center, the Garden of Adonis, is quite unlike the allegorical centers of Books I and II, the House of Holiness and the House of Alma, in that it does not serve as an object lesson for a knight whose virtue it anatomizes. Instead, the Garden of Adonis sets forth the theme of creative love which is developed throughout Book III, particularly in Britomart's quest for Artegall. This quest does not end with the union of Britomart and her knight but with the noble progeny which Merlin has promised will be the fruit of their marriage.

The chief figure in the Garden is Venus, but it is a Venus who is both wife and mother. When we first meet her, she is distraught over the absence of her son Cupid. In search of him, she has left

> . . . her heauenly hous,
> The house of goodly formes and faire aspects,

> Whence all the world deriues the glorious
> Features of beautie, and all shapes select,
> With which high God his workmanship hath deckt. . . .
> [III.6.12.1-5]

She is "halfe weeping" because she has angered her rebellious child. In his stead she takes Amoret and gives her to Psyche, her daughter-in-law, to be raised in "true femininitee," which Spenser contrasts with Belphoebe's education in "perfect Maydenhed."
The Garden is described as the "first seminarie/Of all things, that are borne to liue and die [III.6.30.4-5]." Like the Bower of Bliss, it is with "pleasures fraught;" but unlike Acrasia's bower, the pleasures are not an end in themselves. Adonis is not only Venus' lover but also the Father of all forms. Venus not only "takes her fill" of his sweetness, but also presides over the Garden itself and as "great mother" often "did lament/The losse of her deare brood, her deare delight [III.6.40.3-4]." The Garden of Adonis is a kind of Eden, graced with "all plentie" and sufficient unto itself. Yet its location is earth, over which Mutabilitie rules, and where death is no stranger. Though there is no need of a "Gardiner to set, or sow,/To plant or prune [III.6.34.1-2]," Time "with his scyth" moves the "flowring herbes and goodly things [III.6.39.3-4] ":

> For all that liues, is subiect to that law:
> All things decay in time, and to their end do draw.
> [III.6.40.8-9]

As a celebration of fertility, the Garden of Adonis has a special relation to Spenser's feelings about poetry. Art, a major feature of the Bower of Bliss, delights but to no good purpose. Acrasia's Bower, with its grapes of "burnisht gold," its "painted flowers," and its ivy of "purest gold," is not unlike the Garden of Proserpina in the Cave of Mammon. The famous golden apples which grow there delight the eyes but do not gratify the stomach. During his three-day tour through Mammon's realms, Guyon feeds his eyes at the expense of sustaining nature, and one of the main facts about the Cave is its perverted use of the raw materials of life.[9] C. S. Lewis underestimates the seriousness of the activity with which Acrasia and Verdant are occupied. The Bower of Bliss violates Nature's first law, which is generation. According to Spenser, it is

> ... the mightie word,
> Which first was spoken by th'Almightie lord,
> That bad them to increase and multiply. . . .
>   [III.6.34.4-6]

There are no children in Acrasia's Bower, and while there is notice of decay [III.12.75], there is no mention of birth. The villains of Book III, Malecasta, Malbecco, and Busirane, are all enemies of creative love. Malecasta, whose name means "badly chaste," is dangerous because the rules of Castle Joyous substitute the law of adultery for the institutions which are the basis for fruitful love. Every knight who has a lady must renounce her with "foule defame" or else fight to prove that she is fairer than Malecasta. His reward for winning that trial by sword is not the right to be true to his lady but the favors of Malecasta. It is Malbecco rather than Hellenore or Paridell who receives Spenser's most serious condemnation. Hellenore and Paridell are unfaithful lovers, but Malbecco is "old, and withered like hay,/Vnfit faire Ladies service to supply [III.9.5.1-2]." Malbecco's love for Hellenore is like his love for money, which he hoards for its beauty rather than its productive value. His jealousy perverts the very life processes which Love affirms, since its only fruits are the grief and horror on which it sustains itself.

Spenser's critics have identified Busirane as Destructive Love, Amour-passion, and Courtly Love. He is each of these to some extent, but an overly allegorical reading makes the

mistake of turning him into something separate from
Amoret's tortured consciousness. He is the embodiment of
her fears, and he is the poem's most diabolical representative
of the forces which oppose creative love. We can best
understand Busirane in terms of what we know of Amoret's
preparation for love in the Garden of Adonis. According to
the explanation of Scudamour's claim to Amoret given in
Book III, he won her love after she had come to Faery court
as the example of "true love alone." It would be difficult to
ascribe sexual fears to a woman who has grown up in a
Garden where

> . . . sweet loue gentle fits emongst them throwes,
> Without fell rancor, or fond gealosie;
> Franckly each paramour his leman knowes,
> Each bird his mate, ne any does enuie,
> Their goodly meriment, and gay felicitie.
>
> [III.6.41.5-9]

She would understand natural love far better than Florimell,
who, having grown up in the court, might have reason to
suspect it. But both have in common a dislike for the
attitudes which belong to the tradition of courtly love.
Florimell gives her love to Marinell, who dwells apart from
society on the rich strand. Amoret promises her love to a
knight of the court, and her problems arise when the
traditions of the court threaten the "lore of love, and goodly
womanhead" which she has learned from Psyche. Amoret's
rebellion against the conventions of courtly love ends in an
emotional crisis from which only Britomart can rescue her.

The players in the Masque of Cupid are activated
Petrarchan metaphors and they belong to a tradition which
sees love as a battle in which the woman often becomes
nothing more than the object of a rigorous siege. The figures
which follow Amoret in the procession are the lover's
ammunition, the threat of Reproach, Repentence, and Shame
if the lady refuses love. The "rude confused rout" which

succeeds them personifies the dangers of consummated love,
for when the lady gives in to her attacker she loses the virtue
which made her so desirable. After the lover's victory, the
lady's worst enemies are yet to be conquered:

> Inconstant *Chaunge*, and false *Disloyaltie*,
> Consuming *Riotise*, and guilty *Dread*
> Of heauenly vengeance, faint *Infirmitie*,
> Vile *Pouertie*, and lastly *Death* with infamie.
>
> [III.12.25.6-9]

Cupid, who surveys "his goodly company" with the pride of
a colonel, gloats over the "spoyle" of this game of war.

To call these figures "phantasies/In wauering wemens wit
[III.12.26.3-4]" is not to detract from the very real terror
they arouse. Rather Spenser is asserting that they have no
reality independent of the minds on which they prey. They
do not belong to the reality of nature but to the reality of
conventions which have captured the minds of a society in
which Courtly Love reigns supreme. Because Amoret under-
stands "true love alone"—that is love undistorted by the
trappings of courtly convention—she is horrified by the
wedding masque which offends neither the guests nor the
groom. That she is "conueyed quite away to liuing wight
vnknowen [IV.1.3.9]" suggests both that she is in an
emotional state beyond their reach and that they are not
even aware of the true meaning of the wedding masque.

Britomart can rescue Amoret for two reasons: she is a
woman and she is outside the conventions of courtly love
(since her goal is married love).[10] Busirane recognizes
Britomart immediately as a dangerous opponent and he
attempts to kill Amoret while there is still time:

> Soone as that virgin knight he saw in place,
>   His wicked bookes in hast he ouerthrew,
>   Not caring his long labours to deface,
>   And fiercely ronning to that Lady trew,

A murdrous knife out of his pocket drew,
The which he thought, for villeinous despight,
In her tormented bodie to embrew. . .

[III.12.32.1-7]

Britomart masters him with ease but not before she has received a wound from his hand. As a woman she is also vulnerable to his abuse. When Amoret is restored to complete health, the richly furnished rooms of Busirane's house disappear and the flames which surround it are quenched. Busirane's power over Amoret's mind is ended but Busirane, like the Blatant Beast, does not die. He remains a potent threat in the world.

The theme of creative love which I have traced in Book III of *The Faerie Queene* emerges in a broader context in Book VI. Calidore takes us into a world of pastoral comedy but it is a world which includes tragedy, as Shakespearian comedy often does. C. S. Lewis sees Book VI as a "grave structural fault" in the poem insofar as it "begins with its loftiest and most solemn book and after a gradual descent, sinks away to its loosest and most idyllic."[11] Lewis' comment on the method of Book VI is justified only in that we are faced with a number of unallegorical or barely allegorical scenes. But Book VI is hardly "loose," and in his return to the genre of *The Shepheardes Calendar* Spenser shows a new maturity and a firm grasp of the issues with which he has been concerned throughout *The Faerie Queene*.

Book VI is a fitting conclusion to the whole of *The Faerie Queene* because Courtesy is the virtue which marks the man who has fully awakened to his own humanity:

. . . they that breake bands of ciuilitie,
And wicked customes make, those doe defame
Both noble armes and gentle curtesie.
No greater shame to man then inhumanitie.

[VI.1.26.6-9]

Spenser tells Calidore's story with a new delicacy of insight.
When Calidore takes Pricilla home to her father the morning
after her rendezvous with Aladine in the woods, he conceives
an elaborate scheme to save her reputation:

> There he arriuing boldly, did present
> The fearefull Lady to her father deare,
> Most perfect pure, and guiltlesse innocent
> Of blame, as he did on his Knighthood sweare,
> Since first he saw her, and did free from feare
> Of a discourteous Knight, who her had reft,
> And by outragious force away did beare.˙...
>   [VI.3.18.1-7]

Calidore does not mind a small lie when it is necessary, for
Courtesy is a virtue of the heart. In this sense it is very
different from Justice, a virtue which even an iron man can
understand. Artegall spends the best part of three cantos
weaving and carding after allowing Radigund to master him
in battle, all because "he his faith had plight,/Her vassall to
become, if she him wonne in fight [V.5.23.8-9]." As a result
of his narrow sense of "justice," Terpine is "full shame-
fully ... hanged by the hed [V.5.18.9]" and Irena almost
dies at the hands of Grandtorto: "For she presuming on th'
appointed tyde," Sir Sergis tells Artegall,

> In which ye promist, as ye were a Knight,
> To meete her at the saluage Ilands syde,
> And then and there for triall of her right
> With her vnrighteous enemy to fight,
> Did thither come, where she afrayd of nought,
> By guilefull treason and by subtill slight
> Surprized was, and to *Grantorto* brought,
> Who her imprisoned hath, and her life often sought.
>   [V.11.39.1-9]

Talus, who makes no pretence to human sentiments, "would
not once assay,/To reskew his owne Lord, but thought it iust

t'obay [V.5.19.8-9]." It takes a more human virtue—Love in the person of Britomart—to release Artegall from the bondage he himself has brought about.

Because the major characters in Book VI are less ideas than human beings, love is more free, affection more open. The reunion of Calidore and Pastorella when he rescues her from captivity is unlike any other meeting between man and woman in the entire poem with the exception, perhaps, of the reunion of Amoret and Scudamour which Spenser chose to omit:

> Ne lesse in hart reioyced *Calidore*,
> When he her found, but like to one distraught
> And robd of reason, towards her him bore,
> A thousand times embrast, and kist a thousand more.
>
> [VI.11.45.6-9]

Knights discard their armor and delight in the company of their ladies in Book VI. Lovers enjoy the "goodly merriment, and gay felicitie" which was Venus' law in the Garden of Adonis. Unfortunately these lovers must live in a world where false knights still envy "francke loves" which should be "free from all gealous spyes." The Blatant Beast appears when the lover thinks himself farthest "from envious eyes that mote him spight [VI.3.20.7]."

It is impossible to read Book VI as Spenser's escape from the turbulence of the real world. Its concerns are no less vast than the relationship between love and duty, virtue and society, man and his world. The two characters who withdraw from the world are admirable because they have earned their respite. The hermit who cures Serena and Timias

> . . . had bene a man of mickle name,
> Renowmed much in armes and derring doe:
> But being aged now and weary to
> Of warres delight, and worlds contentious toyle,
> The name of knighthood he did disauow,

And hanging vp his armes and warlike spoyle,
From all this worlds incombraunce did himself assoyle.
[VI.5.37.3-9]

He offers his patients no easy medicine for their ailments, but
teaches them how to cure themselves by abstinence, restraint,
and openness in all their dealings.
Calidore's decision to rest for a time among the shepherds
reflects a new wisdom. He chooses not to

. . . hunt still after shadowes vaine
Of courtly fauour, fed with light report
Of euery blaste, and sayling alwaies in the port.
[VI.10.2.7-9]

Spenser may compliment Elizabeth by asserting that "Of
Court it seemes, men Courtesie doe call,/For that it there
most vseth to abound [VI.1.1.1-2]," but Calidore must learn
that the courtesy of the court is too often "fayned
showes . . . ,/Which carry colours faire, that feeble eies
misdeeme [VI.proem.4.8-9]." The metaphor of the courtier
as a ship that never leaves port suggests that the court has a
narrowing influence on those who choose its comforts over
the trials of the open sea. Busirane is defeated by Britomart,
who stands outside the traditions of courtly love, and the
Blatant Beast ravages the court but leaves untouched the
shepherd grooms who spend their days carolling of love.
Calidore must, of course, leave Pastorella for his quest, but it
is only after he has armed himself with the shepherd's
immunity that he can confront the Beast and bind him. Sir
Pelleas, Sir Lamoracke, and "all his brethren borne in
Britaine land" cannot manage Calidore's feat.
    The culmination of Calidore's education is his glimpse of
the Graces. They are equally the source of his virtue and of
Colin's inspiration, although only the poet is properly
allowed to see them:

These three on men all gracious gifts bestow,
Which decke the body or adorne the mynde,
To make them louely or well fauoured show,
As comely carriage, entertainement kynde,
Sweete semblaunt, friendly offices that bynde,
And all the complements of curtesie:
They teach vs, how to each degree and kynde
We should our selues demeane, to low, to hie;
To friends, to foes, which skill men call Ciuility.

[VI.10.23.1-9]

Poetry's two-fold obligation to delight and instruct finds its apotheosis in the Dance of the Graces. The dance is at once the image of Spenser's art and the essence of his philosophy of virtue. The nakedness of the Graces teaches the importance of simplicity and truth undistorted by disassemblance and malice. The maiden that shows herself "afore" indicates that "good should from vs goe, then come in greater store [VI.10.24.9]." The whole dance celebrates the mortal woman in whom beauty and virtue are properly combined. And since the Graces are *"Venus* Damzels" and the woman around whom they dance is Colin's own beloved, it is clear that love is both the source of all virtue and the fount of poetic inspiration. Calidore recognizes Colin's role as teacher and has "no will away to fare,/But wisht, that with that shepheard he mote dwelling share [VI.10.30.8-9]." But Calidore must return to his love in order to put Colin's teaching in practice.

At the end of our journey through the world of *The Faerie Queene*, we can see that the arrangement of the six books is hardly haphazard. Love is where it belongs, in the very center of a poem which turns about it just as the Graces turn about the poet's human love. And as Love's noblest fruit, Courtesy has its proper place at the poem's end. It remains to consider the way in which the Mutabilitie Cantos bear on Spenser's vision of true humanity—for these Cantos take us out of the realm of man and into the very councils of the gods.

In the context of the Cantos themselves, the gods are
arguing over who should rule the empire of the heavens. In
the context of the poem as a whole, the Cantos provide an
explanation for change in a universe which yet perserves the
security of a benign order. Mutabilitie's evidence for her right
to rule cannot be contradicted:

> Ne shee the lawes of Nature onely brake,
>> But eke of Iustice, and of Policie;
>> And wrong of right, and bad of good did make,
>> And death for life exchanged foolishlie:
>> Since which, all liuing wights haue learn'd to die,
>> And all this world is woxen daily worse.
>
> [VII.6.6.1-6]

Indeed Spenser affirms the truth of her charges in the proem
to Book V and in Canto 8 of Book IV. Even the Garden of
Adonis was not immune to time's ravages. But just as
Calidore gains his mature perspective on the world by
withdrawing from it, Spenser achieves a final perspective by
soaring above it. In the course of the poem's six books, the
universal law that "all things . . . are borne to live and die"
receives ample confirmation. But the law of Mutabilitie has a
corollary in progress, and Nature can assert that this progress
towards perfection is in fact the chief law of the universe. All
things

> . . . their being doe dilate:
>> And turning to themselues at length againe,
>> Doe worke their owne perfection so by fate:
>> Then ouer them Change doth not rule and raigne;
> But they raigne ouer change, and doe their states
>> maintaine.
>
> [VII.7.58.5-9]

She confirms Spenser's belief that the better world of the
past shall be reborn in the future:

> But time shall come that all shall changed bee,
> And from thenceforth, none no more change shall see.
> [VII.7.59.4-5]

Nature's speech is a fitting epilogue to a poem which celebrates an antique age. For Spenser's dissatisfaction with his own world does not end with nostalgia for the past but with a vision of and for the future.

CONNECTICUT COLLEGE

1. A. C. Hamilton, *The Structure of Allegory in The Faerie Queene* (Oxford, 1961), p. 12.

2. Josephine Waters Bennett, *The Evolution of The Faerie Queene* (New York, 1960), p. 3.

3. Thomas P. Roche, *The Kindly Flame: a Study of the Third and Fourth Books of Spenser's Faerie Queene* (Princeton, 1964), p. 50.

4. C. S. Lewis, *The Allegory of Love: a Study in Medieval Tradition* (Oxford, 1958), p. 337.

5. *Ibid.*, p. 334.

6. Harry Berger, Jr., *The Allegorical Temper: Vision and Reality in Book II of Spenser's Faerie Queene* (New Haven, 1957), p. 170.

7. Northrop Frye, "The Structure of Imagery in *The Faerie Queene*," *Fables of Identity: Studies in Poetic Mythology* (New York, 1963), p. 73.

8. Berger, p. 168.

9. *Ibid.*, pp. 23-25.

10. Lewis, p. 344.

11. *Ibid.*, p. 53.

Gerald Grow

Form or Process?

We commonly think of literature as form. But perhaps it is more process than form. Consider a tree. It is not so much a form of *being* as a pattern of *responses* derived from the seed. So human life is not so much the filling up of an empty mold as it is a set of activities which, through repeating certain basic processes—a basic way of dealing with experience which we call "self"—arrives at what, in retrospect, looks like "form." *The Faerie Queene* takes much of its form, similarly, from its processes, and not vice-versa. A tree "is" a certain way of responding to light and soil and water and air, a certain angle the buds take as they come off the branch, a certain series of activities that occur in the leaf, a continual forming of its being. And, at the same time, a tree is always a tree. It has at once full being and constant becoming. A hundred-year-old oak is not more a tree than a seedling is. So *The Faerie Queene* is a complete poem as a tree is a complete tree. Like a tree, *The Faerie Queene* is unfinished but complete. Indeed, according to one wag, Spenser's poem is not only complete, but it also contains five-and-a-half superfluous books. It has established—by the first book—its essential *process* of identity, its basic *activity* of form-ing. It is itself, whole, perfect, absolute. Yet, like a tree, it is constantly in process, constantly changing, growing, expanding into its furthermost reaches, stretching out as far as its massive branches can hold their own weight. Arguments about the completeness of *The Faerie Queene* are senseless. We would do much better to concentrate on its activity as a poem. *The Faerie Queene* is as complete as the beech tree outside my window. The techniques Spenser uses and the progressive range of material he covers expand together in a balance between the fixed, determined form inherent in the seed, and the wayward, accidental development dependent on sun and wind, on characters and historical parallels and poetic movement. The rigidity of the overall framework is balanced by the fluidity of movement within it. The firm unity of moral assertion is balanced by the wide range of human activity covered. The strict movement toward a conclusion of the quest is, even in Book I, modified into unpredictable directions—such as the consideration of pagan heroism and the descent into the underworld. The reasonable Aristotelian virtues are balanced by the non-finite Christian virtues. Temperance is balanced by Charity. Charity, in turn, is channeled through the structures of friendship and marriage and society. This balance is expressed in the very stanza itself, which, within invariably rigid rhyme and meter, slides into a characteristic wandering, expanding movement. The reasonable, planned Aristotelian structure is balanced by the diffuse, eccentric Romantic character of the poem. *The Faerie Queene* branches like any good tree into whatever direction will nourish it, while keeping its basic pattern of growth which makes it recognizable—even miles away—as an oak.

In thinking of people, we too often think of them as having "character" as if it were a thing: a solid, palpable form, like a manner of dress, a suit of armor, a formula in the head. But people are less "character" than they are patterns of action and response. We recognize people by their characteristic ways of dealing with experience. That is what makes us what we are. One man may tackle frustration with

energy and gusto, while another whimpers in defeat. A
woman might only fall in love with men who will be cruel to
her, so she can subsequently revolt and start all over again.
We all live by such processes of action, like Satan's
characteristic rhythm in *Paradise Lost*: transmuting loss and
confusion into hard, narrow, self-centered paradox, such as
"Evil be thou my Good."

  The Faerie Queene is more likely a series of processes of
this kind, a complex of rhythms, than an attempt to fill out
form. It is more like a fugue than a sonata. The lines of its
movement build upon one another, and its chord progres-
sions build up from the internal themes, so that, while the
whole has a unity, it is the unity of development, not the
unity of external form. *The Faerie Queene* is more likely to be
modular than structural. I suspect it is built upon a certain
very complex but whole vision, which is repeated through all
the parts, like a modular form in architecture or in the
cell—repeated again and again to make up the shape of a
building or organism. The poem as we have it is not like an
uncompleted building—for there is no steel framework
sticking up, no empty scaffolding, no naked girders. Everything that is there is whole and complete. It is more like a
tree—stopped in full growth, just beginning to put out its
fullest fruits—the Mutabilitie Cantos—but never reaching an
absolute form that can be called finished. Perhaps we are
lucky Spenser did not complete *The Faerie Queene*. If he
had, we might not find it so fascinating. We might find
ourselves lulled into complacency by a fullness of form—as in
Paradise Lost—so that we overlook the radical humanity of
its activity.

  The Faerie Queene is a little like a comic strip. At any
given time, it could be stopped, and its fundamental
vision—or lack of it—would be apparent. But it can also go on
and on, transmuting the world according to its particular
characters, situations, and conflicts, digesting the cosmos into
a constant battle between Krazy Kat and Ignatz Mouse—in a

sort of divine *elevatio ad absurdum.* Once you have seen a few Krazy Kat strips, you have tasted their essential wisdom, but it is profound enough to hold you again and again. *The Faerie Queene,* far more profound (and far less funny), has an essential wisdom found not in its conclusions, its form, nor its shape, but in its processes, its forming, its rhythms, its shapings of reality. It is one of the limitations of the human mind that we try to blueprint everything—make maps of experience and impose onto life a definite form, give an architecture to our becomings. We are all Platonic, mooning over unattainable forms. But it is the process of living that makes life, it is the process of creating that makes creation. It is the activity of thinking, reading, shaping, concluding, qualifying, analyzing, synthesizing—above all—just *responding* that *makes The Faerie Queene,* or any work of art—and not some absolute ideal form or completeness. There is a certain timidity and fear in our constant search for the reassurance of ultimate form. We are distressed and challenged by organic energy working through its own impulse toward organic form. Spenser's visible design is no sooner perceived than dismissed. The organic, unpredictable element in *The Faerie Queene* is what keeps returning to haunt us on unexpected midnights.

"Every poem must necessarily be a perfect unity," Blake said. And so is every work of art. I would only add: stress the work less and the *working* more. Search for final form in *The Faerie Queene* may be only another way of avoiding the task of responding step by step to its innermost processes, without guide, without goal, and without conclusion. I personally suspect the finished poem would have retained this quality, as *Paradise Lost* does. Spenser is not giving us conclusions, but *experience.* We are more likely to appreciate the poem if we hold off analyzing its gross features of comparative anatomy and immerse ourselves in its very genetic processes, that long twisted stanza that is the DNA of Spenser's verse, and those allegorical creatures that are its

organs. Most poems give us a polished surface, and we rarely
go beyond skin-deep. In *The Faerie Queene* we are forced,
and privileged, to live in the perplexing heartbeat of the
poem's immediate flow.

SAN FRANCISCO STATE COLLEGE

Jean McMahon Humez

"This Richly Patterned Page"

We can compare The Faerie Queene *to a page of medieval illumination, which exhibits a harmonious texture, bright and delicate detail everywhere, many individual miniatures which must be looked at separately—but no very striking general design, and what there is contributes little to the effect of the whole. The unfinished state of the poem therefore matters less than it might. It is a misfortune that half of this richly patterned page is missing; but what is left retains its full vitality.*[1]

Two influential critical introductions to *The Faerie Queene* propose and answer, from different premises and with contrasting results, a perennial problem that troubles each new generation of Spenser's readers: whether the expanse of poetry known as *The Faerie Queene* can be felt and evaluated as a single complete poem.

C. S. Lewis takes the position that the poem is both unfinished (i.e., that it represents only a part of Spenser's design) and incomplete (that it arouses certain expectations in the reader, which it then fails to fulfill). Beginning with his own perception of the poem's strategy, Lewis describes the more important kind of incompletion:

Spenser's whole method is such that we have a very dim perception of his characters until we meet them or their archetypes at the great allegorical centres of each book. . . . Spenser must have intended a final book on Arthur and Gloriana which would have stood to the whole poem as such central or focal cantoes stand to their several books. . . . The poem is not finished. It is a poem of a kind that loses more than most by being unfinished. Its centre, the seat of its highest life, is missing.[2]

Again, in his discussion of Book VI, Lewis asks us to set aside a potential objection to the sequential effects of the six books as we have them, on the grounds that the work is, after all, "unfinished." If the poem had been brought to completion, the argument runs, the desired structure would surely have been supplied.[3] Finally, when Lewis comments on the Mutabilitie Cantos—which he admires greatly—he frankly invites us to value, as he does, an imagined "finished" *Faerie Queene* more highly than the unperfected work before us:

Such poetry, coming at the very end of six books, serves to remind us that the existing *Faerie Queene* is unfinished, and that the poet broke off, perhaps, with many of his greatest triumphs still ahead. Our loss is incalculable; at least as great as that we sustained by the early death of Keats.[4]

Though Lewis is less guarded in his expression of this view than a student of Spenser would be today, the potential *Faerie Queene* imagined by Lewis may still have a secret life. If so, it may be valuable to ask again how Lewis knows that the poem is incomplete, that it is without "its centre, the seat of its highest life."

Spenser's much-discussed letter to Raleigh is the external evidence that the poet at one time planned a work of much greater size than the one he has left us. It seems to show that Prince Arthur was conceived to be the focal character of the fiction, at least at the moment when the letter was written, just prior to the publication of the first three books in 1590. The poem's chosen subject, Spenser writes to Raleigh, is "the historye of king Arthure," and the projected treatment of the subject is compared with the Homeric and Virgilian treatments of major characters.

> By ensample of which excellent Poets, I labour to pourtraict in Arthure, before he was king, the image of a brave knight, perfected in the twelue private moral virtues, as Artistotle hath deuised.

"For the more variety of the history," moreover, the present poet has created a patron knight for each of the twelve virtues. Arthur will enter each of the twelve books to enact those deeds "most applyable to that vertue." As the twelfth book, Spenser will set forth the twelve days of the Faerie Queene's annual feast, which was the chronological beginning of all the action in the poem.

The letter does not mention the need for a separate book on Arthur. Indeed, since Arthur's virtue is said to comprise all the twelve "priuate morall vertues," the implication is that his adventures are most properly to be distributed evenly throughout the twelve books. It is by no means clear from the letter that the quest of the twelfth knight was to have shared the twelfth book with the Annual Feast scene at the Faerie Queene's court. Yet if we do not suppose such a sharing, we then must choose between thirteen books and eleven quests by knights of private virtues, always excluding Arthur's comprehensive Magnificence—and both choices contradict the statements of the letter explicitly.[5]

Even ignoring the numerical difficulties, and allowing ourselves to assume that in 1589 Spenser planned to write a "last" book,

> where I deuise that the Faery Queene kept her Annuall
> feaste xii. dayes, vppon which xii, seuerall dayes, the
> occasions of the xii. seuerall knights, are in these xii
> books seuerally handled and discoursed

it would still be difficult to see in this imagined book Lewis'
missing "allegorical centre, the union of Arthur and
Gloriana."[6] Arthur could not appear at the Annual Feast
where the quests are assigned without drastic revision of the
poem we have, since he has not found Cleopolis even
afterwards, during the performance of the quests assigned at
the Feast. We could imagine, if we wished, that this "last"
book might have begun with a second Annual Feast, where
the knights would have gathered to report on their quests.
Within this framework extensive flashbacks to the earlier
Feast would be possible. We can readily imagine that the
knight of the last quest might bring Arthur back with him to
Cleopolis, after having made use of the Prince's services in
fulfilling his assigned task. In this hypothetical scheme, for
which the letter gives no evidence, we can invent a plausible
meeting of Arthur and Gloriana at Cleopolis.

Since we have already come so far as the path of pure
speculation, it should be remembered that many other
courses, equally plausible or implausible, are not directly
contradicted by the plan sketched in the letter. If Spenser
had lived long enough, and had found that the first twelve
books of the poem were "well accepted," he might, in his
own words to Raleigh, have been "encouraged, to frame the
other part of polliticke vertues in his person, after that hee
came to be king." In this case, perhaps the climactic meeting
of Prince Arthur and Gloriana would have been deferred to
the end of the twenty-fourth book, in the interest of keeping
Faeryland and Britain parallel but separate kingdoms.

Yet, having allowed Lewis that a meeting of Arthur and
Gloriana is conceivable, we could argue, from the six books
we have, that such a meeting would add little to what is
already embodied in the Arthur-Gloriana situation, and

instead lead Spenser into great difficulties. How, for example, would he have tactfully resolved the erotic content of Arthur's quest for Gloriana, explicit enough in the existing description of Arthur's dream-vision?

> For-wearied with my sports, I did alight
> From loftie steed, and down to sleepe me layd;
> The verdant gras my couch did goodly dight,
> And pillow was my helmet faire displayd:
> Whiles euery sence the humour sweet embayd,
> And slombring soft my hart did steale away,
> Me seemed, by my side a royall Mayd
> Her daintie limbes full softly down did lay:
> So faire a creature yet saw neuer sunny day.
>
> Most goodly glee and louely blandishment
> She to me made, and bad me loue her deare,
> For dearely sure her loue was to me bent,
> As when iust time expired should appeare.
> But whether dreames delude, or true it were,
> Was neuer hart so rauisht with delight,
> Ne liuing man like words did euer heare,
> As she to me deliuered all that night;
> And at her parting said, She Queene of Faeries hight.
>
> [I.9.13-14)

The dream-Gloriana here promises that "when iust time expired" she will show Arthur certainly how her love is "bent" to him, and by this Spenser does seem to promise their eventual union, at least in a spiritual sense if not in the physical union of marriage. Such a marriage would make the parallel genealogies of the Briton and Faerie ruling dynasties intersect in an alarming fashion, and would perhaps directly involve Spenser in contradicting the extant Arthurian mythology, rather than (as now) in supplementing that mythology with material invented to deal with the years "before he was king." It seems unlikely, then, that the poet intended to let

the question of marriage, and consequent merger of kingdoms, come up at all; that if Arthur was to have found
Cleopolis and Gloriana, he was also to have returned to rule
the parallel kingdom, perhaps still in the spiritual "service" of
Gloriana. Most probably Spenser would have done after
twelve books something like what he has done after six—that
is, left the outcome of Arthur's search for the living Gloriana
indeterminate. Only in this way, perhaps, could he have
avoided answering the question raised by his own fiction:
whether the Faerie representative of England's Virgin Queen
had actually, through some enchantment, sent that dream of
herself to spend the night on the grass with the Prince, in
order to woo him into the service of her ideal moral realm.

The indeterminancy of Arthur's search for Cleopolis does
not seriously interfere with the communication of the
thematic significance of the Arthur-Gloriana threading of the
narrative, such as it is. Though Lewis looks to his hypothetical last book for an explanation of such questions as arise
when Arthur rescues the Red Crosse Knight, it seems only
fair to let the problem of defining Arthur's virtue, which is
created by the letter, be solved by the letter. Thus Lewis
objects,

> If Arthur is Aristotelian 'Magnanimity,' in search of
> earthly glory, his deliverance of St. George is arrant
> nonsense. 'Magnanimity,' in this sense, cannot come to
> the rescue of Holiness; for whatever in the pagan
> character of the *megalopsychos* is not sin, belongs
> already to the Saint. And the error is one which Spenser
> is the least likely of all poets to have committed: distrust
> of 'the World' and worldly ambition, even to a fault, is
> the essence of the man.[7]

To this somewhat dogmatic objection, without involving
Aristotle, Spenser's own formulation makes a clear enough
response: "I labour to pourtraict in Arthure, before he was
king, the image of a brave knight, perfected in the twelve
priuate morall vertues." Evidently Holinesse is conceived as

one of the virtues "perfected" or contained in what Spenser calls "magnificence." Why then should not a questing and imperilled abstract Holinesse, temporarily in the dungeon of spiritual pride, be rescued by the perfected Holinesse that resides in Arthur's Magnificence?

Arthur appears in each of the six books we have, and his deeds on behalf of the various Faerie Knights may be variously interpreted, without recourse to the letter, as an accumulating revelation of his versatile heroism and complicated prowess. His search for Gloriana need not be read so flatly as a form of "wordly ambition." After Arthur has recounted his dream of Gloriana to Una, we are specifically told through the judgment of Una—a relatively unimpeachable source—that Arthur has no desire to conquer or possess her (allegorically "to win or gain glory" in the eyes of the world), but only to serve her interests, the way a lover smitten with a lady's beauty would do:

> O happy Queene of Faeries, that hast found
> Mongst many, one that with his prowesse may
> Defend thine honour, and thy foes confound:
> True Loues are often sown, but seldom grow on ground.
> [I.9.16.6-9]

The poem tells us, then, what the relationship of this Glory to this Magnificence is to be—the queen of the realm embodies the glory of the realm, and is served by the united virtues of the private subject, which on the narrative level are embodied in the prowess of Arthur "before he was king." By coming to the aid of Gloriana's knights, the Prince is already serving the highest earthly form of Glory in every book. So far as the allegorical usefulness of the Arthur-Gloriana situation goes, then, the meeting is irrelevant. The difference for the plot would be slight as well: Arthur would afterwards have the consoling knowledge, as a faithful lover, that his service is known and accepted by his lady-liege. But again, since such acceptance in the romance terms of the narrative would most naturally be represented in Gloriana's gift of herself, it is clearly in the best interests both of allegory and narrative plotting to keep Arthur and Gloriana apart.

Graham Hough approaches the reconcilement of the letter with the poem from the other direction, arguing that the first three books of the poem came first, and that the slippery plan in the letter was devised to impose a single coherent subject on an already "multiple scheme," with Arthur chosen as the vehicle of that desired sense of unity. For Hough Arthur's "position in the scheme is never more than half-heartedly worked out":

> As a unifying factor he is of no effect whatever on the poem as we have it, though he might have acquired a retrospective importance by the time we arrived at the Faerie Queene's court at the end, where doubtless he would have been finally united to her.[8]

Hough proposes that we assume that the plan outlined in the letter "would never have become the real structural principle of *The Faerie Queene*,[9] thus freeing us from the necessity of missing that ephemeral final book on Arthur and Gloriana. At the same time he locates what Lewis calls "the seat of its highest life" elsewhere. We should not have done justice by Lewis' candid and intelligent dissatisfaction with the poetry, however, without discussing briefly his internal evidence for its fatal incompletion. The letter merely confirms, by suggesting that the poem was incomplete by Spenser's own standards, what Lewis finds in reading the poem itself, that it finally leaves us with major promises broken.

From an analysis of Spenser's "method" in the single books, Lewis infers that an analogical method of organization characterizes the overall structure—or would have character-ized it when the poem should have been finished. Thus on the level of the single book, the "method" is to have

> an allegorical core, surrounded by a margin of what is called 'romance of types,' and relieved by episodes of pure fantasy. Like a true Platonist, he shows us the

Form of the virtue he is studying not only in its transcendental unity (which comes at the allegorical core of the book) but also 'becoming Many in the World of phenomena.'[10]

If we correctly take "core" to refer to "content," and "centre" to "locus," there would presumably still be substantial agreement among students of Spenser that each book of *The Faerie Queene* does indeed have (or very nearly has) a single, highly allegorical scene which serves positively to define the nature of the Book's controlling virtue. Nor would there be much dispute as to which scenes these are, perhaps: The House of Holinesse (I), The House of Alma (II), The Garden of Adonis (III), The Temple of Venus (IV), Mount Acidale (VI). In the case of Book V, it might be questioned whether the positive allegorical center should be located at Mercilla's Court[11] or in Isis' Church—neither scene, perhaps, does for the virtue of Justice what the other allegorical centers do for their virtues.

Once we have questioned the idea that each allegorical center fits its book in the same way—as we begin to do the moment Book V breaks Lewis' pattern—the clarity of the pattern itself begins to fade. If Spenser had approached composition in the way Lewis' description implies—writing an "allegorical core" first, and then "draping the rest round" it, or at any rate methodically intent upon the single scene that sets the virtue forth in its "transcendental unity"—then why choose the Temple of Venus as the heart of a book about Friendship? Obviously even the central allegorical scenes, if we still agree that this is what they are, in all the books but V differ in kind and in degree of centrality. The Dance of the Graces on Mount Acidale does not really tell us so much about what Courtesy or Civility is, as where it comes from and what it feels like; and though the scene is indisputably "central" in some way both for the reader and, we may guess, the poet, it is by no stretch of the imagination as allegorical as Mirabella's train, nor does it illuminate the quality of Courtesy in a positive way nearly so well as the actions of Turpine, Crudor, Blandina and the Brigands do by negation. On the other hand, if we did not have the Garden of Adonis in Book III, our notion of the virtue of Chastity would be radically wrong, composed only of Florimell fleeing, Amoret undergoing torture at the hands of Busirane, and Britomart fiercely unhorsing every knight that crosses her path. The Garden of Adonis makes the startling connection of Chastity with the generative aim of sexuality, opposing the fertility of natural love to the sterile sensuality in the Bower of Bliss. The scene allies itself, through the identification of Venus and innocent love, to the Temple of Venus in Book IV, making the allegorical "cores" of Books III and IV as difficult to discuss or understand separately as the narrative events in the two books. Yet the House of Holinesse and the House of Alma are significant places without reference to any other books of the poem; and perhaps each is exhausted of its usefulness when we have considered its relationship to the discrete book in which it occurs.

Lewis may have wanted to find a single "allegorical centre" to the whole poem because he had already found such a center to each book. It would be intensely gratifying if the macrocosm were to reflect the microcosm so sharply. The method Lewis saw in *The Faerie Queene* has illuminated the poem for countless readers, yet other descriptions of its workings are possible. It would be particularly desirable to find one that can restore the existing *Faerie Queene*, rather than its twelve- or twenty-four-book counterpart in our imaginations, to the center of value.

As indicated above, Hough takes the view that the "concern over construction" shown by Spenser's letter to Raleigh is relevant only "formally and externally to the kind

that Spenser believes himself to be practising, but not to the
real nature of his work."[12] Admitting that the poem is
probably unfinished in some trivial, historical sense, Hough
suggests that its readers nevertheless "feel it as a whole,"[13]
and gives a summary of its book-by-book thematic patterning
that is perhaps as sympathetic and skillful a description of
the "organic" unity of the public poem as we have.

> It begins with the book of Holinesse, because for
> Spenser this is the necessary ground of all human
> development. . . . Spenser's placing of it as he does
> corresponds to the Protestant theology of prevenient
> grace—without it all other activity is worthless. Next
> comes Temperance, as the first condition of any possible
> integrity. . . . These books are self-contained, complete
> within themselves . . . yet they are in a sense preliminary
> to Spenser's main preoccupations.

> Then we have Books III and IV, called the legends of
> Chastity and Friendship, but really to be taken together
> as the poem's great central area, concerned with Love.
> . . . The celebration of Love, the distinction of its
> different tempers and varieties, the portrayal of the
> conditions which foster it, and of its enemies in the
> heart and in the outer world—it is this that forms the
> main substance of *The Faerie Queene*. . . . Love is the
> active source of value.[14]

In the fifth book, Hough, like Lewis, finds the representation
of Justice inadequate, "the only grave fault" in the poem,
though he can still justify the place of the virtue in the
growing pattern ("Since man is a political animal, the force
of concord must be prolonged into the social and political
sphere").[15] The book of Courtesy, in his view, seems "the
final enhancement of a spontaneous natural grace." Though
Hough evidently finds Book VI attractive, he implies that it is
less than thematically climactic, almost a delightful super-

fluity. By the end of Book V, "the main lines of Spenser's view of life are laid down."[16]

If we were to follow Hough's lead in expressing a somewhat subjective sense of the relationship among the virtues of the six books, the only major addition, perhaps, would be in observing the implicit relationship between Justice and Courtesy. If, as he says, the first two books are about the constitution of the individual soul, and its primary dependency on God; and if the second two books consider the potential harmony of two such souls in union (particularly through love that leads to marriage); then the final pair seem to be about the foundations of the next largest human union, the social contract, with Courtesy perhaps taking over the adumbrated role of Mercy from Book V.

As Hough's reading indicates, the theme of Love (most notably romantic or heterosexual love, but also the kinds of loving represented in Concord, Civility, Courtesy, and to a lesser extent, even Friendship) does indeed make itself felt as the major subject of the poem. It is not only the explicit, thematic concern of Books III and IV, but is also the appropriate narrative metaphor for assembling other thematic structures as well. I am of course thinking of the way an emotional attraction between two characters of thematic significance arouses our expectations of the union of their corresponding values, as in the betrothal of Una and St. George, or in the foreseen marriage of Britomart and Artegall.

In this context it is interesting to notice that Book II, the Legend of Temperance, is the only book of the six which does not make use of the love-betrothal-marriage narrative metaphor to bring about an important thematic union. Undoubtedly this is because of the self-sufficient, even distinctly standoffish, nature of the virtue of Temperance itself, as Spenser conceives it. Guyon skillfully resists temptation, mediates between extremes, defeats and destroys dangerous excesses, aided only by the Palmer and by Prince Arthur, but never strengthened or weakened by a lady-love—

though he is said to have a lady somewhere, we never learn more of her. There are evident difficulties, of course, in dramatizing within the romance conventions the love affair of the champion of Temperance. In Book II, Alma, the soul, is a "virgin bright,"

> That had not yet felt *Cupides* wanton rage,
> Yet she was woo'd of many a gentle knight,
> And many a Lord of noble parentage,
> That sought with her to lincke in marriage.
>
> [II.9.18.2-5]

This passage suggests that if Alma had been a character in any other book of the poem, we might have had her wedding to a knight representing something like Love of God, or Charity. But it is her role, in this book, as the sober governess of the body, that requires that we meet her in the virgin state.

Though the Medina of Book II bears some relation to Concord (whom we meet in the Temple of Venus making peace between the brothers Love and Hate), the narrative metaphor used to express the essential operations both of Medina and Concord is peace-making. The reconciliation of two opposed parties, representing principles which are eternally opposed, might seem a less powerful dramatic action than the betrothals and promised weddings and procreation of the characters in the other books. Yet it is notable that in this book of mediation and compromise, the Golden Mean can appeal to Concord as a higher power:

> But louely concord, and most sacred peace
>   Doth nourish vertue, and fast friendship breeds;
>   Weake she makes strong, and strong thing does
>   increace,
>   Til it the pitch of highest prayse exceeds:
>   Braue be her warres, and honorable deeds,
>   By which she triumphes ouer ire and pride,
>   And winnes an Oliue girlond for her meeds:
>
> [II.2.31.1-7]

The Concord described by Medina at this juncture is recognizable as simply Peace (the warrior against the causes of war, as line 5 tells us). But when we meet Concord herself in the Temple of Venus, she is clearly Spenser's *Natura*, a cosmic power representing the principles ordained by God to govern the physical world:

> By her the heauen is in his course contained,
>   And all the world in state vnmoued stands,
>   As their Almightie maker first ordained,
>   And bound them with inuiolable bands;
>   Else would the waters ouerflow the lands,
>   And fire deuoure the ayre, and hell them quight,
>   But that she holds them with her blessed hands.
>   She is the nourse of pleasure and delight,
>   And vnto *Venus* grace the gate doth open right.
>
>   [IV.10.35]

Therefore, although Book II makes no explicit use of love as the narrative equivalent of the fusion of separate values into some transcendental unity, perhaps it argues implicitly that the separateness and indeed opposed natures of elemental things in the created order gives stability to the pattern, and even special value to the instances of fusion that can occur. If Concord personifies the "inuiolable bands" of Nature, she opens the gate to Venus's grace precisely because sexual union depends upon the initial and continuing separation of male and female. Obviously if the sexes were not distinguished and even opposed, like warring elements, in Nature, the mystery of their impulse toward union would not exist, and could not be Spenser's most useful mirror for other, invisible unions.

But these considerations do not really arise within Book II itself. There we have no heterosexual love as a narrative metaphor. Moreover, since the Palmer's advisory role seems to represent accurately the frequently unattractive promptings of Reason, we do not even have a vivid friendship on the narrative level to suggest the perpetual importance of self-transcending, personal alliance. Hough is undoubtedly right, then, in taking Book II to establish prerequisite moral integrity for the intensely isolated individual. Though we will feel Spenser's Temperance, or Self-Discipline, to be a minor virtue at best (when compared with Holinesse or with his peculiarly untranslatable Chastity), and a negative virtue even among the minor ones (in contrast, for example, to Courtesy), it is useful to remember that Temperance is "government" of the minor and potentially negative parts of the Christian man—the vegetable and animal aspects of his mixed being. If in the context of the resources of the spirit, the human body is seen as corruptible and corrupting, then an absolutist and heroic champion of its government would no doubt strike us as a curious failure in decorum. The Book suggests that if we concern ourselves with the demands and frailties of the body alone, our sphere of reality will be as limited and negative as are Guyon's actions.

Finally, as Hough's reading of the thematic development in the six books indicates, we are asked to take Book II together with Book I, as paired images of the spiritual and bodily houses put in order, and put into right relation. Our sense of the right relation between the two houses of the individual being thus delineated will be the foundation for understanding one of the poem's central distinctions: that between healthy, fertile, and innocent heterosexual love and its sterile, false, and inverted parodies. To understand the origins of the multiple imitations of love we will encounter in the remaining four books, we need Book II.

This is particularly true since Spenser's method is often to make the negative concrete and multiple, and the positive single and abstract. The ideal love which we are to suppose is planted and nurtured in the Gardens of Adonis, and won in the Temple of Venus, after all, has no single embodiment in the narrative level. All of the love relationships pictured in action demand the redress of some more or less serious failures in self-government, by at least one of the parties,

before Spenser will award them consummation. And the
consummations are typically deferred, for one reason or
another, to a future not within the scope of the poem: St.
George has six more years of service to Gloriana before his
marriage can take place; Britomart and Artegall separate
twice, to perform different tasks, and during the latter
separation Spenser leaves them; Amoret and Scudamour were
to be reunited in the 1590 version of Book III, but were
deprived of this consummation when Books IV-VI were
added; Calidore leaves Pastorella with her parents; and, again,
Arthur does not meet Gloriana in person within the poem.

If we are attempting, with Hough, to evaluate the
significance of the six books we have, it will not be sufficient
to explain all these unconsummated unions by inventing a
future Book full of marriages. We can only assume from the
pattern before us that the poem promises eventual union, but
is unwilling to imply that union of this sort is available here
and now, visibly, perfectly, comprehensibly. We might even
feel that the incompletion of all the major love-narratives is
actually one of the more positive and significant aspects of
their metaphoric function. Without the often oppressive
sense of the limitations of the flesh and of wordly enter-
prises, which is so strong in Book II, we would be in danger
of dismissing the fact that even the positive love-relationships
of the poem are left imperfect and unconsummated—we
might say that the pattern was "merely" required by the
romance conventions, or that it is an accident reflecting the
poem's fragmentary condition. When we take Book II into
account, however, the pattern makes considerable metaphoric sense.

Hough and Lewis, along with many other good readers of
Spenser, find it necessary to apologize for the failures of
Book V. Hough's statement of the poem's "organic"
thematic unity pauses frankly to admit that the Book does
not accomplish in fact what it means to accomplish. It has

long been a staple, even a commonplace, of Spenser criticism to observe that the vision of Justice is a severe and uncongenial one, especially to the modern reader who finds that his own egalitarian political prejudices differ greatly from Spenser's (presumed) hardnosed Elizabethan assumptions. There are signs that a thaw in the relations between critics and Book V is in progress.[17] And Book V is of particular importance if we are interested in the operations of the love-situation in the narrative as a metaphor for what we have been calling, somewhat too loosely perhaps, "thematic fusions." This is so because in Book V Spenser gives us, most compactly and at the same time most ambiguously, in the Britomart-Artegall-Radigund triangle, an explicit contrast between "right" and "wrong" male-female power relationships. Like Book II, Book V has suffered neglect for the comparative unattractiveness of its hero and its virtue. Yet if a case is to be made for an integration of the themes of the six-book *Faerie Queene*, with Love as its central subject, there is a clear need for discussion of what this book has to do with the subject.

Justice, we have assumed above, is concerned with the viability of a social contract, or with the possibility of harmonizing the conflicting demands of individuals when more than two individuals are involved. Though acts of justice are clearly related to acts of temperance, since each virtue is governmental, regulative, and by definition requires as much denial as assent, the champion of Justice immediately differs from Guyon in having a love-relationship which not only does not interfere with his virtue, but actually redefines it when its initial definition proves inadequate.

If *The Faerie Queene* can be said to have a central character, it is not Arthur nor the invisible Gloriana, but Britomart. She is the heroine of what Hough has called "the poem's great central area," Books III and IV, and it is therefore of immense interest that in Book V she should split in two, or meet her travestied self, the Amazon Radigund, in a conflict which has at stake the marriage of "Chastity" and "Justice," and the generation of the Tudor royal race. In a

poem full of mirrors of Elizabeth, it is perhaps not surprising
that a female character should be central, or that a virtue
called "Chastity" should be so defined as to become very
nearly the opposite of virginity. Nor is it surprising that
Britomart should be royal, martial, very nearly the most
self-sufficient quester in the poem, or that the expanded
significance of her virtue should seem second only to
Holinesse among those the poet treats. It is somewhat
surprising, however, that Spenser chooses to treat the
Britomart-Artegall-Radigund triangle in the way he does, and
we may profitably consider the events and their implications
here.

Artegall's training and temperament, as has often been
noticed, associate him closely with Spenser's view of
savagery. He has no existence in the Golden Age, during the
reign of Saturn, when Justice is embodied in female form, as
the goddess Astraea:

> For during *Saturnes* ancient raigne it's sayd,
> That all the world with goodnesse did abound:
> All loued vertue, no man was affrayd
> Of force, ne fraud in wight was to be found:
> No warre was knowne, no dreadfull trompets sound,
> Peace vniuersall ray'd mongst men and beasts,
> And all things freely grew out of the ground:
> Iustice sate high adorn'd with solemne feasts,
> And to all people did diuide her dred beheasts.
>   [V.proem.9]

The female embodiment of divine Justice trains up a male
champion of human justice when social organization degen-
erates from this original perfection; Artegall is trained in "a
caue from companie exilde" and practices his discipline
"Vpon wyld beasts, which she in woods did find,/With
wrongfull powre oppressing others of their kind
[V.1.7.8-9]." Artegall's first appearance in the poem in
person has already made the same point. At the tournament
[IV.4.39] he entered "in queynt disguise,"

For all his armour was like saluage weed,
With woody mosse bedight, and all his steed
With oaken leaues attrapt, that seemd fit
For saluage wight, and thereto well agreed
His word, which on his ragged shield was writ,
Saluagesse sans finesse, shewing secret wit.

Artegall has been shown "savage" not only by costume, but also by motive, long before we know him to be champion of Justice. Because Britomart defeated him in their first joust, he pursues her "full of despiteous ire,/That nought but spoyle and vengeance did require [IV.6.11.4-5]." Clearly Spenser is making sure we do not mistake him for a complete man, let alone for a complete champion of Justice. His original virtue is one which human beings share with the better beasts, the raging courage to attack when provoked. He is an exaggerated, nearly travestied, version of what we would now call "virility." To assure ourselves that Spenser explicitly makes Artegall one-sided, we need only think of Calidore's behavior in situations that confront his judgment, calling for tact, self-restraint, wit, sympathy, and finally even personal renunciation. When we do so, it is clear that civilization ("ciuility") does represent for Spenser a notable advancement from the human iron age. Calidore has his weaknesses, and makes mistakes, but there is no denying the positive contrast that his uniquely human application of intelligence to social problems makes with Artegall's "instinctive" aggressiveness.

There are good reasons for calling Radigund a double, or infernal parody of Britomart. The careful parallelism of Artegall's two scenes of defeat by a woman warrior is designed to show us that the champion of Justice cannot distinguish between Britomart and Radigund. In both cases, he is rendered powerless at the sight of a beautiful woman's face, arrested for a moment in the heat of combat, perhaps superimposing a particularly masculine beauty on a feminine one. Britomart's "angels face"

Like to the ruddie morne appeard in sight,
Deawed with siluer drips, through sweating sore,
But somewhat redder, then beseem'd aright,
Through toylesome heate and labour of her weary fight.
[IV.6.19.6-9]

At the equivalent moment in the combat with Radigund, he unlaces her helmet and her face strikes him as

A miracle of natures goodly grace,
In her faire visage voide of ornament,
But bath'd in bloud and sweat together ment;
Which in the rudeness of that euill plight,
Bewrayd the signes of feature excellent:
Like as the Moone in foggie winters night,
Doth seeme to be her selfe, though darkned be her light.
[V.5.12.3-9]

Both women elicit the same reaction from Artegall, though neither is capable of physical conquest in hand-to-hand battle. Since each of the female warriors overcomes Artegall through her beauty, the combat between Britomart and Radigund will be like a tie-breaking contest, and is as necessary as the third proposition of a syllogism. Britomart and Radigund are linked not only as contenders for Artegall's allegiance on the narrative level, but also surely as warring forces within him, since the woman that wins will be allowed to define his mode of life thereafter. Artegall dropped his sword at the sight of each woman, overcome by the terror of doing any further combat with, or injury to, Beauty. The sword, let us remind ourselves, was not representative of power—that belongs to Talus's iron flail—but of judgment:

For there no substance was so firme and hard,
But it would pierce or cleaue, where so it came;
Ne any armour could his dint out ward,
But wheresoeuer it did light, it throughly shard.
[V.1.10.6-9]

Artegall's judgment is not really necessary when beauty happens to reflect goodness, and therefore we cannot seriously fault him for his reaction to Britomart. But his judgment fails again when beauty does not bear so close a relationship to goodness. Like the satyrs who respond to Una's radiance "naturally," but lack the means for understanding it, and so are as ready to worship her donkey as herself, Artegall is as primitive a state government as they are a tribal religion. If Radigund resembles Britomart in Artegall's eyes, she may more closely resemble Artegall himself in our own. Her humiliating treatment of conquered males is similar in spirit to Artegall's own distribution of punishments that with crude sarcasm reveal the crime. Just as he had made the knight who murdered his lady carry her head with him from that time on, as a visual token of the nature of his offense, so Radigund the as the knights whom she regards as male supremacists in women's clothing, as a symbol of their scorn for her sex turned back on them. Both Artegall and Radigund confuse justice with revenge, and do not care to be loved, so long as they are feared. Radigund has, and to some extent successfully, taken on the most "virile" or "saluage" characteristics of knighthood ("Through vengeful wrath and sdeignfull pride half mad [V.4.43.3]"). Spenser ironically emphasizes the resulting dilemma when she falls in love with Artegall, describing her initial reluctance to love in the classic terms from romance literature, where the rebellious victim of Cupid is a proud young male:

> Yet would she not thereto yeeld free accord,
> To serue the lowly vassall of her might,
> And of her seruant make her souerayne Lord:
> So great her pride, that she such basenesse much abhord.
> [V.5.27.6-9]

As so often in the poem, we are reminded of Sidney's great prose romance, here particularly of the comically didactic scorn with which Musidorus, who has not yet fallen in love, lashes Pyrocles, who has:

... for as the love of heaven makes one heavenly, the
love of vertue, vertuous; so doth the love of the world
make one become wordly, and this effeminate love of a
woman, doth so womanish a man, that (if he yeeld to it)
it will not onely make him an *Amazon*; but a launder, a
distaff-spinner; or what so ever vile occupation their idle
heads can imagin, & their weake hands performe.[18]

Radigund, like the exaggerated male she has tried to become,
fears loss of power and status in offering herself as servant to
the womanized Artegall—a very nice irony since she herself
has womanized him, and unwomanized herself.

Despite the poet's frequent coaching of a negative attitude
toward Radigund,[19] the Amazon is given a moment of
almost tragic insight into her situation, in her speech to
Clarin:

> *Clarin* (sayd she) thou seest yond Fayry Knight,
> Whom not my valour, but his owne braue mind
> Subiected hath to my vnequall might;
> What right is it, that he should thraldome find,
> For lending life to me a wretch vnkind;
> That for such good him recompence with ill?
> Therefore I cast, how I may him vnbind,
> And by his freedome het his free goodwill;
> Yet so, as bound to me he may continue still.
>
> [V.5.32]

It is as if she has realized the futility of the "virile" or
enslaving strategy for compelling love, and is seeking a return
to "natural" courtship. The last line, of course, undercuts the
rest. Yet it could be argued that Radigund is only self-
deceived here, and not too far from the mark at that. Love is
bondage or binding—she forgets only that it is freely elected
mutual binding. She knows at this moment that she is already
caught, and we can understand why she should want Artegall
also enmeshed before she reveals her own vulnerability a
second time.

It is the use of Clarin as the intermediary that constitutes Radigund's real failure, or perhaps represents her essential moral blemish. Whatever Clarin's ancestry in Italian romance epic, and whatever covert implications her name may bear, her role on the narrative level seems relatively clear. She is an elaborate chain of disguised communications, rumors, indirect and partially falsified information. She betrays both parties to the negotiations, and herself as well. Perhaps her role represents the attempt to accomplish politically what cannot be accomplished by martial methods. Radigund has replaced her strategy of forceful conquest with one which aims to entrap through illusion or guileful persuasion. We might see this as a reversion to "feminine" strategy from "masculine," if it were not for one of Spenser's most puzzling passages, in which he seems to deny that "force" is masculine and "fraud" feminine:

> Here haue I cause, in men iust blame to find,
>   That in their proper prayse too partiall bee,
>   And not indifferent to woman kind,
>   To whom no share in armes and cheualrie
>   They do impart, ne maken memorie
>   Of their braue gestes and prowesse martiall;
>   Scarse do they spare to one or two or three,
>   Rowme in their writs; yet the same writing small
> Does all their deeds deface, and dims their glories all.

> But by record of antique times I find,
>   That women wont in warres to beare most sway,
>   And to all great exploits them selues inclind;
>   Of which they still the girlond bore away,
>   Til enuious Men fearing their rules decay,
>   Gan coyne streight lawes to curb their liberty;
>   Yet sith they warlike armes haue layd away,
>   They haue exceld in artes and pollicy,
> That now we foolish men that prayse gin eke t'enuy.
>   [III.2.1-2]

These reflections are designed ostensibly to lead to the explanation, in the next stanza, that Britomart is the fictional representative of this "warlike puissance in ages spent," just as Elizabeth herself is the historical example of feminine superiority in "all wisdome." Yet "artes and pollicy" is suspiciously different from wisdom. Spenser's presentation of himself here as a feminist author, who is willing to contradict the version of sexual history provided by most male writers before him, is also unconvincing. The point of the passage may be to indicate that men and women are equally capable of pursuing power over the opposite sex through direct physical compulsion and through artfull "pollicy." It may also suggest that women are historically in the forefront of both pursuits, i.e., that they are more eagerly adaptive to the conditions of degenerated social organization after the Golden Age than are men. In Christian terms, this is a familiar statement: Eve was more likely to fall than Adam, and indeed fell first, and tempted him to follow. The irony does seem to cut both ways, however, since men are indeed "foolish" to "envy" the superiority of women—or their priority—in these brazen or iron age activities.

However we interpret the moral significance of Radigund's sojourn in the politics of courtship, it clearly fails. Britomart's arrival for the final combat with Radigund is understandably a relief for the Amazon, who has been out of her depth in political swamps:

> Whereof when newes to Radigund was brought,
>   Not with amaze, as women wonted bee,
>   She was confused in her troublous thought,
>   But fild with courage and with ioyous glee,
>   As glad to heare of armes, the which now she
>   Had long surceast, she had to open bold,
>   That she the face of her new foe might see.
>   [V.7.25.1-7]

Radigund seems by now to have realized that she has shut off one side of her nature, and so the opportunity to engage in the simplicity of physical combat fills her with joy. In passing we might notice that here, as when she first encountered Artegall, Radigund displays not only personal courage, but the protective instincts of a good leader as well, in both cases recognizing the threat Talus represents in a pitched battle:

> There she resolu'd her selfe in single fight
> To try her Fortune, and his force assay,
> Rather then see her people spoiled quight,
> As she had seene that day a disauenterous sight.
>
> [V.4.47.6-9]

> But when they of that yron man had told,
> Which late her folke had slaine, she bad them forth to hold.
>
> [V.7.25.8-9]

In the ensuing battle between the two women, imaged as a combat between Lionesse and Tygre over "some hungry pray [V.7.30.1-2]," the poet emphasizes, perhaps for the sake of our pity and terror, the unnaturalness of the sight:

> The Trumpets sound, and they together run
> With greedy rage, and with their faulchins smot;
> Ne either sought the others strokes to shun,
> But through great fury both their skill forgot,
> And practicke vse in armes: ne spared not
> Their dainty parts, which nature had created
> So faire and tender, without staine or spot,
> For other vses, then they them translated;
> Which they now hackt and hewd, as if such vse they hated.
>
> [V.7.29]

So long they fought, that all the grassie flore
Was fild with bloud, which from their sides did flow,
And gushed through their armes, that all in gore
They trode, and on the ground their liues did strow,
Like fruitles seede, of which vntimely death should
grow.

[V.7.31.5-9]

Since this scene calls attention to the likenesses of the two
women warriors, their battle-madness and their joint disregard for the reproductive purpose of nature in creating "their
dainty parts," the reader may feel that in killing Radigund
Britomart is actually destroying the false version of herself
that has subjugated Artegall. Britomart is no Amazon but a
princess temporarily disguised as an Amazon, and Spenser
makes it perfectly clear that she will retire from the field of
battle when she conceives a child.

In the Isis Church episode, significantly placed between the
scenes in which Britomart hears of Artegall's captivity and in
which she rescues him, she dreams that she is in the position
of the Isis figure, and the priests tell her that the crocodile-
Osiris under her foot is Artegall. When the crocodile has
devoured the flames, and threatens to consume her as well,
she beats him back with her rod. Only after this discipline,
and his renewed humility, will their marriage be consummated, and a lion engendered. If there are any narrative
equivalent of Britomart's "clemency" subduing Artegall's
"sterne behests, and cruell doomes [V.7.22.9]," it must be
her beheading of Radigund, whose unnatural tyranny is
founded on revenge. The final situation is replete with
paradox: Justice has been "womanized" by cruelty; cruelty is
born a woman, but makes herself into a ruler "halfe like a
man [V.4.36.8];" clemency "wrothfull" and "in revenge"
destroys mercilessness; and a conquering woman restores
manliness to Justice, who has been able to do nothing for his
own restoration.

The story is complicated, and perhaps susceptible of many interpretations. In essentials it shows Artegall learning a lesson from Britomart: how to distinguish between the attractions of cruelty and the attractions of equity or clemency, and how to destroy the first through the second. In both of Spenser's myths of "antique" justice, the principles represented by the womanly figure are superior to those embodied in the male: Isis stands over Osiris, and Astraea's Golden Age divinity is replaced by Artegall's iron age bestial courage. Artegall's courage and cruelty both are mirrored in Radigund, the usurper of authority. This side of his nature as Justice has been allowed to usurp the ultimate authority that actually resides in clemency. The initial conflict between Artegall and Britomart, followed by the conflict between Radigund and Britomart, is a narrative metaphor suggesting that it is as difficult (and as necessary) to combine rigor and mercy in government as it is to reconcile the naturally warring male and female principles in marriage. As the sexes try to subdue one another, so do the values of the Old Law and New Dispensation. If the eventual marriage of Britomart and Artegall is to subordinate Britomart as a woman to Artegall as a man, it is also to subordinate Artegall as Old Law to Britomart as New. This is the way Spenser achieves factional "equity" between the sexes, through making the power relationship on the narrative level reverse the power relationship on the symbolic or allegorical level. Artegall is to rule in the here and now, but Britomart is to rule in the ideal state or in the ideal prince. We do not witness the marriage of Britomart and Artegall in the poem, but we are assured that it is coming.

It should be admitted that the representation of love between Britomart and Artegall is as perfunctory and unconvincing on the narrative level as it is imaginatively appealing in the abstract. Perhaps because it is so unlikely a match, if we restrict our interest to the fictional personalities of the couple, we are compelled to feel that their union must

be taken on faith, if it is to be taken at all. Spenser could
easily have made Artegall more attractive and admirable as a
person. We therefore must assume, I think, that we are to
admire Artegall only in the most grudging and limited
fashion, and to find his behavior as representative of human
justice as repellant as it is necessary. Again, there is precedent
for this disabusing presentation of "justice" in the last book
of Sidney's *Arcadia*. There the great trial scene shows the
best human justice to be wretchedly ignorant and inhumane,
better in some ways and worse in others than the prejudicial
passions that boil around it.

Book V of *The Faerie Queene* examines relations between
the sexes in political terms. It also proposes an ideal solution
to political or governmental problems in terms of a sexual
metaphor. The hermaphroditic Venus of Book IV, Canto 10,
remains veiled. The closest approach to this mysterious
fusion of the sexes that can be reached in the human world is
in the love-bethrothal-marriage progression. In the Britomart-
Artegall-Radigund triangle, Spenser frankly presents the
power struggle between male and female, and indicates that
"equity" will consist of balanced subordinations, the actual
female to the actual male in power, but the male principle to
the female principle in goodness. Mercilla's tears are represented as better than the "iust verdict" that condemns
Duessa, yet "strong constraint" subordinates the better
(mercy) to the worse (justice). Britomart is certainly presented as better and wiser than Artegall, yet she restores him
and the "fleshly force" he represents to political sovereignty
over women. Given that the concrete, wordly order of things
and the abstract, ideal or divine order seem inversions of one
another, we can either attribute the contrast to unexamined
ambivalence, and call it a failure in consistency, or argue that
the poem is fully aware of the ways in which the world's
solutions to political problems fail to mirror the imagined
ideal. The latter choice has the advantage of making sense
within the Christian perspective, and is perhaps an acceptable
temporary expedient for reopening Book V for contem-

porary consideration. The poem forces us to take the potential union of justice and mercy on faith, through showing us that in men's actions justice dominates mercy, though in men's imaginations mercy is superior to justice. In the world we know, opposite values are at war. In a mental world we create through desire, they would fuse. In that world Red Crosse and Una, Arthur and Gloriana, Britomart and Artegall, would come together in the mysterious permanent embrace which Spenser originally arranged for Amoret and Scudamour, but cancelled on further consideration:

> Lightly he clipt her twixt his armes twaine,
>   And streightly did embrace her body bright,
>   Her body, late the prison of sad paine,
>   Now the sweet lodge of loue and deare delight:
>   But she faire Lady ouercommen quight
>   Of huge affection, did in pleasure melt,
>   And in sweete rauishment pourd out her spright:
>   No word they spake, nor earthly thing they felt,
> But like two senceles stocks in long embracement dwelt.
>
> Had ye them seene, ye would haue surely though,
>   That they had beene that faire *Hermaphrodite*,
>   Which that rich *Romane* of white marble wrought,
>   And in his costly Bath causd to bee site:
>   So seemd those two, as growne together quite, . . .
>   [III.12.1590.45-46]

It seems to me that Spenser did not "forget" to reinsert this scene in his six-book *Faerie Queene* of 1596. He simply transferred it from the narrative level of visible human events to the symbolic level of invisible and imagined events, by making it the central icon in the Temple of Venus. In doing so, he made a serious alteration of design in his poem. What he once considered an appropriate "conclusion" to a "story" of three-book *Faerie Queene* came to be perhaps the most resonant symbol at the heart of the six-book poem; and at the same time physical consummation of the love-narratives seems to have become impossible.

These partial attempts to find grounds for asserting a thematic cohesiveness in *The Faerie Queene* are necessary if we wish to test Hough's argument for the poem's "organic" completion. But Hough's statement of this argument, though attractive, finally gives a stronger sense of thematic wholeness than I find satisfying. Under pressure, the poem does split in half, with Books I, II and V felt as one "piece," and III, IV and VI as the other. It is surely futile, in any case, to pretend that as much poetic fiction as the work (or any of its Books) is made of can be reduced to thematic statement. The diversity and breadth of concern in *The Faerie Queene* are perhaps more truly impressive achievements than would be the "unity" we look for. As Hough says, the poem is "composed of many relatively small parts, each commanding our appreciation by itself and all harmonious with each other; and this is its structural principle."[20] To "complete" anything so long and so comprehensive in its progress may be simply to stop at a good moment. A formalistic conclusion—something that serves to summarize or speak definitively for a poem of such great length—may not be an important requirement. The materials will have had to organize and subordinate themselves in the reader's memory during the many sessions he has spent with the poem, and the reader will no doubt have his own sense of fullness of experience when the poem ceases. For this sense of fullness, no "last word" on the part of the poet would really suffice.

Yet the poem does not break off in mid-thought or mid-sentence. We should remind ourselves, first, that each Book has its own formal resolution in the narrative completion of its quest (with the single exception of the questless Book IV). Though Britomart has been assigned no official quest by Gloriana, she nevertheless discovers that she has one, and fulfills its purpose admirably. At the same time, every book leaves certain narrative threads untied when it ends. Many of these may have been forgotten or ignored because they had served their local purposes. Both Lewis and Hough point out that this uncompulsive plotting of minor stories is characteristic of the sixteenth century Italian romance epics Spenser was following. Others of these loose threads are, of course, narrative bridges between one book and the next. "Completion" for any one of the books, then, is only partial on the narrative level, yet more than adequately serves to separate the major narrative/thematic subdivisions of the work from one another, as an aid to the reader's memory in its job of retrospective organization.

The resolution of the last book is particularly interesting in itself, and even more intriguing if we ignore the Mutabilitie Cantos for the moment (which Huron suggests are "the perfect epilogue"), to see how Book VI will serve if considered as the "last" element of the poem. Calidore's quest is the only one in *The Faerie Queene* which although successfully "completed," may also be said to fail. Prior to Book VI all of the poem's central offenders are (so far as we are told) removed from the action permanently.[21] St. George kills the Dragon; Guyon destroys the Bower and takes Acrasia captive; Britomart makes Busirane undo his spell, and then chains him and leads him captive "to wretchedness and wo;" and Artegall kills Grantorto and frees Irena. But at the end of Book VI, we are told explicitly that the capture of the Blatant Beast was a transitory triumph only:

> Thus was this Monster by the maystering might
> Of doughty *Calidore*, supprest and tamed,
> That never more he mote endammadge wight
> With his vile tongue, which many had defamed,
> . . . .
> So did he eeke long after this remaine,
> Vntill that, whether wicked fate so framed,
> Or fault of men, he broke his yron chaine,
> And got into the world at liberty againe.
>
> [VI.12.38.1-4;6-9]

So now he raungeth through the world againe,
   And rageth sore in each degree and state;
   Ne any is, that may him now restraine,
   He growen is so great and strong of late,
   Barking and biting all that him doe bate,
   Albe they worthy blame, or cleare of crime:
   Ne spareth he the gentle Poets rime,
But rends without regard of person or of time.

Ne may this homely verse, of many meanest,
   Hope to escape his venemous despite,
   More than my former writs, all were they clearest
   From blamefull blot, and free from all that wite,
   With which some wicked tongues did it backebite,
   And bring into a mighty Peres displeasure,
   That never so deserved to endite.
   Therefore do you my rimes keep better measure,
And seeke to please, that now is counted wisemens
                      threasure.
                      [VI.12.40-41]

Speaking out of a present situation ("So now he raungeth . . ."), the voice of the poet tells how he personally is injured by the escape of the Beast. This is an unusual, perhaps unique, note in the poem. As the "bard," Spenser has previously addressed the Muses, in his formal invocations, and Queen Elizabeth, in the prologue to each Book. But this new aspect of his persona is reminiscent of the posture assumed in the apology for *The Shepheardes Calendar*:

Go little booke: thy selfe present,
As child whose parent is unkent;
To him that is the preseident
Of noblesse and of chevalree,
And is that Envie barke at thee,
And sure it will, for succoure flee
   Under the shadow of his wing. . . .

It seems to me no coincidence that the whole of Book VI has much in it that is personal for the poet, and much that is reminiscent of Spenser's other poetry. The Dance of the Graces on Mount Acidale is not only an "allegorical centre" of the Legend of Courtesy, but also a compliment to Spenser's ("Colin's") lady. As the vision begins we are reminded of the refrain from his *Epithalamion* in the line describing the sound of the nymphs' dancing feet ("That through the woods their Eccho did rebound," VI.10.10). And the poet presents his intention after the vision ends, in the well-known tactful address to Gloriana-Elizabeth:

Sunne of the world, great glory of the sky,
    That all the earth doest lighten with thy rayes,
    Great *Gloriana*, greatest Majesty,
    Pardon thy shepheard, monst so many layes,
    As he hath sung of thee in all his dayes,
    To make one minime of thy poore handmayd,
    And vnderneath thy feete to place her prayse,
    That when thy glory shall be farre displayd
To future age of her this mention may be made.

[VI.10.28]

The Spenserian disillusionment with the Court, familiar from his pastorals and satires, emerges naturally in the Book of Courtesy, where he has taken up the pastoral conventions again. Meliboe, telling Calidore of his youthful visit to "roiall court," strikes the keynote of *Colin Clouts Come Home Again*:

Where I did sell my selfe for yearely hire,
    And in the Princes gardin daily wrought:
There I beheld such vainenesse, as I neuer thought.

With sight whereof soone cloyd, and long deluded
    With idle hopes, which them doe entertaine,
After I had ten yeares my self excluded

From natiue home, and spent my youth in vaine,
J gan my follies to my selfe to plaine,
And this sweet peace, whose lacke did then appeare,
Then back returning to my sheepe againe,
I from thenceforth haue learn'd to loue more deare
This lowly quiet life, which I inherite here.

[VI.9.24.7-9;25]

In this last book of *The Faerie Queene*, the poet emerges into
that pastoral setting that has stood, rather more directly than
the romance-epic setting, for the realm of his personal and
professional experience. By the concluding stanzas of Book
VI, Canto 12, the poet has come fully out of the "antique"
world of Faeryland into the present, in his own person. The
Blatant Beast, an inhabitant of the romance fiction, has
chased the poet first into the pastoral setting, and finally out
into contemporary London—in essence, out of the poem. We
can take the last stanzas of Book VI as Spenser's subscribed
signature to *The Faerie Queene*.

I have ignored the Mutabilitie Cantos until now because
they make a treatment of the resolution of the poem more
difficult. They hold together so well, independently of the
rest of *The Faerie Queene*, that they virtually make a
complete and separate poem. It is notable that they are set in
an ancient mythological past. The poet (or whatever the
first-person voice represents here) claims to have found the
story they contain himself, "registred of old,/In *Faery* Land
monst records permanent." We can be almost sure that the
first-person verbs with which the Cantos begin refer to the
same persona of the poet (or perhaps his shepheard-poet
guise, Colin Clout), rather than to a new character, simply by
listening to the voice when the setting becomes pastoral.
Thus, the trial of Mutabilitie's case takes place on

... *Arlo-hill* (Who knows not *Arlo-hill*?)
That is the highest head (in all mens sights)

Of my old father *Mole*, whom Shepheards quill
Renowmed hath with hymnes fit for a rural skill.

And were it not ill fitting for this file,
    To sing of hilles and woods, monst warres and
        Knights,
I would abate the sterneness of my stile,
    Monst these sterne stounds to mingle soft delights . . .
                        [VII.6.36.6-9;37.1-4]

The rhythm established by the parenthetical comments gives
this passage something of the flavor of the narrative style in
The Shepheardes Calendar, as exemplified by these lines from
the seventh eclogue, for July:

For he was proude, that ill was payd,
(no such mought shepheardes bee) . . .   [149-150]

This had a brother, (his name I knewe)   [161]

But now (thanked by God therefore)
The world is well amend, . . .   [169-170]

Ygyrt with belts of glitter and gold,
(mought they good shepheards bene) . . .   [177-178]

To Rome, (if such be Rome) and then
he sawe thilke misusage.   [183-184]

And the interlude of Diana and Faunus reinforces our feeling,
suggested originally by Book VI, that the poet is turning
increasingly to pastoral mythology as a relief from the
sustained "heroic" romance style and world, and from
allegorical mythology.

    It is worth observing that in the six books of *The Faerie
Queene*, there is no passage, of length comparable to the

Mutabilitie Cantos, which excludes as they do any of the characters of the surrounding romance-epic narrative. The great allegorical Houses and Gardens and Temples are all integrally connected to the "plot"—that is, Red Crosse enters the Houses of Pride and Holinesse, and Guyon does the same for the House of Alma and the Bower of Bliss. Amoret is present, however small her part may be, when the Garden of Adonis is described, and the House of Busirane is penetrated by Britomart. Even the interludes that do not carry forward the action are rather carefully linked to the narrative: Marinell attends the wedding of the Thames and Medway, Arthur and Guyon read the chronicles of British and Faerie Kings. (In the latter interlude, we are given Arthur's reaction to the abrupt conclusion of his chronicle before Guyon reads his):

> . . . that so vntimely breach
> The Price him selfe halfe seemeth to offend,
> Yet secret pleasure did offence empeach,
> And wonder of antiquitie long stopt his speach.
>
> [II.10.68.6-9]

Thus the Mutabilitie Cantos are unique, in their independence from the demands of the continuing narration and in their recurrent testimony to the direct presence of the poet (and no one else) as narrator and auditor. The two-stanza reflection and prayer, with which the fragment ends, seem to express the poet's own reaction to his material ("When I bethinke me on that speech whyleare,/Of *Mutabilitie*, and well it way:/Me seemes . . ."), and in their presentation of the direct relationship between the poet and "that great Sabbaoth God," are again unlike anything else in the fiction of the first six books.

There are grounds for thinking, then, that the whole Mutabilitie fragment demonstrates continuation of the tendency we found at the end of Book VI, for the poet to break out of his own frame. He drops here, as there, the carefully established illusion of authorial impersonality, the public voice of the romance-epic "bard" which controlled the narration of the first five books. This is the sense in which the Mutabilitie Cantos can be felt as an "epilogue" to *The Faerie Queene*. They are not quite of a piece with it, though they were obviously written under the strong influence of its themes, structural habits, and its mode of vision. They seem to have more to do with the concerns of the lyric poet than with the stated ends of *The Faerie Queene*. What important quest could be successfully completed, after all, by a hypothetical Knight of Constancy, when Mutabilitie is the law of the sublunar world? Surely he could not defeat Death or Decay; even Fickleness, the human equivalent of cosmic mutability, must persist (like Adonis, "eterne in mutabilitie") until

> ... time shall come that all shall changed bee,
> And from thenceforth, none no more change shall see.
> [VII.7.59.4-5]

As they stand, the Mutabilitie Cantos can perhaps be read as the poet's search for consolation for a sense of futility and loss, perhaps touched off for him by the recent escape of the irrepressible Blatant Beast back into the world. If the Beast cannot be destroyed, how was Calidore's sacrifice of the pastoral world to his sense of social mission justified? Perhaps by this time Spenser had come to consider his own project of setting forth in a comprehensive fiction the most important personal virtues of a man as vain as Calidore's quest, and was willing to end the effort with an expression of faith in the stability, immutability, and incorruptibility of a world imaginatively higher and more gratifying than Faerie Land.

I do not claim to have found any more than a partial completion in my sense of the poem's resolution. To allow Book VI and the Mutabilitie fragment to echo against Spenser's other poetry in a somewhat fanciful fashion is merely to find for the whole *Faerie Queene* the same kind of

resolution that the single books of the poem have: a major
quest is complete, but certain strands connect the poem on
either side with the surrounding story. Like Lewis, I have
looked for a macrocosm that will reflect the microcosm. But
more like Hough, I have tried to find ways of valuing the
existing *Faerie Queene*, rather than its imagined "finished"
counterpart.

BOSTON UNIVERSITY

1. Graham Hough, *A Preface to the Faerie Queene* (New York, 1963), p. 94.

2. C. S. Lewis, *The Allegory of Love* (New York, 1958), pp. 336-7.

3. Lewis, p. 353. Lewis finds that Book VI is "distinguished from its
predecessors by distinct traces of the influence of Malory (a welcome novelty)
and by the high proportion of unallegorical, or faintly allegorical, scenes." Rather
than seeing this individuality of the Book as evidence of a "terminal modifica-
tion" that prepares for conclusion, however, Lewis suggests that "this last feature
easily gives rise to the impression that Spenser is losing grip on the original
conception of his poem; and it suggests a grave structural fault in *The Faerie
Queene* in so far as the poem begins with its loftiest and most solemn book and
thence, after a gradual descent, sinks away into its loosest and most idyllic. But
this criticism overlooks the fact that the poem is unfinished. The proportion of
allegoric core to typical, or purely fictional fringe has varied all along from book
to book; and the loose texture of the sixth is a suitable relief after the very high
proportion of pure allegory in the fifth. The only fragment of any succeeding
book which we have proves that the poem was to rise from the valley of
humiliation into allegory as vast and august as that of the first book."

4. Lewis, p. 357.

5. The most relevant passages from the letter are these: "So in the person of
Prince Arthure I sette forth magnificence in particular, which vertue for that
(according to Aristotle and the rest) it is the perfection of all the rest, and
conteineth in it them all, therefore in the whole course I mention the deedes of
Arthure applyable to that vertue, which I write of in that booke. But of the xii.

other vertues, I make xii. other knights the patrones, for the more variety of the history..... The beginning therefore of my history, if it were to be told by an Historiographer, should be the twelfth booke, which is the last ... "

6. Lewis, p. 353.

7. Lewis, p. 337.

8. Hough, p. 89. Hough, we should note, despite his insistence on distinguishing the "organic" development of the poem from the plan in the letter, still imagines that the union of Arthur and Gloriana would "doubtless" have occurred if Spenser had arrived at Booke XII.

9. Hough, p. 91.

10. Lewis, p. 334.

11. In Lewis's view, Mercilla's Court *should* have been the "allegorical centre" of the Book, and he calls its inadequacy in this respect Spenser's "one great failure in this kind—a failure which paralyzes the whole book because that canto should have been its heart (p. 349)."

12. Hough, p. 93.

13. Hough, p. 234.

14. Hough, pp. 234-5.

15. Hough, p. 235.

16. Hough, p. 235.

17. I regret that I cannot deal in this paper with two recent studies in which this Book has received fresh critical attention: Donald Cheney, *Spenser's Image of Nature: Wild Man and Shepherd in The Faerie Queene* (New Haven 1966), particularly Ch. 4, "Astraea: The Golden Age and Artegall's Savage Justice" and Ch. 5, "Wild Man and Shepherd"; and Jane Aptekar, *Icons of Justice: Iconography & Thematic Imagery in Book V of The Faerie Queene* (New York 1969). Cheney argues in Chapter 4, however, that "the very unattractiveness of Artegall's justice might suggest that the apparent 'simplicity' of Book V ... is in fact a function of Artegall's limited role as the champion of earthly justice (p. 147)." And Aptekar also suggests, in her chapter on "Force and Fraud," that Artegall is designedly an unlikeable hero, whose methods are scarcely less unattractive to the Elizabethan reader than to us ("That these means are neither godly nor good Spenser is as well aware as is the twentieth-century democrat," p. 124).

18. Albert Feuillerat, *The Prose Works of Sir Philip Sidney*, (Cambridge, 1965 and 1968), Vol. I, *The Countess of Pembrokes Arcadia*, p. 78 (Lib.1, ch. 12).

19. Notice the negative attitude toward Radigund as seen in the stanza of the bald editorializing about the cruelty of womankind, V.5.25., or in the prejudicial use of the word "lust" to characterize her attraction to Artegall.

20. Hough, pp. 93-4.

21. I am not regarding Archimago as one of the "central offenders" (by which I mean the official villains assigned to the questing knights). Even if he were to be so regarded (since he is in many respects more prominent and dangerous than the "official" villain of the Book, the Old Serpent, at least on the narrative plane), he is not really an exception to the pattern I am attempting to establish, since he simply disappears from the action, and is not explicitly said to be a permanent threat. Duessa, who is resurrected at least twice more after her stripping in Book I (in Book IV, and in Book V) for minor roles in the actions, is finally dispatched in a curiously offhand manner, so that Mercilla can show "more than needfull naturall remorse" in "yeelding the last honour to her wretched corse [V.10.4.8-9]."

Paula Johnson

Literary Perception and
The Faerie Queene

Is *The Faerie Queene* as we have it a shapeless fragment or
is it, as has been argued by more than one critic in the last
few years, perceivable as an artistic unity?[1] Even though this
vast poem is admittedly unfinished when we measure it
against Spenser's stated plan in the letter to Raleigh, if it can
nonetheless be perceived as a unity, then for the practical
purposes of criticism it is complete, and does not need for its
full understanding the projected latter half that Spenser never
wrote. A preference for treating *The Faerie Queene* as an
integrated whole is prompted by two qualities of recent
criticism. The first is an attitude toward art, too pervasive to
be fully documented, that can be summed up in Robert
Frost's definition of a poem as "a momentary stay against
confusion." To many thinking people in this multifarious and
contradictory world, art is one of the few (if not the only)
sources and sites of comprehensible order. Being a human
product, it is our surest testimony to the value of human
endeavor, a value constantly threatened on one side by the
efficiency of complicated machines and on the other by the
absurd vagaries of irrational and uncontrollable forces. Art in
such a context comes to seem the last best hope of man on
earth. If it is to satisfy that hope, it must at the very least
offer a consistent and self-sufficient organization of human

experience—in short, unity of form.[2] For those who read it, Spenser's poem is either a looming threat to this hope or a peculiarly glorious fulfillment of it. To have encompassed so much, and made sense of it all! One reason, then, for seeing *The Faerie Queene* as complete (if we do) is that we desperately need to perceive it so.

The other factor that appears to be influencing recent critical studies like those of Northrop Frye, A. C. Hamilton, Graham Hough,[3] Thomas Roche, and Kathleen Williams is a change in the methods of interpreting literature in general and Spenser's poem in particular. In the particular case, this change is to some extent a reaction against the elaborate studies of Spenser's literary sources and historical allusions so amply represented in the *Variorum Spenser* of a generation ago. The current trend in Spenser studies seems to be a determination to attend first of all to the surface of *The Faerie Queene*—to the stories, images, language, and so forth. Hamilton justifies this emphasis by an appeal to Reformation Protestant concern with the literal meaning of scripture, and equates the "literal level" with the "visual image."[4] Similarly, Williams points out that in the opening lines of Book I "we meet at once not two abstractions but two romance characters, a knight and a lady. . . . "[5] The allegory thus becomes not so much a matter of point-for-point correspondence of single items in the poem with isolated moral ideas, as a global analogy between the world of the poem and the moral and physical universe. The combination of holistic interpretation and concern with *The Faerie Queene* as a verbal structure has put the question of unity, effective completeness, in the foreground of Spenser criticism.

Once it is granted that Spenser's failure to carry out his whole intention does not necessarily imply that his poem cannot have a unified form, the locus of its possible unity becomes its perception by the reader. Thus before any attempt to validate objectively by critical exposition a unity or completeness that the reader may subjectively perceive, we must inquire about the nature of literary perception itself. In regard to *The Faerie Queene*, critics who try to demonstrate the work's integrity as we have it do so on the basis of an unquestioned intuition. Fortunately (since to guess at another person's subjectivity is hazardous) the critic nearly always makes at some point an explicit statement about his intuitive impression. In order to keep even this more general phase of the discussion related to the specific literary work in hand, I shall use a few of these brief statements as examples of literary perception—as experimental data, so to speak. They fall naturally into two categories, of which the first includes such as the following:

> It is only on looking back at the end of the journey that the fairyland of Spenser's imagination seems to dissolve into its constituent parts. Trying to organize his impressions and comparing notes with others, the disenchanted traveller asks himself whether the unity of atmosphere and purpose which he thought he experienced in the poem was more than illusion created by the continuity of its slow and elaborate music and its intricate and resplendent tapestry.   (Hans P. Guth)[6]

> When the poem is studied as a whole, incompleted indeed, but not mutilated, there emerges a pattern too large and intricate to be fully perceived with one glance, but all the more satisfying for that very reason. . . .
>   (M. Pauline Parker)[7]

> *The Faerie Queene* is composed of many relatively small parts, each commanding our appreciation by itself and all harmonious with each other; and this is its structural principle. Its essence is immanent in these multitudinous local effects, not in an overriding plan which could be abstracted and schematically displayed.
>   (Graham Hough)[8]

Each of these comments describes a static impression—which does not at all mean a stiff or sterile one. Guth, who seems honestly bewildered by *The Faerie Queene*, gives the

clearest hint about the nature of the impression: "looking
back at the end of the journey. . . . " What in fact all these
writers are dealing with is the way the poem seems in
retrospect, after one has stopped reading. We always do have
this kind of perception of literary works when we get to the
end, put the book down, and look back in memory at the
work as a whole. The total form of the work then becomes
for us a single mental configuration, which may be more or
less visual, clear, or simple, and more or less satisfying as a
form. Readers for whom this retrospective configuration is
strongly visual are often prompted to compare literature with
the graphic arts: Guth likens *The Faerie Queene* to a
tapestry; Roche envisions it as a triptych or diptych.[9] The
perception itself, however, is not really visual, but simply a
mental event, even though its static quality suggests the use
of visual images as analogues for it, and of visually-based
metaphors to describe it.

The clarity of the configuration depends mainly on the
degree to which details of the work as perceived are
subordinated to its main outlines; in this connection Hough's
remarks are illuminating. If indeed the structural principle of
The Faerie Queene is that merely of "multitudinous local
effects," then the poem does not and never could present a
clear total shape, no matter how much of it Spenser had
succeeded in finishing. We may in the end have to concur
with this view, and adopt a radical agnosticism about the
form of the poem; but there are other possibilities, one of
which is adumbrated in Parker's comment. While Hough is
saying that *The Faerie Queene* as a retrospective configuration lacks clarity, Parker is saying that it lacks simplicity:
"too large and intricate to be fully perceived with one
glance." One defining characteristic of the retrospective form
is its simultaneity: it is not extended through time, but is
exactly what *can* be perceived at a glance. That is its chief
limitation. One can only be fully conscious of just so much at
a given moment, and no more. In order, therefore, to
perceive a large and complex work at a glance of memory, we

must simplify it. No matter how careful the poet may have
been to construct a clear form by integrating all details into
it, the form may still defy unitary apprehension because of
its complexity, and the reader who wants to see it as a whole
is forced to carry out the necessary simplification for himself.
Simplification means suppressing details and substructures
to allow the appearance of a configuration limited to what
this one spot of awareness (the critic's mind at the moment)
can possibly contain. Suppressed items however are not
altogether blotted out; they are only relegated to what Freud
called the "preconscious": that twilight region of the mind
the contents of which, unlike those of the *un*conscious, are
mostly accessible to voluntary recall; the region in which
things exist simultaneously and prelogically, and to which we
abandon ourselves when we go to sleep. In relation to the
simplified retrospective form of a poem, the preconsciously
remembered details are a shadowy fringe, helping to give the
main outline its individual quality and capable at any point
of coming to the full light of present awareness as soon as
one shifts the focus of one's attention to them. Since no one
denies that *The Faerie Queene*, whatever else it may be, is
large and complex, it is possible that Guth's frustration and
Parker's resignation at what they seem to have felt as a failure
to perceive unitary design in the poem are due to not having
carried the process of simplification far enough. It may be
that we have only to stand farther back, as it were, and the
hidden form will materialize for us in all its archetypal
grandeur. Northrop Frye, whose metaphor of "standing
back" from a poem I have borrowed, assumes "as a working
hypothesis, that the six books we have form a unified epic
structure," that the Mutabilitie Cantos bring us "to the poet's
'Sabbath's sight' after his six great efforts of creation, and
there is nothing which at any point can be properly described
as 'unperfite.' "[10] The way in which Frye goes on to validate
this unitary perception suggests that he is indeed standing a
long way back from the poem. That is a consideration I shall
return to. For the moment Frye's remark, like that of Roche

about the triptych, establishes the possibility of a perceptible complete form in Spenser's fragment—whether an accurate perception of a satisfying form remains to be seen.

These, then, are some of the ways in which *The Faerie Queene* may appear to a critical reader in retrospect as a static configuration; but there is still another mode of literary perception. The most influential modern commentator on Spenser has undoubtedly been the late C. S. Lewis, who was not willing to consider *The Faerie Queene* as more than a fragment: "The poem is not finished. It is a poem of a kind that loses more than most by being unfinished. Its centre, the seat of its highest life, is missing."[11] But while he denied it retrospective unity of form, Lewis testified to a different kind of satisfaction in the poem:

> . . . a feeling that we have before us not so much an image as a sublime instance of the universal process . . . not so much a poet writing about the fundamental forms of life as these forms themselves spontaneously displaying their activities to us through the imagination of the poet.[12]

This type of statement concerns the second kind of general impression a reader has of a literary work, that of its progressive form.[13] This in subjective terms is our perception of the work while we are in the process of apprehending it. The process is more than simply incremental; even the first few words of the poem set up a *gestalt*, a form perceived as form. The reader does not merely add up items as he goes along, but experiences a constantly transforming pattern that is varied, developed, and complexified as the reader follows its temporal progress. A reader whose most vivid imagination is aural will be apt to draw analogies between the temporally perceived literary work and musical forms. Like the retrospective form, the progressive forming of the work may be more or less clear and simple, and more or less satisfying.

To summarize one's progressive apprehension is very difficult, partly because it is primarily in the progression of

the work that its emotional values, so hard to recapture or
define, inhere; and partly because the perception is by its
nature dependent on an extended temporal process of
reading. For both these reasons brief comments of the same
general type as that of C. S. Lewis quoted above are relatively
rare. Worse yet, the pair of statements that offer themselves
happen to be diametrically opposed:

> If plot is soul, the poem cannot escape damnation. . . .
> The constituent elements are not sequential in their
> arrangement; they are truly episodic, obeying no law of
> progress or development. They are not tied to each other
> but to the principal subject of discourse. . . . One may
> take hold of the meaning of a book almost anywhere in
> it.   (William Nelson)[14]

> [Spenser is able] to present the poet's vision of ordered
> nature without doing violence to the moment by
> moment experience which is itself part of the nature to
> be ordered. . . . Spenser marshals all his organizing prin-
> ciples as one; the poem moves altogether, and moves
> unerringly towards unity.   (Kathleen Williams)[15]

Whereas Lewis was content to suggest how the ongoing
perception of *The Faerie Queene* consisted of a coherent
series of ever-developing forms, Nelson denies that the
progressive form provides any satisfaction whatever. Like
Hough's perception of the retrospective form, Nelson's of the
progressive aspect is one of radical fragmentation. Williams, it
is evident, finds herself at the opposite extreme. Just as Frye
sees the retrospective form as completely satisfying, so does
she perceive the progressive form, the unfinished state of
which "does not prejudice that much of its order which it
does reveal, since each aspect of the final unity is developed
in itself."[16]
   From the various bits of testimony now before us, and
from our own subjective apprehensions of form, it is possible
to infer certain minimal criteria for satisfying form, both in

the progressive and the retrospective aspects. Both types of pattern are felt to be more or less satisfying as they exhibit closure, balance, coherence, and the fruitful resolution of tensions set up within the work. The way each type of pattern can exhibit these characteristics differs, naturally, as the two modes of experience differ. Even taken together, they do not, I hasten to admit, entirely account for the full impression the poem makes on a reader. The analytic system I am trying to outline has to do with what critics call the structure and what a psychologist might call the *gestalt* of a work, its formal characteristics and organization. My inquiry is not designed principally to explain the work's emotional impact, nor how it "speaks to our condition," except rather indirectly. This is therefore a special, partial way of looking at literature, but one that is I think the most capable of dealing with questions of the completeness or formal unity of Spenser's poem. The four criteria for satisfying form just mentioned must be explained more at length:[17]

1. *Closure.* Psychologists investigating visual perception have discovered that if a simple shape, say a circle, with a small break in its outline is flashed briefly on a screen, people will identify it as a complete, closed shape. Similarly, if a person looks fixedly at the slightly broken circle for a few seconds, his visual afterimage will, again, be a closed circle. The preference for finished forms—forms that show closure— becomes also a tendency to supply closure in our perception even in some cases when it is not objectively there in the form to be perceived. When a form lacks closure, we feel a twinge of impatience, the impulse to say, "Drop the other shoe." When the form in question is literary, we demand two sorts of closure, corresponding to the two aspects of literary form. This is most obvious in the progressive aspect of narrative: we want a story to arrive at some end (even if it is not a happy one). Cases in point are Chaucer's *Hous of Fame*, the two versions of Keats's *Hyperion*, and Dickens' *The Mystery of Edwin Drood*. The last example is the most

tantalizing because it suggests its continuation and ending with clearer hints, and belongs furthermore to a genre that makes use of material suspense to urge the reader onward.

No one denies that *The Faerie Queene* lacks progressive closure: Scudamour and Amoret never get reunited, Arthur never does find Gloriana, poor Serena is left without clothes, and so in any number of less glaring instances. The only real issue here is not whether the poem lacks closure, but to what extent its admitted lack impairs the reader's sense of unity and completion. Since there are other qualities of organization that also make for satisfying form, it is possible—for Frye and Williams, as we have seen, it is actual—for those other qualities to overrule in the total perception the partial absence of progressive closure. The danger is that, as in the case of simple visual shapes, a reader may supply the missing parts from his own need of them. In extreme cases this may even be done deliberately—witness the attempts to write an ending for Dickens' novel; or (since the need for progressive closure affects any sequential form) the fact that most listeners are willing to accept in performance the half or more of Mozart's *Requiem* that was supplied by Sussmayr, simply to round out the experience.

Closure in the retrospective configuration is less easy to define. It must be achieved by filling out whatever form the reader has been led to expect, as for instance, the cycle of the days of creation that Frye alludes to for the six-plus books of *The Faerie Queene*. The question here is of course whether the reader has actually been prepared by cues in other parts of the poem to accept "that Sabbath's sight" as the final missing part of a pattern already almost finished. A poem may also suggest a pattern peculiar to itself, not dependent on some form already familiar to the reader such as the seven-day cycle. Often a poem's pattern will achieve closure by the use of balance, the next criterion for satisfying form to be discussed.

2. *Balance.* Henry James wrote in reference to *The Wings of the Dove* of "the author's scarce more than half-

dissimulated despair at the inveterate displacement of his general centre," of "my regular failure to keep the appointed halves of my whole equal;" of the "make-shift middle" and the "false and deformed [latter] half" of the novel.[18] Balance has to do with the sense of just proportion and of symmetry. Though almost impossible to define in abstraction, the presence or absence of balance (largely a feature of the retrospective configuration) is perhaps the most quickly and surely recognizable aspect of artistic form. The criss-cross of the falling and rising careers of Richard and Bolingbroke in *Richard II*; the nearly geometric interplay of the phases of temptation and the division into books of *Paradise Regain'd*; the parallel-with-contrast of the first and final stanzas of Blake's "The Tyger," are obvious instances of formal balance.

On the other hand, balance may be conspicuous by its absence, as when Samuel Butler in *The Way of All Flesh* deserts Shandean satire for contrived wish-fulfillment, or when the last three acts of *The Jew of Malta* seem a different sort of play from the first two. Balance, then, concerns both offsetting structures of events, words, images, and so forth, and the giving to each element of the work a kind and amount of treatment that seem appropriate to it in its context. When we judge that a topic or event is either slighted or overstressed, or that a metaphor is overworked, we are identifying a perceived imbalance.

When a critic—Roche or Frye for instance—speaks of the six books of *The Faerie Queene* as constituting a pair of triads or a triad of pairs, he is maintaining that the poem shows large-scale balance and is therefore a satisfying form. The danger here again is that the critic's perception may distort the work in the direction of a greater regularity than it really has. Such general perceptions must in every case be objectively validated by showing exactly what in the poem is symmetrical or in just proportion with what.

3. *Coherence* in a literary form normally implies continuity and consistency. Consistency at the crudest level can be defined negatively, as the absence of self-contradiction; that

is, of irresolvable multiple statements having the same reference. See, for instance, I. 8.10 and 18—just which arm of Orgoglio *did* the Prince cut off? But of course a large work can absorb a few minor bloopers of this sort. Inconsistencies in a character's behavior or in the author's philosophic ideas are usually less disturbing, since personality and speculation leave such ample room for acceptable paradox; and paradox becomes acceptable insofar as a work contains it by consistencies of language, narrative sequence, imagery, tone, and so on. When these fail, the work can seriously frustrate our desire that it "make sense."

When Vinaver edited the rediscovered text of Malory as eight separate tales under the title *Works*, he was in effect (and explicitly) denying continuity and therefore coherence to *Le Morte d'Arthur*. If the parts of a work show closure separately, and do not contain important elements that link up with other parts, coherence is lacking. In the progressive mode, the coherence of a narrative usually depends on a believable temporal sequence of events; but the absence of progressive continuity by no means implies that coherence is absent from the retrospective configuration. A good example of this is Faulkner's *The Sound and the Fury*, in which continuity (though not consistency) is deliberately broken up for the sake of coherence of a different, non-sequential kind in the retrospective form. Progressive coherence is generally speaking more emphasized in narratives showing a developmental sequence, like many nineteenth century novels. In such cases the retrospective form is of less importance than a sense of the probability and relevance of moral processes. But coherence in one or the other aspect of a work is necessary if we are to perceive it as a satisfying form.

In either formal aspect, in any kind of literary work, coherence is the successful articulation of parts. Thomson's *Seasons* is a negative example, since in its final, most expanded version, this poem shows neither continuity nor consistency; the only source of coherence is progressive and aural: the same poetic voice goes on in the same metre for

4,000 lines. In Spenser's *Fowre Hymnes* we are led to expect
a development and complementary interrelation of ideas that
hardly exists in fact, but a sense of coherence is nevertheless
provided by the interlinking of words and images and by the
rhetorical crescendo that sweeps through all four poems. It is
no surprise then to find that coherence is the quality most
often attested to in *The Faerie Queene*. The puzzled Guth,
whose remarks were quoted a few pages back, speaks of a
"unity of atmosphere and purpose" in the poem's progressive
form. Hamilton is putting much the same impression into
more sophisticated terms when he writes of "our single vision
of the poem as fiction."[19] If *The Faerie Queene* meets any
of the criteria for satisfying form, it is most likely to meet
that of coherence, "bringing the greatest possible variety into
compleat Unity by the never interrupted interdependence of
parts."[20] This quality is most striking while we read, that is
to say, in its progressive aspect; but it is present also in the
retrospective configuration.

One further criterion remains to be discussed:

4. *Resolution.* The resolution of tensions set up within the
work is a self-evident requirement for satisfying form, and is
intimately related to closure. The reader is constantly being
led to project hypothetical resolutions, though he is probably
not fully aware of his activity. If no adequate resolution is
offered, the form cannot be perceived as a satisfactory whole.
As an extreme example, illustrating how resolution differs
from closure, suppose that Oedipus in Sophocles' play had,
upon discovering his crime, merely blushed a little and
cleared his throat, then arranged to settle a pension on
Jocasta as queen dowager, and himself gone on to reign
happily ever after. This would provide closure, but hardly the
resolution of internal tensions. The horror aroused by the
hero's archetypal misdeeds demands that Oedipus meet with
an appropriately terrible retribution. Or to approach the
nature of resolution in another way, if no tension were
present in it, a poem might show all the first three criteria for
satisfying form—closure, balance, coherence—but no one

would care. Because form, as I am using the word, is not an abstractible quality, but rather the work itself perceived as a whole, it is not possible to subclassify the tension-resolution category. Whether the tension to be resolved is rooted in the depth of our feelings about our family, or in our equally deep need to make sense of the world we live in, its resolution in the work of art is a quality of the whole work as we perceive it. "The sense of control," Blackmur once wrote, "is perhaps the highest form of apprehension," and if there is no internal tension, no difficulty overcome, the most orderly form can be no more than a dead symmetry. In any work of art, for form to be satisfying, it must seem to be *achieved*. The order must proceed from energy.

I have gone to this length in discussing the perception of literary form, because from the general disagreement about *The Faerie Queene*—a disagreement that the selection of published remarks I have quoted amply illustrates—it is clear that the question of the poem's completeness cannot be adequately dealt with if we pretend that the poem exists in some ideally objective universe of which our minds are mere passive reflectors. On the other hand, to say that *The Faerie Queene* exists only as it is perceived, and that all perceptions are equal, so that no critical statement can rightly be preferred to any other, is solipsism—a defeatist position that I for one am not yet discouraged enough to take. The critical reader's immediate perception of the poem is indeed his primary datum, the place where he must start; but in itself it should not be, and so far as I know never is, the place he is trying to get. Once that primary subjective datum is understood, the critic's task is to show precisely to what in the poem his perception is the faithful response; or, more accurately, he must find some way to communicate the experience that includes both his response and the poem.[21] The critic does in a sense end where he began, with the whole form; but by the end of his study, if both the initial perception and the analytic process are accurate, the critic's insight has become common property in which other readers can share. This can only be done, in prose discourse, by dealing with the poem part by part, even though the whole form is more than the sum of parts that a critical analysis can point out.

The definition of what is to be considered a "part" is therefore the key to a particular critic's analytic system. Thus Nelson chooses to consider a thematic symbol expressing a moral or philosophical idea as a part; that being so, "one can take hold of the meaning of a book almost anywhere in it." Such an approach ignores the progressive aspect of form almost entirely and reduces retrospective form to seven equal aggregates of equal elements; it does not help very much towards an understanding of formal organization. Analyses that accept verbal structures (in one way or another) as parts come much closer to validating formal perception. It is hardly possible to discuss all such analyses, so I shall choose only two: the first, A. C. Hamilton's, considers as a part any sequence of events that presents an analogy to some mythic pattern. As a fair example of how this system works, Spenser is said in Books III and IV to "reduce the nightmare world of romance to the ordered dream of faery land by treating thematically two classical myths, Venus and Adonis, and Cupid and Psyche."[22] Promising as this sounds, it becomes in the working-out a process of identifying every episode with one or the other archetype and thus of identifying the episodes with each other. Hamilton's method has the distinct advantage of taking into serious consideration both the retrospective and the progressive aspects of form, by granting that the sequence of elements is important, and by giving at the same time an intelligible way of perceiving analogies between different sequences. Nevertheless he does not avoid the peculiar weakness of archetypal criticism, its tendency to become reductive. When every element is conceived as not merely analogous to, but ultimately identical with every other element, as in Northrop Frye's vision of the apocalyptic logos, the fruitful internal tension of the whole disappears. *The Faerie Queene* may in fact be a satisfying total form, but this method does not succeed in demonstrating it.[23]

The opposite problem is presented, or so it seems to me, by William's study. This scholar's impression of the progressive form of the poem has already been quoted; throughout her book it is this aspect with which Williams is most concerned. As a result, for all the local flashes of illumination her analysis provides, she tends to follow Spenser's progression so closely that the reader loses sight of the forest among the trees. A scrupulous attention to detail here obscures the greater outlines that must be present if *The Faerie Queene* is a unified form. As Thomas Roche remarks, "understanding almost requires the momentary staying of the onward push of the poem to make those significant moments or phrases (that become our own vision of *the* structure) our limited means of attempting to hold the total poem."[24]

The immense range and complexity of *The Faerie Queene* do indeed contribute to the difficulty of seeing it whole; but then, Dante's *Commedia* is proof that range and complexity alone need not defeat the reader's hope of an intelligible form. Still, to look for retrospective unity in Spenser's poem is a deceptive business, and for a good reason. This is the problem of "standing back" from the poem mentioned earlier: in order to perceive *The Faerie Queene* in retrospect as any sort of satisfying total shape, one has to accept the six books, plus the Mutabilitie poem, as its building blocks. The best supported configuration of these seven blocks seems to be one that divides them into either two or three groups. My own preferred metaphor for the possible shape thus presented is that of an arch, resting on Books I and VI, with Books III and IV at the top, and leaving the Mutabilitie Cantos as a forever yet-to-be-placed keystone. If we move in a step closer, and revive some details that had to be suppressed in the interest of this simple figure, it still seems in most respects to hold up. The parallel dramatic structures of Books I and II that Hamilton works out so carefully can

justify their placement one on top of the other; Book III,
since the Garden of Adonis is evidently the good counterpart
of the wicked Bower of Bliss, builds up the figure more than
acceptably; and this entire semi-arch rests firmly on the
redeemed Eden of Book I. So far, so good.

But the other half is not so satisfactory. The narrative links
in the stories of Amoret and Scudamour, Florimell and
Marinell, and Britomart and Artegall set Book IV in place as
in effect the second half of Book III, though one could
scarcely maintain that the two are coupled by parallel
internal structures. After this, coming down the second side
of the arch, Book V must be in some sense the opposite
number of Book II, a supposition that at first seems
defensible. Not only is Justice the only other of the four
cardinal natural virtues besides Temperance that appears by
name in the poem, but there are also unmistakable echoes of
Guyon's sequence of adventures in Artegall's. The most
obvious of these are in the final cantos of the two books:
Mercilla's court corresponds to the House of Alma; in each of
these places Prince Arthur receives an appeal for help that he
will respond to by carrying on a major battle, and in each the
book's quest-hero is shown the source and paradigm of his
particular virtue, and is rested and fortified for his final
struggle. Arthur's fight with Gerioneo parallels his fight with
Maleger, since in both cases he is defending a woman's claim
to her castle. Guyon on the way to the Bower of Bliss meets
with sundry difficulties, as does Artegall on the way to rescue
Irena. Both heroes, when their final conquest is made, have a
freed populace to cope with.

All this is as tidy as one could reasonably desire.
Unfortunately, however, the first eight cantos of Books II
and V do not fit into the plan. Artegall's sojourn with
Radigund may with not too great a distortion be taken as his
version of a visit to the Cave of Mammon; perhaps one could
even maintain that Britomart who rescues him is a surrogate
for Arthur. But in Book II it is Guyon, not Arthur, who visits
the house of Medina (the minor allegorical set-piece that

foreshadows the major one of the house of Alma), while in Book V it is Britomart, not the book's hero, who spends a night in Isis Church (related to Mercilla's court as Medina's house is to Alma's). Further, Britomart's visit to Isis Church and Guyon's to Medina are both differently placed and differently motivated. Then, too, what are we to make of the Souldan and Adicia? Can they be corollaries of Maleger's host, or of Pyrochles and Cymochles?

A similar kind of difficulty, only compounded, awaits the attempt to find parallels between Books I and VI. At the haziest level of generality we might be able to say that whereas I and II treat of grace and nature, V and VI treat of nature and grace. Even coming a little closer in, Mount Acidale is surely another Eden—or is it a secular version of the Red Crosse Knight's vision from the Mount of Contemplation? Serena has affinities with Una: she is befriended by the "saluage man" as Una was by the satyrs, and she is brought back to civilization, so to speak, by Arthur. But Serena is the one in need of healing from the hermit, whereas Una was a guest not a patient at Coelia's house; and Calepine (whom we might consider a secondary image of the book's hero, Calidore) is not even present.

This kind of game can obviously be played as long as one's patience and ingenuity hold out, but I think I have already carried it far enough to show that it is subject to the law of diminishing returns. Only if we suppress details in the most comprehensive way can we convince ourselves that the six books offer anything like a parallel, mirrored, or otherwise symmetrically balanced and closed form. We must, to take up Frye's metaphor again, stand so far back from the poem that its total shape is a mere blur, to be interpreted after the manner of the Rohrschach inkblots as whatever the reader needs or likes to see. But when we begin to focus attention on parts smaller than whole books, the real elements of the poem come back into light, and those elements do not tend on the whole to validate what one hoped was an accurate perception of balanced closure. That, I imagine, is why Frye never tries to explain what Artegall has to do with Thursday or Calidore with Friday, in his days-of-creation scheme.

Although I cannot agree with Hough that the structural principle of *The Faerie Queene* is nothing more closely organized than multitudinous local effects, I do think that the poem's retrospective form appears to hold out promises of balance and coherence that it does not fulfill. This is no novelty for Spenser; witness the *Fowre Hymnes*, in which the rhetoric covers over inconsistencies in the progression of ideas. *The Shepheardes Calender* is an even clearer case, as is the less readable *Teares of the Muses*. In all of these minor works however an intended formal scheme is present—two kinds of beauty and love, or the months of the year, or one lamentation per Muse. But even when a clear frame of this sort is given, Spenser is far from meticulous about making the parts of the work conform to it. In *The Faerie Queene*, so far as I am aware, we have no reliable evidence for such a framework. It is clear from what portion of the poem we have that Spenser's avowed plan of twelve books, one for each of the "twelve private morall vertues," was being treated with so great a freedom that the stated scheme has very little to do with the poem's practical organization. Scholars so far have not been able to agree even on what twelve virtues Spenser may have meant, much less on how the extant six books illustrate them. Another problem arises with regard to the quest of Prince Arthur. The prince does indeed make an appearance in every book, but his importance varies so much and his activity is so discontinuous that as far as retrospective unity is concerned, we can only accept Lewis's conclusion that Arthur is of no use.[25] In this aspect, then, *The Faerie Queene* remains an unresolvable ambiguity.

The aspect of progressive form is I believe more satisfying. *The Faerie Queene* may not show a kind of form that can with any assurance be judged unitary or complete; but it does show coherence, the quality that accounts for the reader's conviction that faery land is a self-sufficient imaginative world. To illustrate this fully within the limits of this essay is impossible, but as an indication of how coherence is achieved, let us define as "parts" the poem's thematic focal points, the chief *places* that important characters visit. These are always governed by one or both of two complementary principles: the concept of order and the concept of profusion. Each of these concepts includes a moral polarity: order is good and disorder is bad; fertility is good and sterility is bad. In the evil Palace of Pride, for instance, Lucifera's deadly counsellors ride on "six vnequall beasts [I.4.18.1]," and in the evil House of that vile enchanter Busyrane, the Mask of Cupid is again a procession of unequal pairs in an "euill ordered traine [III.12.23.4]." As against these, Fidelia and Speranza approach with "euen steps and equall pace [I.10.12.5]," and the foundation of Alma's House is mathematically proportioned [II.9.22]. These small details contribute to a consistent moral outlook, in which whatever is orderly in a man's body or his character, in the social structure or in the universe, is recognized as good; whatever is disorderly is bad. So pervasive are these ideas that we assimilate them smoothly as part of our orientation to the poem.

But the notion of order can by no means deal with all the world's possible moral phases, and it is no less than all that Spenser tries to include. As the poem progresses (regardless of the chronology of its composition), the simple dichotomy between order and disorder is revealed to be inadequate, and the complementary theme of profusion is made more prominent. Here the moral dichotomy is more subtle. It is first presented in the opposed descriptions of the Bower of Bliss and the Garden of Adonis; in the former, we are expected to see a spurious version or parody of the latter. One of the reasons why the Bower looks so good is that it comes first, before the reader has an example of good profusion by which to evaluate the bad. The other reason for its ambiguity is that, while disorder clearly implies an order that is being violated, profusion is first of all simply an abundance too great to be intellectually schematized—is, in fact, the creation itself as a living process. The only imaginable parody of the true (God's) creation is a false (diabolical) creation: thus the true and false Florimells. But although Spenser tries to give the Bower of Bliss an evil aspect by stressing its admixture of artificiality, its sterility, and its bestial consequences, its beauty is unlike Duessa's or the snowy Florimell's. It is genuine, and so far indistinguishable from the beauty of the Garden of Adonis or of Arlo Hill.

This subtilizing of the poem's moral groundwork yields not only coherence, but also the fruitful resolution of real tensions. Like the poem itself, the sites of good profusion always submit to an ordering principle: the rows of creatures in the Garden of Adonis, the patterned dances of the ladies on Mount Acidale, even Mutabilitie's cycles of months and seasons. Similarly, the verbal surface of the poem is a combination of spontaneity and control. Spenser used language with a free hand, reviving old-fashioned words and making new coinages, transforming words as sounds. The variations in spelling that indicate an accomodation of phonetics to the stanza's exacting rhyme scheme represent a continual metamorphosis of language itself, unpredictable but always in obedience to the poetic pattern, in the same way as the episodes and thematic sites in the narrative are related by loose analogies and an ongoing sense of exuberantly inconclusive, yet orderly development. That the development never issued in a closed symmetrical design is perhaps a misfortune; but the sense of control is never quite lost. Victories of any kind in the poem are always partial and costly. Yet Britomart rescues Amoret, even though she is wounded in the process; Calidore restrains the Blatant Beast, even though it is sure to escape before long. Although Arthur never reaches Gloriana, he is on the right way towards her, and the Cleopolis that the reader cannot locate is nonetheless the invisible center of the poem's moral geography. Unity in its most rigid definition, as a quasi-geometrical regularity of the retrospective form, is not to be had, but the poem's progressive coherence exorcises for the time being the specter of a random universe.

YALE UNIVERSITY

1. I have in mind especially Northrop Frye, "The Structure of Imagery in *The Faerie Queene,*" *Fables of Identity* (New York, 1963); Thomas Roche, *The Kindly Flame* (Princeton, 1964); and Kathleen Williams, *Spenser's World of Glass* (Berkeley and Los Angeles, 1966).

2. Morse Peckham, *Man's Rage for Chaos* (New York, 1967), argues that art's function is not to create but to violate order; but this is impossible unless art fundamentally implies an order against which "violation" takes on meaning. Cf. Catherine Lord, "Unity with Impunity," *Journal of Aesthetics & Art Criticism*, XXVI (1967), 103-106.

3. A. C. Hamilton, *The Structure of Allegory in The Faerie Queene* (Oxford, 1961); Graham Hough, *A Preface to The Faerie Queene* (New York, 1963).

4. Hamilton, p. 33.

5. Williams, p. 1.

6. "Unity and Multiplicity in Spenser's Faerie Queene," *Anglia,* LXXIV (1956), 1.

7. *The Allegory of the Faerie Queene* (Oxford, 1960), p. 305.

8. Hough, p. 93.

9. Roche, pp. 200-201.

10. Frye, p. 71.

11. *The Allegory of Love* (New York, 1958), p. 337.

12. Lewis, p. 358.

13. My notion of "progressive form" is indebted to Kenneth Burke, *Counter-Statement* (New York, 1931), pp. 157-184; and to Leonard Meyer, *Emotion and Meaning in Music* (Chicago, 1956).

14. *The Poetry of Edmund Spenser* (New York, 1965), pp. 134, 145.

15. Williams, pp. xiii, xix.

16. Williams, p. xix.

17. The following discussion is based mainly on Kurt Koffka, "Problems in the Psychology of Art," *Art: A Bryn Mawr Symposium* (Bryn Mawr, 1940), pp. 180-273; David Katz, *Gestalt Psychology* (1950); Rudolf Arnheim, *Art and Visual Perception* (Berkeley, 1954); Lawrence Kubie, *Neurotic Distortion of the Creative Process* (Lawrence, Kansas, 1958); and Norman Holland, "Literary Value: A Psychoanalytic Approach," *Literature & Psychology*, XIV (1964), 43-55. A similar approach to literary form, directed principally to lyrics, is that of Barbara H. Smith, *Poetic Closure: A Study of How Poems End* (Chicago, 1968).

18. *The Art of the Novel* (New York, 1934), p. 302.

19. Hamilton, p. 43.

20. Coleridge; quoted by Hamilton, p. 14. Cf. the statement in the eighteenth chapter of *Biographia Literaria*: "*all* the parts of an organized whole must be assimilated to the more *important* and *essential* parts."

21. On the analytical constructs "subject" and "object" and their limitations in literary criticism, see Erwin W. Straus, "Aesthiology and Hallucinations," *Existence: A New Dimension in Psychiatry and Psychology,* ed. Rollo May, Ernest Angel, and Henri F. Ellenberger (New York, 1958), 139-169; and Louise M. Rosenblatt, "Towards a Transactional Theory of Reading," *Journal of Reading Behavior*, I (1969), 31-50.

22. Hamilton, p. 138.

23. See the criticism of Frye and Hamilton by Rudolf B. Gottfried, "Our New Poet: Archetypal Criticism and *The Faerie Queene*," PMLA, LXXXIII (1968), 1362-1377.

24. Roche, p. 199.

25. Lewis, p. 336.

Susanne Murphy

Love and War in Spenser's
The Faerie Queene

At the opening of *The Faerie Queene*, in the proem to the first book, the poet Spenser speaks in his own voice, introducing himself and the creation which is to follow:

> Lo I the man, whose Muse whilome did maske,
>   As time her taught, in lowly Shepheards weeds,
>   Am now enforst a far vnfitter taske,
>   For trumpets sterne to chaunge mine Oaten reeds,
>   And sing of Knights and Ladies gentel deeds;
>   Whose prayses hauing slept in silence long;
>   Me, all too meane, the sacred Muse areeds
>   To blazon broad emongst her learned throng:
> Fierce warres and faithfull loues shall moralize my song.
>   [I.proem.1.1-9]

Again in the Mutabilitie Cantos, usually accepted as parts of books which were to follow the sixth, the poet addresses his readers personally:

> Then gin I thinke on that which Nature sayd,
>   Of that same time when no more *Change* shall be,
>   But stedfast rest of all things firmely stayd
>   Vpon the pillours of Eternity,
>   That is contrayr to *Mutabilitie:*

> For, all that moueth, doth in *Change* delight:
> But thence-forth all shall rest eternally
> With Him that is the God of Sabbaoth hight:
> O that great Sabbaoth God, graunt me that Sabbaoths
> sight.

[VII.8.2.1-9]

Perhaps the most obvious conclusion to be drawn from this juxtaposition of the opening and closing stanzas of *The Faerie Queene* is the use of the concept of change in both instances. The poet clearly places himself and his artistic ability within the sublunar sphere in which mutability rules. Like all living things he participates in the cycle of development and decline, and like them, too, he requires assistance from others outside himself. In the light of the rest of the poem it would be fair to say, I think, that the poet's appeals to the Muse, to Cupid, to Venus and to Mars in the opening section are more than the mere mechanical fulfill-ment of an artistic convention. For Spenser's acceptance of the world as one of universal change is special in that it also includes a belief in a stability which exists beyond that change. The particular emphasis of the Mutabilitie Cantos as a whole is precisely that mutability and permanence depend upon each other. Nature warns Mutabilitie that her desire for total power would result in her own destruction; and the poet affirms that it is through the very fact of change that he is led to a belief in the steadfastness behind it.

It seems reasonable to assert, therefore, that Spenser's thought in its generalized form is squarely within the tradition of Neoplatonic theory. This theory itself has two aspects: first, that proper contemplation of the world below leads the contemplator to the truth which lies beyond it; and second, that each discernible lack in this world guarantees the existence of the ideal form in which that lack will be fulfilled. We have on one hand an assertion of worth for the things of this world, and on the other, an unequivocal positioning of them on an inferior level. St. Augustine and Petrarch discuss precisely this duality of values in the *Secretum Meum*.

> Petrarch: I pray you make no rash judgment. The love which I feel for her has most certainly led me to love God.
> St. Augustine: But it has inverted the true order.
> Petrarch: How so?
> St. Augustine: Because every creature should be dear to us because of our love for the Creator. But in your case, on the contrary, held captive by the charm of the creature, you have not loved the Creator as you ought. You have admired the Divine Artificer as though in all His works He had made nothing fairer than the object of your love, although in truth the beauty of the body should be reckoned last of all.[1]

Petrarch here is using love as a metaphorical means of expressing a theory about the union of opposite principles. Plato's Aristophanes had suggested an explanation of love as the force driving male and female halves back to their original and more ideal unity. According to Aristotle motion implied desire and desire implied lack. Throughout the Renaissance which took so many of its philosophical cues from Plato and Aristotle, then, the belief prevailed that life was a quest to bring about the unification of opposites: body with spirit, physical values with spiritual ones. God and the Good were understood and frequently represented as a harmony of opposites, the resolution of polarities. Man, on the other hand, was fallen out of harmony, and somehow split. This division was seen as existing within man himself, in the mind/body conflict, for example; and externally as well in the notion that man even at his best was incomplete— requiring union with his own opposite (symbolically either the male or the female) in order to achieve perfection. A good human being recognized his own partiality. An evil one, in contrast, failed to see this truth and stagnated in his own incompleteness. The importance of *quest*, or motion toward something outside the self, in a virtuous life, is clearly a crucial concept.

The paradox of Ficino's ladder and Aristotle's motion, as we have seen in the selection from Petrarch, is the intrinsic two-directionality. Ladders are means of descent as well as of ascent, and motion can as easily be inspired by evil desires as by good ones. Not every union of opposite principles, therefore, is an ideal one. Similarly, not every sexual relationship between a man and a woman is a meaningful symbol for the unifying power of love. Spenser's ideal stasis, represented in terms of mutability and permanence, is one of mutual giving in which each member depends for perfection upon a fruitful relationship with the other. The two together constitute a formal pattern in which the whole and the parts give meaning to and take meaning from each other. Mutability exists in a relationship with permanence, knowledge of eternity through knowledge of time, the pattern of the song through the interaction of different notes.

This musical metaphor for the ideal harmony of the divine, which sometimes can be present on earth, is as important for Spenser as it will be later for Milton. In both *Paradise Lost* and *The Faerie Queene*, moreover, the greater part of the action takes place in a fallen world—one, that is, in which harmony is something to be sought, rather than something which is given. Despite the apparent unreality of the setting, therefore, both works are far more real in their statement of the human situation than other poems which are perhaps more superficially in the realistic tradition. At its outer edges *The Faerie Queene* is an epic-romance, overflowing with dangerous dragons, brave knights, ladies-in-distress and mysterious forests. Just inside those edges it is an unfinished moral allegory describing only six of what were eventually to have been twenty-four classical virtues. Yet another step closer to the still-distant center, however, even these six books begin to take on a meaning apart from formalized moralizing and contemporary social comment—a meaning which is both complex and beautiful just as it stands.

"Fierce warres and faithfull loues," the poet tells us, shall moralize his song. The reader is advised at the very outset that the old standbys of chivalric tradition, bravery in war and loyalty in love, are present in this work for more than their own dear sake. However the poet emphasizes equally the literal manner in which the subject will be handled in his prayer to the particular deities of love and war later in the proem. On one hand, then, the particular loves and battles of the narrative are announced as poetic symbols intended to "moralize" in the direction of something beyond themselves. On the other, the patrons of love and war, in real life as well as in art, are called upon to assist in the moralizing. This duality, as C. S. Lewis points out, is typical of Spenser's allegorizing technique in general. Not only do the characters in the work achieve their meanings with reference to virtues or historical personages outside of them, but also these same virtues or personages are explained with reference to the characters within the narrative pattern.[2] In one half of the movement, therefore, the wars and loves of St. George constitute a pleasant vehicle for a statement about the nature of holiness and its achievement by the Christian saint. In the second part of the pattern, though, the legend of holiness itself forms part of the larger statement on the nature of life on this earth and the decisions, battles and romances which it involves. What complicates the attempt to paraphrase the poem, of course, is the magic whereby both things go on at the same time. A critic leaves chivalric love behind, follows the progress of the symbol, and arrives back at love in the real world of strife all over again.

We have no way of knowing what the whole of *The Faerie Queene* would have been like had the poet completed all twenty-four, or even twelve, of the books described in the letter to Raleigh. A union of Arthur and the Queen as symbol for the ideal magistrate perhaps is a tempting speculation, but

remains a speculation all the same. Then again, in a structure
as rich as the one with which we are dealing here, it is
possible that the addition of more material would have
evoked different interpretations of the events of the first six
books—qualifying some, altering others. This measure of
doubt, however, in no way implies that the six books just as
they are now are some meaningless jumble of episodes, or
even that they should be compared with a detective story
before the discovery of the vital clue. Elaborately related
themes are evident as soon as the six books are considered
together. Examination of these themes, in addition, makes it
possible to formulate a poetic statement which has relevance
to each of the books and to many of their several episodes.
Had the work been completed, more themes would probably
have presented themselves. Possibly, too, several of these
themes would have found places within a still larger
framework hints of which are already present (however
darkly) in the material now before us. With reference to a
fabric as dense as that of *The Faerie Queene*, any attempt to
trace themes, to derive meanings, is bound to convey only a
limited impression of the poem itself, since what the critic
sees in *The Faerie Queene* is his vision and not Spenser's.
That there are a great many themes is unquestionable. That
of love and war, however, as symbols (and somehow more
than symbols) for the vital interaction of all opposing forces,
is such an important one in the Renaissance that it will be
useful to develop it here.

The task of Red Crosse throughout Book I can easily be
expressed as prowess in battles and faithfulness in love. Two
of his major failures are the original desertion of Una
prompted by his acceptance of Archimago's interpretation of
their love, and his defeat by Orgoglio after he had willingly
surrendered his identity as a man of warfare. The great
success at the close of the book, of course, represents love
and war too. The victorious fight with the dragon illustrates
Red Crosse's worthiness to be Una's husband and the ritual
betrothal confirms the success of his two-fold quest. Operat-

ing seemingly at odds with this simple statement, however, is
the episode at the House of Holinesse in which Jerusalem is
revealed to the saint:

> But when thou famous victorie hast wonne,
> And high emongst all knights hast hong thy shield,
> Thenceforth the suit of earthly conquest shonne,
> And wash thy hands from guilt of bloudy field:
> For bloud can nought but sin, and wars but sorrowes
> yield.
>
> [I.10.60.5-9]

Battle, St. George is told, although it is most necessary for
the affairs of this world, is rather more evil in itself than
good. It is a part of earth rather than of heaven, and when
final victory has been achieved, all conflict will cease. The
case of love, however, is more complicated. "As for loose
loues are vaine, and vanish into nought [I.10.62.9]." The
sexual relationship which remains earthbound is a particular
sort of relationship, a "loose loue." Even in pursuit of
heaven, Red Crosse is reminded, he is not justified in
deserting Una. "That may not be (said he) ne maist thou
yit/Forgo that royall maides bequeathed care [I.10.63.6-7]."

Clearly, then, within the context of this first book, Spenser
seems to imply that there are at least two sorts of love, one
bound to the earth and one appropriate to the pursuit of
heaven. In the course of the narrative, Red Crosse's relationships with the two women, Una and Duessa, serve to
emphasize this distinction. In the best of the courtly
tradition, Red Crosse's battles are frequently inspired by the
love relationship. And these battles too are ambiguous,
deriving either worth or futility from the love with which
they are involved.

It is a tribute to the poet's ability to portray the human
situation that Red Crosse so frequently cannot tell what is
good and what is bad, and that he can so often do precisely
the wrong thing for precisely the right (or the nearly right)

motive. The struggle of life for him is to join the form with
the reality, the right deed with the right motive, and most of
his wrongs are committed (as has often been remarked, too
late) with all of the best intentions in the world. Spenser's
moralizing technique, as any good poet's must be, is very
concrete. He does not say, in effect, this is the *theory* of
virtuous warfare, or of an ideal romantic relationship. He
provides instead two blatantly similar situations—one an ideal
and the other a typical distortion of the ideal, and in the
context of the poem (but only there) makes his point—of
which is to be admired and which rejected—eminently clear.
The subtlety of the approach is remarkable. Like Thomas'
fourth temptation in Eliot's *Murder in the Cathedral*, the
worst evil is not an obvious, cloven-footed, red-tailed,
black-hatted villain whom it would be difficult to misinter-
pret. He is instead a more insidious persuader, possessing
many characteristics of the genuine good, whose hat is
perhaps only the palest shade of gray, and who is only
revealed as evil under the closest and most large-minded of
scrutinies. Red Crosse's faithfulness to Duessa, his victorious
battles for her sake, are as worthy in themselves as is his
similar loyalty and bravery for Una. Only from a point of
view beyond his own is it possible to say that those deeds are
only half right.

Similarly the concrete forms which are given to virtue in
the course of the poem are frequently given to vice as well.
The interaction between mother and offspring, which with
Charissa operates as a symbol of an ideal love relationship,
parallels that illustrated earlier in the case of Error, whose
children drew both life and death from their parent. Allegory
as a poetic device is always reversible because it must always
be a merely imperfect symbol for what essentially cannot be
expressed at all. The numerous disguises in *The Faerie
Queene* and the ease with which characters change material
identities reveal the basic imperfection of sense experience. If
Red Crosse had understood more of Truth than what was
expressed in the physical nature of Una—if he had seen her,

in other words, as we do, as a poetic symbol pointing toward something beyond itself—he would not have been deceived by Archimago's false image of her. The false Una can duplicate only the physical appearance; she cannot duplicate the nature of the original, which would be contrary to the sexual looseness of the vision.

The most intriguing question of this first book, and one which is repeated throughout the poem, is the poet's emphasis upon heroic battles on one hand, and his denial of their ultimate worth on the other. There are clearly good and bad battles, as we have already seen, but even these good battles will disappear in the New Jerusalem. Red Crosse's Christian armor, given to him by Una, was unworthily laid aside before his battle with Orgoglio. Spenser implies, however, that the unarming in itself is not an absolute fault. In certain contexts, those of lovemaking, for instance, war equipment may justly be removed. Even after his greatest victory, however, Red Crosse cannot cease his knightly career.

> Of ease or rest I may not yet deuize;
> For by the faith, which I to armes haue plight,
> I bounden am streight after this emprize,
> As that your daughter can ye well aduize,
> Backe to returne to that great Faerie Queene,
> And her to serue six yeares in warlike wize.
>
> [I.12.18.2-7]

The ceremony at the close of Book I, then, is, significantly, a betrothal rather than a wedding. It is a familiar romance motif that the marriage cannot take place until the quest, warfare, has been laid aside, an ideal union thus associated symbolically with the formal end of all conflict (although this does not hold true in every case).

The important thing to notice here, in any case, is that the vision of permanent cessation of warfare is connected only with heaven. As long as Red Crosse remains on earth the need to fight and to distinguish between good and bad battles continues. Life-as-battle and life-as-quest are both persistent metaphors and, I think, perhaps essentially identical. As long as life remains fallen, as long as we exist in a sublunar sphere, there must be motion and lack. And there must then be conflict with evil which must continue to exist merely as one of the givens in the human situation. The battle, in itself, is neither an ultimate good nor evil. Spenser's heaven is not one in which heroes fall one day only to rise and continue the fun on the next. Neither is his earth one in which battles are always right or always wrong. Knights who indulge in random conflicts or warfare for unworthy causes are consistently condemned. Strife among men is seen clearly as an unavoidable element of earthly existence, but one which must be made valuable as a means to an end higher than itself. To refuse battle when battle is necessary, to impose an artificial peace upon elements which should naturally conflict, signifies for Spenser a breakdown in the ideal scheme of things—even though true perfection is characterized by the cessation of warfare. This complexity of subtle parallels between the real solution and the patent solution which almost does the same thing, continues in Spenser's treatment of love in Books II and III.

C. S. Lewis has illustrated carefully the parallels in the descriptions of the Bower of Bliss and the Garden of Adonis. He has given very cogent arguments for the implication of these artistic parallels. Both places, he contends, are meant to represent attitudes toward human love. The Bower illustrates perverse stagnation and self-interest, while the Garden is a haven of happy interaction and mutual giving.[3] Although I agree essentially with what Lewis has to say about these two "allegorical centers," I should like here to stress a slightly different aspect of Spenser's treatment of the Bower. I am troubled primarily by the fondness which the poet seems to display for Acrasia's home country, even though his ideal hero is made to condemn and destroy it in the end. Parts of the description do convey a surfeit of lushness and pure sensuality, and Lewis is justified in pointing them out. But there are other aspects here, just as there were others in the description of the Idle Lake, which are quite simply appealing, and I cannot convince myself that the appeal is due only to a misreading of the poet's intention. It seems to me, rather, that we are meant to have a more complex understanding of the Bower than, for instance, of the Cave of Mammon. The Bower is more dangerous than the Cave because it is so close to being right, because it represents a positive good only slightly altered, an ideal made to fit into a situation which cannot contain it. The Bower can be seen, then, as an ultimately evil refusal to accept the natural given of reality. The relationship between art and nature in the Bower may be only one small step away from Spenser's concept of an ideal relationship, but the effect of that small step is enormous.

Good art reveals the truth about nature and this power of revelation and illumination is at the heart of any mimetic theory of literature. Art may imitate realities which are somewhat beyond the ordinary everyday ones and for this reason it can be used as a means of instruction; but what it imitates must ultimately be valid human reality. Art uses what is; it affirms and gives meaning to it, but it may not deceive or falsify reality even for a seemingly good end. Yet this last is what occurs in the Bower, in a distortion which functions in two ways. Primarily the art in the Bower creates an independent nature, refusing to accept the real one.

> And ouer all, of purest gold was spred,
> A trayle of yuie in his natiue hew:
> For the rich mettall was so coloured,
> That wight, who did not well auis'd it vew,
> Would surely deeme it to be yuie trew:
>
> [II.12.61.1-5]

The second and more important falsification, however, concerns the determination not to accept *what is* on a far larger scale. It involves a refusal to affirm the mixture of bad and good in this world. Symbolically the peace between the opposing forces achieved in the Bower is not one of meaningful interaction, but of an artful cease-fire. It is the harmony represented by Artegall's giant who measures quantitatively but cannot judge qualitatively. The weather of the Bower undergoes no change, "rude and fine parts" are joined without distinction, and the captured knight is deprived of his identity as a warrior and of his necessary human activity of choosing between right and wrong which is part of that identity. The carefully constructed metaphor of life-as-quest, as a constant struggle to distinguish between bad and good, which Spenser had established in Book I, breaks down in the Bower. And the breakdown occurs, the poet emphasizes, at the expense of reality. The proper goal of human life, revealed in the vision at the House of Holinesse, may be a stasis, but it is one which must grow out of a willingness to deal with natural conflicts. Ideal harmony is achieved by a careful blending of discordant sounds. The Bower, in contrast, represents only one note which has been extended artificially.

According to the Renaissance interpretation of the "great chain of being" man is half angel and half beast, a combination of body and mind. The movement toward perfection is a constant battle of one half against the other, and since perfection itself is not attainable on this earth, the only way to halt battle here and now is to reduce both halves to their least common denominator, that of the animal. In the symbolic terms of poetry, knights who want to remove their armor *permanently* before the end of the war must either kill themselves to destroy the body or become beasts to destroy the mind. Either alternative is merely an artificial imitation of the final peace associated with the New Jerusalem.

The synthesis achieved in the Bower is an invalid one, a step down rather than up on the ladder. Yet it is a synthesis just the same and this accounts for its superficial desirability. Like Red Crosse's bravery on behalf of Duessa, it is the right effect achieved through the wrong means, the form is correct but the matter is unreal. Change and death, at the core of Spenser's conception of reality, must be given a meaningful place in any system which pretends to offer an explanation for life. Yet this is exactly what does not occur in the Bower. Mutability here is not explained in terms of a larger perspective. *It* is not given a place in a greater scheme. Instead in the "Song of the Rose" mutability becomes a kind of ultimate itself, a justification for a *carpe diem* morality. Mutability here may be accepted as a fact; but that acceptance, like Verdant's acceptance of Acrasia's love, leads downward into despair. Conflicts of opposing forces within the scheme established in the Bower ultimately can neither be justified nor completely removed (although the attempt to abolish the seasons illustrates an effort in that direction). In order to maintain itself the Bower must work against rather than with reality. The peace achieved there, consequently, cannot be a true one, even though the forms of "peace," "harmony," "union-through-love," are the valid symbols for the ideal life. As a foil for the false situation of the Bower Spenser provides the Garden of Adonis in Book III.

One of the first aspects of the description of the Garden to strike the reader is the emphasis placed upon its power of generation. Whereas the Bower had been primarily a place of retreat unto itself, the Garden is pictured as a vital source of life.

In that same Gardin all the goodly flowres,
   Wherewith dame Nature doth her beautifie
And decks the girlonds of her paramoures,
   Are fetcht: there is the first seminarie
   Of all things, that are borne to liue and die,
   According to their kindes. . . . .

[III.6.30.1-6]

The method in which life comes about, too, the perpetual interaction between changing forms and eternal substance, is treated in the following cantos in great detail. The general impression of the Garden is of a place in which reality in all its complexity is made to function harmoniously without any distortion of truth. In contrast to the Bower, for instance, there is no need to falsify or to negate. Even Chaos, living "in hatefull darkenesse and in deepe horrore [III.6.36.7]," is allowed a purposeful place in the whole. The stasis achieved in the Garden is one of continuous conflict, of perpetual death and rebirth, of unending interaction of opposites. It is the same world which, under different circumstances, could be used as an incitement to despair or as a sermon on the vanities of this world. The perspective from which it is viewed here, however, serves to make of it an affirmation of the meaning behind the process of life and death. Time here is the "troubler" of earthly joys, just as in the Bower; but like the dual-natured Genius who guards the Garden gate, it is made to fulfill a double purpose. Time both permits of individuality and guarantees the permanent succession of individuals. "There is continuall spring, and haruest there/Continuall, both meeting at one time [III.6.42.1-2]," the poet tells us. On one hand importance is given to each particular life cycle and, on the other, the end of each individual does not necessitate pessimism. Each rose and each lover is important for his own sake and within his own time span. Each is given an opportunity to grow and develop; but the process of aging and death which finally destroys the individual also makes new creation possible. Realities are not hidden in the Garden as they were in the Bower. Seasonal changes, death and decay, are openly present and are given a meaningful place within a larger system. The emphasis upon the creativity of the Garden over and above the stagnation of the Bower has to do with the overall system of imagery in *The Faerie Queene.* What is good moves outwards, including more and more reality within it, combining opposites in meaningful patterns, seizing upon all aspects of human experience. What is evil, in contrast, revolves around itself,

limiting realities within artificial boundaries, imitating the
apparent patterns of the ideal, but unable to fill them with
actual substances.

Warfare, love and art in Spenser's *Faerie Queene* all occur
in the real world—the world, that is, in which good and evil
are mixed and difficult to distinguish. There can be, as we
have seen, both bad and good war, love, and art. Bad in the
examples given here, and I believe, throughout the entire
poem can usually be associated with a falsification of reality,
a willingness to accept the pleasing surface rather than an
effort to create a system which will accommodate the more
difficult parts of human life. Here as in *Paradise Lost* the
most dangerous evils are those which imitate genuine goods.
Physical love as a symbol for divine harmony lies at the
bottom of both the Garden and the Bower. Satan's temptation of Adam and Eve is an offer of fuller knowledge of their
position with regard to God and the angels. This is the same
knowledge which God himself wants to share with them and
which he sends Raphael to impart. In Book V God directs the
Angel to converse with Adam "as friend with friend":

> As may advise him of his happie state,
> . . . . .whence warn him to beware
> He swerve not too secure; tell him withall
> His danger, and from whom, what enemie
> Late fall'n himself from Heav'n, is plotting now
> The fall of others from like state of bliss;
>
> [*Par.Lost*.V.234;237-241]

And in Book IX the serpent offers Eve a similar share in the
divine knowledge of the world.

> Ye Eate thereof, your Eyes that seem so cleere,
> Yet are but dim, shall perfectly be then
> Op'n'd and cleer'd, and ye shall be as Gods,
> Knowing both Good and Evil as they know.
>
> [*Par.Lost*.IX.706-709]

Good, in contrast to evil, is represented as an orderly arrangement of opposing forces within some larger scheme which gives them meaning without distorting their individual reality. The virtuous love relationships of the main characters in *The Faerie Queene* share the outward movement of the Garden of Adonis. Male and female principles come together in an active interchange, and it is only from a larger point of view that the emphasis can be placed upon what binds rather than what separates them. Neither surrenders his own identity as Verdant in the Bower and Artegall under Radigund's power are forced to do. Rather each in all his complex reality contributes to the whole which encompasses them. The character of the warrior, associated on earth with the need to judge bad and good, becomes, as well, the first qualification for the ideal lover. Perpetual conflict, eternal change, are the very elements which finally make possible the ideal stasis of love. But the virtuous Mars can surrender justly only to the Venus who is worthy of him—who justifies rather than negates his quest.

Spenser's peace on earth is never finally established. Evil individuals are overcome but the process of evil by which they are affected and infected remains. The ideal Venus may be a stable hermaphrodite,[4] but earthly love requires two eternally separate individuals for completion. The elaborate pattern of dancing Graces in Book VI disappears when Calidore comes into view. Like the harmony of art which imitates it, heavenly peace is final only in heaven. A proper earthly peace points to it, imitates its form, embodies it in poetic symbol, but cannot replace it. Each apparently idyllic love in *The Faerie Queene* is forced into a relationship with the dubious world outside it. The pastoral world has no permanent immunity in the world of thieves.

The structure of *The Faerie Queene*, then, makes a larger pattern out of the various romantic and military conflicts. Like Dame Nature in the Mutabilitie Cantos, the poet makes use of perpetual change to express the permanence which lies hidden behind it. And in this paradoxical sense, too, the

openendedness of the work is meaningful. Adam and Eve in
the final lines of Milton's epic stand at the very beginning of
human reality as we know it. Similarly Spenser's battles are
"more real" exactly because they are not, and cannot be,
completed during life. An unfinished poem can be made,
among other things, to illustrate the perpetual process of art.

NEW YORK CITY

1. Petrarch, *Secretum Meum*, translated by William H. Draper, *Prose and Poetry of the Continental Renaissance in Translation*, ed. Harold Hooper Blanchard, 2nd ed. (New York, 1955), p. 41.

2. C. S. Lewis, *Spenser's Image of Life*, ed. Alastair Fowler (Cambridge, 1967), Chapter 1.

3. *Ibid.*, Ch. 3.

4. The notion of Venus in the Temple of Venus and of the Goddess Nature in the Mutabilitie Cantos as veiled because of their hermaphroditic natures is suggested by the poet himself as one possible reason for the veiling [VII.7.5-6]. C. S. Lewis, *op. cit.*, and Donald Cheney in *Spenser's Image of Nature* (New Haven, 1966) both discuss the relationship of these figures to the larger themes of love in the work.

John E. O'Conner

Prince Arthur

The Cohesive, Tempering Grace

> The general end therefore of all the booke is to fashion a
> gentleman or noble person in vertuous discipline: . . . So
> have I laboured to doe in the person of Arthure.

The question of unity, which so often arises in discussions of
the six books of *The Faerie Queene*, is answered partially by
Spenser himself in this statement of purpose. The poem is an
allegorical treatment of specific virtues. And the ennobling
power of virtue, as an abstract ideal, is embodied in the figure
of Arthur. Arthur's relation to the specific virtues allegorized
in each book is the factor which most appreciably contributes to the unity of *The Faerie Queene*.

Prince Arthur makes his first appearance in the poem at a
point in Book I when the Red Crosse Knight has just
succumbed to the evil forces of blustering and arrogant pride
(Orgoglio) and Una has just learned of the series of
deceptions which led to Red Crosse's imprisonment
[1.7.21.2]. An investigation of the events leading up to Red
Crosse's submission to pride and the immediate context in
which Arthur first appears will help explain how the
intervention of the Prince affects the virtue of holiness,
embodied in Red Crosse.

Partly as a result of evil forces beyond his control
(Archimago) and partly due to his own naivete, the Red

Crosse Knight allows himself to be overcome by a kind of showy pride when he willingly accompanies Duessa to Lucifera's castle. Once there he indulges in ostentation and self-satisfaction at having triumphed over Eros and Sansfoy in the first two battles of his knightly career. While at Lucifera's superficial and gaudy castle, Red Crosse finds himself in the limelight. His pride is not obsessive and he has the presence of mind to reject the vain publicity that is offered him in the form of Lucifera's joy ride. Finally, after discovering the dangers to which the pretentious atmosphere of Lucifera's castle expose him, Red Crosse flees.

It is not long, however, before the Knight is once more overcome by the same beguiling influences, i.e. Duessa, that earlier led him to Lucifera's castle. Duessa finds Red Crosse unarmed and slumbering lazily in a cool shade. She immediately takes advantage of his carelessness and begins to dally with him. Red Crosse's weak spiritual condition is enfeebled further when he drinks from a nearby stream without realizing that the water is polluted. Since there is no way he could have known of the water's pollution and since drinking is a natural act, this brief episode demonstrates how naturally resistence to temptation, on both a spiritual and physical level, diminishes once man has exposed himself to sin. Red Crosse does nothing to counter what his own self-deception, in the person of Duessa, is leading him into; and he is eventually seduced:

> Yet goodly court he made still to his Dame,
> Pourd out in loosnesse on the grassy grownd.
>   [I.7.7.1-2]

This is the moment of total lack of resistance. Pride, the gravest of sins, strikes. Red Crosse is deceived by his own self-satisfaction at having earlier withstood the onslaughts of sin. His mistaken notions of his own virtue have now trapped him and subjected him to pride, antithetical to all virtue.

Just before Arthur comes on the scene, Una learns of her knight's total self-deception and blustering, arrogant pride.

She learns that the knight she loves has allowed himself to be seduced by self-deceit, her "onely foe, mine onely deadly dread [I.7.50.7]." One would expect a woman, after having learned of her lover's faithlessness, to reject and scorn the disloyal lover; and, in Una's case, to give up her search for him. Una's reaction, however, is quite the opposite. Although she suffers when she hears of Red Crosse's downfall, she sees his sinful condition as a reason to love him all the more. "And loue fresh coles vnto her fire did lay [I.7.27.5]." Ironically, suffering prompts Una to continue both her love and her search for her unfaithful lover with renewed vigor and resolve.

It is at this moment of Una's magnanimous response to her knight's sins that she encounters Arthur and finally enlists his aid. Due to Arthur's mysterious origin, his supernaturally virtuous upbringing, and the celestial brilliance and durability of his armor, he can be seen as a personification of heavenly grace intervening at a time when Una most deserves its aid and Red Crosse most needs it. Arthur's appearance at this particular point in the story suggests a twofold function of divine grace: in Una's case, it serves as a kind of reward for the deliberate continuation of love in the face of adversity; and in Red Crosse's case, it is a redemptive force that is freely available and is even imposed, in a time of despair. This latter aspect of grace is brought out in Canto 8 when Arthur, upon hearing of Red Crosse's despairing plea for death, furiously rips open the cell door, falls headlong into the hole and "After long paines and labours manifold [I.8.40.5]," manages to lift the spiritually limp knight out of the dungeon of sin and despair. Thus can grace which is unsought serve as an active force supplying the initial impulse toward the acquisition of virtue.

Arthur's rescue of Red Crosse is significant in that the latter's vain pride is overcome, and he is freed from the influence of the gravest of sins. Yet it is also significant that this is as far as Arthur goes in his intervention into the affairs of Red Crosse and Una. For as active and unsought as his help has been, Arthur does not offer to accompany Red Crosse on his mission to rescue Una's parents. The redemptive grace that Arthur's help signifies does not compel Red Crosse to behave in any prescribed manner after he has received it. His independence of action, as well as his own responsibility for the accomplishment of his mission, is respected. Thus, when Arthur and Red Crosse part company, the latter immediately and deliberately exposes himself to the dangers of despair and quickly comes as close to death under its power as he did under the influence of pride. The assistance of grace therefore does not resolve all moral conflicts. In Red Crosse's case it constitutes the first step of his renewed journey toward the accomplishment of his mission; it reunites him with "steadfast truth" which saves him from despair and guides him to spiritual perfection. The active assistance of grace embodied in the intervention of Arthur is the first and most important step in the process of making Red Crosse a better and greater man. Indeed he becomes a great man, as the aged Contemplation prophesies, he becomes "Saint George of merry England, the sign of victory." And Arthur, as the embodiment of "magnificence," accomplishes his allegorical task: he makes George "great," which is what "magnificence" literally means; and he refines him spiritually, thus exhibiting the unique power of grace.

Arthur's second appearance in the poem occurs when he accidentally interrupts Pyrochles and Cymochles as they begin to strip the sleeping Guyon of his armor [II.8.23.1]. Prior to this scene the irascible Pyrochles and the angry, lascivious Cymochles had been subdued in battle by Guyon. Now finding him asleep and believing him dead, they decide to take their vengeance by stripping and thus dishonoring his corpse.

Guyon, the knight whose adventures are to illustrate the exercise of temperance, has fallen asleep as a result of his tedious three-day passage through the cave of Mammon. No temptation presented to him in the cave ever seriously threatened his temperance because nothing offered by

Mammon was of any interest to him. Guyon's trip through the cave is not unlike that of a husband who is dragged endlessly through the woman's section of a department store and constantly offered things for which he has absolutely no use or interest. After three consecutive days of such a trip, it is little wonder that Guyon faints when it is over. Of course his faint signifies a relaxation of his temperance; and since his temperance has never been in the slightest danger until now, this relaxation could very well be the natural result of having constantly led an excessively temperate life. Such a rigidly temperate life is very virtuous but also very boring and tedious, and conducive to over-confidence. When one is bored and at the same time deceptively presumptuous of his own virtue, he is particularly vulnerable to the onslaughts of irascibility and concupiscence. This is Guyon's condition at the point of Arthur's arrival in the second book.

Upon learning of the dishonor that Pyrochles and Cymochles are about to commit against Guyon, Arthur calmly (one might say, temperately) points out that all knights owe each other mutual respect. Pyrochles responds by angrily attacking Arthur with his sword and the latter finds himself compelled to fight and finally kill the vengeful knights. Thus grace preserves the honor and value of temperance when exposed to irascibility and concupiscence. It is important to note that Arthur battles with the two angry knights in defense of Guyon's honor and not his life. Grace sustains the value inherent in the virtue of temperance without implying that temperance imposes an absolute obligation on man. In other words, for as much as temperance is to be esteemed, occasions arise when a little intemperance and irascibility are justified. One such occasion was Christ's angry expulsion of the bankers and stock brokers from the temple. Another is Arthur's current battle with anger and concupiscence.

In that battle there is a curious incompatibility between the arms that the respective knights use and the virtues or vices they each represent. In the first part of the fight Arthur defends himself using only his lance, which is broken during the course of the battle, and his shield, which he never unveils. Pyrochles fights with Arthur's magic sword, Morddure, earlier acquired by Archimago, and Guyon's shield. At a desperate moment in the battle, the Palmer rescues Arthur by handing him Guyon's sword, the sword of temperance. With this new, significant weapon Arthur's strategy changes drastically. Before receiving the sword, he had been fighting by evasion; he now begins fighting with aggression:

> As a saluage Bull, whom two fierce mastiues bayt,
> When rancour doth which rage him once engore,
> . . . .
> Breathing out wrath, and bellowing disdaine,
> . . . .
> So rag'd Prince *Arthure* twixt his foemen twaine.
>   [II.8.42.1-2,6,8]

Arthur's rage, endorsed by grace, is in this case an element for the conquering of rage itself. In some instances the exercise of temperance calls for a little healthy anger in order to preserve grace and sanity and temperance itself. But this requirement is temporary as seen by the fact that Arthur uses a sword that is not his own and which he will return to its owner at the end of the battle.

Whereas grace and temperance can make use of anger in specific instances to attain their ends, rage is incapable of serving its ends by means of grace and temperance. Pyrochles has Arthur's sword in his hand during the fight but it is totally ineffective against grace. He defends himself with Guyon's shield, but in the end he is overcome. Grace reaffirms the basic soundness of the virtue of temperance while demonstrating that temperance itself can at times be tempered by a just anger.

Once irascibility is defeated, Guyon awakes and, in the company of Arthur, goes to Alma's castle. The two knights experience some difficulty in gaining admission to the castle, since it is under the siege of Maleger, Impatience and Impotence. Eventually, the two knights do enter and spend a pleasant evening being entertained by Alma's borders. The following day Guyon leaves to continue his mission against Acrasia, leaving Arthur to deal with the problems of Maleger's siege.

Notwithstanding Guyon's separation from Arthur, the latter's battle with Maleger helps explain further the notion of temperance and the role that grace plays in the balanced exercise of the virtue. The strategy employed by Maleger in his siege is to mount particular attacks against the five senses in an effort to lay waste to the soul. Inside the castle an attitude of self-protection mixed with dismay prevails and it issues in a defensive rather than offensive policy toward all who appear outside the castle. Even when grace and temperance called, there was initial fear and apprehension about admitting them.

The castle of the soul is pictured as a self-contained establishment which provides its own entertainment and possesses its own institutions of intellectual activity. Yet what goes on inside is entirely estranged from what happens outside. The whole scene of the castle under siege and subject to Maleger's specific attacks against the five senses represents a mentality hypersensitive to the dangers of sin and prone to isolate itself from the rest of the world in order to avoid temptation. Maleger—his long, bony, pale body crowned with a skull—represents a kind of spiritual malingering. A soul afflicted with such a malady naturally suspects all that it perceives, and fears that all is sinful and evil. Impatience accompanies Maleger in the siege in order to demonstrate the lack of self-tolerance experienced by the moral hypochondriac that results from his excessive guilt. Misguided spiritual impatience ultimately leads to a hesitancy to act for fear of falling into sin. That is why Impotence also attends Maleger in his assaults against the soul. Impatience with oneself in the face of Impotence can only lead to spiritual paralysis and frustration. Arthur's victory over Maleger and his debilitating lieutenants is the influence that grace has in keeping the soul from judging itself too severely. Grace tempers the conscience with mercy.

One of the important aspects of grace brought out in the first two books of *The Faerie Queene* is that, in order to function effectively, those who are to be helped by grace must be disposed to receive its assistance. If they do not seek grace directly, neither do they reject it when it is offered. Grace was obtained for both Red Crosse and Guyon through the intercession of faithful advisers who were intimately involved in the lives of the respective knights and who recognized the efficacy of grace. The role played by grace in the third book differs from that in the first two books because the person whom grace attempts to help, Florimell, flees from its assistance. Arthur first sees Florimell when she is being chased by an evil forester. In an effort to rescue her, Arthur pursues the forester and succeeds in forcing him to give up the chase. Florimell, not recognizing Arthur's good intentions, now flees from him and eludes his efforts to overtake and comfort her. Florimell's flight from grace is emblematic of the indiscriminate fears which prevent one from facing the moral risks that give value to virtue. Florimell's unwillingness to risk meeting Arthur deprives her of the saving influence of grace. Not accepting the aid of grace has painful consequences for Florimell. Her fear intensifies and becomes increasingly unbearable as she continues her flight.

The last seven stanzas of Canto 5, Book III, contain Arthur's lament for failing to overtake Florimell and offer her his assistance. His bitter castigation of night, as the "mother of annoyance sad, sister of heavy death and nurse of woe," can be read as a diagnosis of Florimell's fearful attitude toward the natural risks of life. Arthur, whose armor is the antithesis of darkness, accuses night of being the root of a "heavy heart," "the nurse of bitter cares" and "the renewer of old smarts." He sees that these are the inner discomforts that afflict Florimell because fear has darkened her soul. Fear has caused her to reject unwittingly the saving light which Arthur, as grace, so eagerly tries to provide. The efficacy of grace depends on the willingness of those in need to accept its aid.

Whereas Arthur's actions in Book III demonstrate how grace seeks to temper the exaggerated fears that render grace ineffective, his intervention in Book IV shows grace trying to mitigate the excessive liberty that certain passions are sometimes allowed to have. As Arthur comes on the scene, he encounters Amoret and Aemylia suffering the consequences of a frightening and painful bout with the evils of lust [IV.8.19]. He immediately administers the comforts of grace in the form of some "precious liquor," thereby gratuitously offering forgiveness in case the ladies feel at all guilty about their unpleasant experiences. Furthermore his mere company provides the ladies with the strength to sustain the unavoidable onslaughts of slander and calumny that afflict even the innocent.

No sooner has Slander's backbiting been nullified by the presence of grace when envious lust again appears in the form of Corflambo in hot pursuit of Placidas. The latter cries to Arthur for help and the lustful monster is quickly dispatched. Then at the instigation of Arthur Placidas tells the long story of how his good friend Amyas was on his way to a rendezvous with his fiancee, Aemylia, when he was kidnapped by Corflambo's son and imprisoned in lust's dungeon with a large number of other young men. He tells how Corflambo's daughter, Paeana, a whore, persistently but vainly tried to seduce Amyas and how he, Placidas, managed to get himself mistaken for his friend and thrown into prison in an attempt to substitute himself for Amyas and help the latter escape. Curiously enough, only the first part of his plan worked; that is, Placidas was mistaken for his friend and substituted himself for Amyas in those sessions with Paeana that had been so trying and distasteful for Amyas. So while Amyas remained below in the dungeon waiting to escape, chastely faithful to his Aemylia, Placidas was busy deceiving Paeana and supposedly "To my firends good, more then for mine owne sake [IV.8.60.8]," allowed himself to be seduced by the beautiful whore. Placidas' devotion to friendship is enviable.

Aemylia, upon hearing that Amyas is still alive, asks Arthur's help in freeing him. It is significant, in light of Placidas' story, that it is Aemylia and not Placidas himself who asks for Arthur's help. Not only is affection pictured here as being more concerned with the plight of a loved one, but the profundity of Placidas' friendship is brought into question. In any event Arthur frees Amyas and all the other prisoners of lust as well, thereby demonstrating the unquestioning forgiveness with which grace is bestowed, especially when love is the basic reason for its intervention. When all are free and Amyas is reunited with Aemylia, Arthur takes Paeana aside and, in a further gesture of forgiveness, mollifies her burning lust with friendly and graceful speech. Then he does something that seems very strange: since Paeana is still very much attracted to Amyas, Arthur persuades the latter to take the one-time whore for his wife. And we are told that from that day forth they lived in peace and joyous bliss and Paeana reformed her ways. Whatever happened to Aemylia, who also loved Amyas, remains a mystery. Oh, the power of grace to reconcile chaste and faithful Amyas to the daughter of lust; and oh, the mystery of its ways.

The intervention of Arthur in the fifth book differs from his earlier interventions in that here he is not called upon to assist the titular knight of the book, Artegall. Instead Arthur becomes his companion and peer in their successful efforts to restore justice. The scene of Arthur's entrance into the book is designed to show the equality of strength and effectiveness of grace and justice. As Canto 8 opens Samient is being chased by two evil knights. Arthur and Artegall, independently, subdue one of Samient's pursuers. Then, not recognizing each other, they fall into battle and suffer identical consequences: both break their spears, neither is unhorsed,

but both totter equally in the saddle. Spenser draws a parallel
between the nature of grace and of justice, yet he also
describes justice as the more sacred virtue, resembling God in
His imperial might. It will be remembered that the unsur-
passed brilliance of Arthur's armor and sword is also of divine
origin. Finally when each knight discovers the identity of the
other, they "both them selues full eath perswade/To faire
accordaunce" and "[swear] either others cause to maintaine
mutually [V.8.14.4-5,9]."

The revenge that is taken on the Sultan and Adicia for
their hostile behavior toward Samient is a joint effort of
Arthur and Artegall. They use a certain amount of deception
in order to enter the Sultan's castle and Arthur subdues the
Sultan while Artegall protects Samient against the rage of
Adicia and causes the latter to flee to the woods where she is
transformed into a tiger. A similar joint effort is undertaken
by Arthur and Artegall when they set out to overcome
Malengin, the figure of guile and deceit who lives in a deep,
dark cave. Again the knights employ deceptions, this time in
order to entice Malengin from his cave. He is dispatched by
Artegall who chops him into minute pieces with his sword,
thereby imitating the type of death that the Sultan received
earlier at the hands of Arthur—i.e., the Sultan was chewed to
rags in the wheels of his chariot after the horses had been
driven crazy by the light of Arthur's shield.

Samient leads Arthur and Artegall to Mercilla's court and
they enter just as Duessa is being tried for attempting to
usurp Mercilla's crown. The two knights are invited to share
the judge's bench with Mercilla, suggesting that the three
elements necessary for judging others are justice, mercy and
grace. The presence of these three allegorical figures on the
same bench also serves to show the equality of their natures.
Just as grace and justice have been described as having a
divine origin, so too is mercy: "Sith in th'Almighties
euerlasting seat/She first was bred, and borne of heauenly
race [V.10.1.7-8]." The fact that justice is tempered by grace
and mercy is born out in the results of Duessa's trial.

Artegall's reaction to Duessa's lawful sentence is stern; he sees no reason why she should not be punished rightfully according to the law. On the other hand Arthur is moved to pity when he hears Grief, Nobility, Pity, and Regard for Womanhood testify in Duessa's behalf. As for Mercy, she is moved to tears upon hearing the final sentences and ends the trial by mitigating it. So, just as grace, in the person of Arthur, has served as a tempering influence before, so now does it combine with mercy to help temper justice.

But lest the reader think that Arthur personifies that grace which the Roman Catholic Church teaches, Spenser has the magnificent knight undertake the reconquest of Belge's territory which had been usurped by the tyrant Geryoneo. It is obvious from Spenser's description of Geryoneo's chapel and its altar that the tyrant is a representation of the Roman Catholic Church. The altar stone is the most significant feature of a Roman Catholic altar. The religious sacrifice is performed over the altar stone, which rests within the altar; and the sacrifice derives much of its validity from it. Spenser's portrayal of this important element as a cowardly, cannabalistic monster to whom Geryoneo offers the bodies of his subjects in sacrifice is a condemnation of the Roman Catholic Mass in particular. Since the monster is a female, it is also a condemnation of Holy Mother the Church in general. Arthur's final victory over Geryoneo and the monster is the victory of true grace over the false tyrannical "grace" for which the Roman Church is the agent.

The equality of strength and effectiveness earlier established between grace and justice is maintained to the end of Book V. Arthur's restoration of Belge to her rightful position was accomplished without the help of Artegall, just as Artegall's assistance to Sir Burbon and his victory over Grantorto are accomplished without Arthur's help. Arthur's entrance into Book VI is significant in that it constitutes a departure from the pattern established by his entrances into the earlier books. In contrast with those other entrances, all of which occurred at moments of crisis, that of Book VI occurs at a relatively relaxed moment in the narrative. Arthur comes upon Serena and the "saluage man" as the latter is accompanying the former in her rather aimless wanderings in search of Calepine. It is true that the "saluage man" and Serena have both been wounded and could very well use grace's assistance, but they are not in as dire a need for it as were Red Crosse, Guyon or Florimell when Arthur appeared on the scene in their respective books. Arthur comes across Serena and her escort at a moment when courtesy, the titular virtue of the book, is being exercised in probably its most fundamental way.

The "saluage man," who has never been exposed to the fancy life at court where courtesy is so refined as to be an art, and who indeed is barely human at all, is found accompanying and ministering to Serena in the simplest, most unaffected way possible. His concern for Serena is entirely gratuitous, unforced by any social custom and based solely on a natural and innate generosity of spirit. Therefore Arthur's entrance in this scene does not constitute a rescue as in the previous books, but serves as grace's endorsement of courtesy at its most natural and fundamental level.

As it to further emphasize grace's association with the exercise of unaffected and unpompous courtesy, Arthur leads the "saluage man" and Serena to the shack of a humble hermit where their wounds are cured. This hermit was once a courtly knight but had forsaken the ostentation of the court in his maturer days and settled upon a simple, rustic existence of which prayer formed an essential part. As Arthur and his new companions pass by the hermitage, the old man invites them to stop for a rest and offers them the humble facilities of his shack and the spiritual comfort of his own simplicity. In the end it is the hermit who shows Serena and the "saluage man" how to cure their wounds. Arthur then leaves Serena in the care of the hermit. When he departs the "saluage man" insists upon accompanying him and serving as his squire. In so doing he ratifies the association between grace and simplicity.

It is a fortunate accident that Arthur's last appearance in the poem makes this association. His contribution to the different virtues in the poem has been manifested in his simplifying and stabilizing influence. His interventions have served to uncomplicate and dismantle the difficulties that are the effects of deviation from virtue. Each of Arthur's interventions illustrates that there is "care in heauen" for the conflicts with evil that man constantly faces on earth. They show the many facets of grace and the myriad ways in which grace can affect human behavior. The fact that Arthur is the only figure common to all books of the poem suggests that his series of interventions serves as a strong unifying thread running through the complicated tapestry of the romance. It is through his periodic reappearances that the various virtues become linked to one another. Common to all his appearances is the underlying principle that grace is always at the disposal of those who are willing to receive it. Common also is the tempering influence that his interventions seek to provide, as much in moderation of excessive virtue as in the correction of vice.

WASHINGTON UNIVERSITY

Richard Pindell

The Mutable Image
Man-in-Creation

The letter to Raleigh shows Spenser's concern for unity in *The Faerie Queene* and many critics, thus challenged, have set out under the banner of unity to capture this long, beautiful, intricate, and somewhat sprawling poem. Many critics have been unable to resist composing some plan of organization for the poem which explains and justifies the sequence of books in it. A. C. Hamilton, for instance, responds, and succumbs, to the challenge of the quest for unity this way:

> Its [the poem's] unity may be seen also in its relation to the whole life of man: the adventure of the Red Cross Knight shows that pattern into which human life is born; Temperance defines that primary virtue through which man first establishes an equation with the external world; Acrasia is that mother-figure whom the child must destroy in order to enter manhood; Chastity is that virtue whereby the adolescent keeps his integrity, Amoret's release being the preparation for marriage which is shown in Book IV; Friendship shows the mature man establishing social relationships, the chief one being marriage; Justice is the concern of middle age when the right social relationships are consolidated into

the just state; and Courtesy is that maturing of human virtue in the complete man. If Book VII treats Mutability, it would show how old age and death bring the completion of one cycle and the beginning of another.[1]

More recently Richard Neuse, keying on the concept of chivalry, finds a progression along the lines of comedy:

> If the first two books are basically comic in that they assert a beneficent world order, the third might be called a problem comedy: its looser structure reflects the wider net the poet is casting as he deals with more broadly social problems, but it also marks the beginning disintegration of the earlier framework. Chivalry is losing its determinate, purposive character, and chastity comes to be defined almost entirely in opposition to the bad faith of society.
>
> Book IV introduces the bitter or dark comedy of the last three books, in which chivalry as a formative force breaks down almost completely.[2]

Terminating this progression in Calidore, Neuse sees the latter as "radically inadequate to his task. He never penetrates to the essence of courtesy, seems in fact incapable of doing so. And his conquest of the Blatant Beast, if it is not meaningless, fails to have exemplary value because he never comes to an understanding of its nature. He is incapable of dealing with the social evil it represents, being himself one expression or symptom of that very evil."[3] Calidore, "far from redeeming the failure of the court, actually sums it up in his person."[4] Does Calidore really invert to this extent the ideal that he represents, or is he only the victim of this particular scheme? Could not one draw just as plausible, and sketchy, a plan for the poem by taking a very different tack? Book I, with its steep vicissitudes and its vision of man's heavenly reconstitution, charts the course of man's pilgrimage, while the other books test his innate ability to travel. In

Book II man shows his ability to resist evil, in Milton's words, to "see and know, and yet abstain." Books II and IV, which can be considered a unit, reveals man's power to pursue the good, to envision the One, when the eyesight must include the Many. Book V portrays man's ability to apply the good, to make public his private vision of the good in a way that brings to the world a measure of order and meaning. In Book VI all these elements conspire to make a man, Calidore, who possesses the temperance of Guyon [VI.1.30.4-9], the fortitude of Britomart [VI.1.6.1-5], the discernment of Artegall [VI.2.23.5-9] and in general the magnanimity, if not the magnificence, of Arthur and, like these knights who are also guilty of some lapses, a measure of human frailty.

Such schemes are interesting but finally reductive and disappointing. Their sponsors generally subscribe, as a probably necessary act of faith, to Northrop Frye's suggestion that the six books of *The Faerie Queene* "form a unified epic structure, regardless of how much might have been added that wasn't."[5] Critics tend to give Frye the benefit of the doubt of which this remark takes advantage: we after all will never know how the completion of the other books would have affected the existing ones. I am more cautious than Frye. I believe that *The Faerie Queene* has unity, or rather *a* unity, but if it is present on the level of structure—by which I mean both its general organization and its imagistic patterns—it is certainly not prominent. The fact that "in Canto 10 of each book the knight receives a vision of his virtue—the House of Holinesse, Alma's Castle, the Temple of Venus, Mercilla's Court, Mount Acidale" and that "Arthur's first appearance in the various books occurs in either Canto 7 or Canto 8 (except in Book VI)"[6] or that at the beginning of Books II, III, and VI the knight of the previous books passes the baton of quest to his successor contributes very faintly indeed, given the size and complexity of the poem, to any sense of unity. Such recurrences are more a statement of the intention of unity than of its achievement.

Unity also proves a will-o'-the-wisp in the matters of character, theme, episode, and imagery. Thomas Greene remarks that "the status and meaning and concreteness of all the manifold figures of the poem shift and fade and recombine."[7] At some point the natures of the good knights overlap. They are all generally temperate, pure, courageous, just, and courteous. As Joanne Field Holland remarks, "their attributes are pooled, their differences a matter of stress."[8] Spenser uncharitably adds to the confusion in the similarity of many of the names of his characters, especially in Book VI, where we find Serena, Mirabella, Priscilla, and Pastorella and Calidore, Crudor, Coridon, and Colin, and when he famously forgets in the first cantos of Book III whether Britomart is accompanied by Red Crosse or Sir Guyon.

As for unity of theme, many hoary commonplace truths recur in one form or another: "Much dearer be the things, which come through hard distresse [IV.10.28.9];" "What other meed then need me to requight/ . . . That is the vertue selfe, which her reward doth pay [V.11.17.7-9];" "In vaine he seeketh others to suppresse,/Who hath not learned him selfe first to subdew [VI.1.41.5-6]." Such truths, however simple, succinct, and universally proven, inevitably prove slippery in their application to hard realities. In the total context of the poem they are subject to numerous modifications, equivocations, and contradictions. For example, granted that self-mastery is desirable, how is it achieved? On the one hand we have to reckon with the poet's statement near the point of Red Crosse's entrance to the House of Holinesse that "If any strength we haue, it is to ill,/But all the good is Gods, both power and eke will. [I.10.1.8-9]" and on the other hand with the Hermit's equally confident assertion to the Squire and Serena:

> For in your selfe your onely helpe doth lie,
>   To heale your selues, and must proceed alone
>   From your owne will, to cure your maladie.
> [VI.6.7.1-3]

How do we square these two statements? The reply that one is a Christian and the other a pagan response to human weakness is little help. Why are two such radically different responses in the same poem?

The maze of episodes also tends to blur any total image of the poem. The episodes, taken singly, are highly artificial; but taken as a whole, they are extremely lifelike. (As C. S. Lewis puts it, "the things we read about in [the poem] are not like life, but the experience of reading it is like living.")[9] They repeat, but do not duplicate, each other. They are so similar, yet so subtly and crucially different.

Finally images are always shifting between positive and negative values. Spenser appropriates for allegorical purposes the traditional opposition of iron and gold. But iron is not always the metal of the foe, nor is gold always the possession of the righteous. The combat between Red Crosse and Sans Joy is generally seen as one between right and wrong, but both warriors are protected by "yron walles [I.5.6.9]." Similarly, if Fidelia has a golden cup, so does Duessa. Arthur's scabbard is made of ivory but so is the gate in the Bower of Bliss. Duessa in Book I wears scarlet but so does Britomart in her dream in Isis Church. Sometimes an image is not only so mutable, but in addition, like the image of the "girlond," also so frequent that it dissolves in the reader's grasp, having no more significance, he might think, than the indefinite article.

All this shows the extent to which the principle of mutability penetrates and informs the poem.[10] Perhaps it is significant that the Titanesse Mutabilitie has the spotlight, both in heaven and on Arlo Hill, in the same cantos where Spenser mentions certain sources of inspiration for his poetry: " . . . Dan Geffrey (in whose gentle spright/The pure well head of Poesie did dwell [VII.7.9.3-4])," Nature, and the Irish countryside. Is he not also recognizing Mutabilitie as a kind of Muse when he sets her upon this mountain? He dramatizes not only her importance in the scheme of things but also, in spite of her shrillness and arrogance, her essential

attractiveness, her "louely face [VII.6.31.1]," which turns
Jove's wrath to desire, and her winsome nerve and verve.
Critics who over-schematize the poem in search of unity tend
to neglect the operation of mutability, just as they tend to
emphasize the statement of design in the letter to Raleigh at
the expense of the letter's penultimate paragraph:

> But by occasion hereof, many other aduentures are
> intermedled, but rather as Accidents, then intendments.
> As the loue of Britomart, the ouerthrow of Marinell, the
> misery of Florimell, the vertuousnes of Belphoebe, the
> lasciuiousnes of Hellenora, and many the like.

Too often critics attend Spenser the teacher and overlook
Spenser the entertainer. They try to separate the delight and
the instruction, when for educational purposes the poet
cunningly makes them inseparable. Such critics fasten on
Spenser the geometrician and forget Spenser the impres-
sionist. Disarmed by their schemes, critics invading Faery
often suffer the fate of Napoleon in Russia. They are simply
overwhelmed by the relentless flood of events which leaves
knights like Red Crosse, Guyon, or Arthur in a swoon of
fatigue and which separates Guyon's loss and recovery of his
horse by the space of thirty-six cantos. The discursiveness
and ingeniousness of critics soon founder on Spenser's
excursiveness and casualness. Spenser criticism, perhaps more
clearly and quickly than others, shows criticism to be a
dissective discipline and creation an integrative discipline.

Yet, if the evidence for disunity is formidable, it need not
be overwhelming. The fact remains that in the course of the
poem a subtle but persistent impression of unity gains upon
the reader. It is a unity that operates on all levels but escapes
schematization on any one. It is a hovering and amorphous
unity that is always in the process of evolving from flux. Its
presence is most clearly felt in the poem in the great mass of
unshaped material—material to which no secure meaning may
be attached—which permits the poem in spite of its artifice to

recede steeply into reality and to meet life on the level of life. It is something like a unity of feeling or what Graham Hough calls a "unity of atmosphere" (which he sees as the definitive unity of *The Faerie Queene*), but it is more definite, more demonstrable.[11] It is the unity of an attitude toward life possessed by the model man as he emerges from the poem.

To discuss this unity without violating the variegated life of the poem, we must catch it close to its source: the germinal instant in the poem, the moment of truth—a man confronting an image. Characters see and seek in an image an omen of their destiny. Immobilized by the blinding rays of Arthur's shield, Orgoglio "has read his end/In that bright shield [I.8.21.4-5]." Britomart, with promptings from Cupid and especially Merlin, sees in the image of Artegall in the magic mirror compelling visions of her future which send her off in quest of him. Images in the poem, regardless of any allegorical meaning they might have, tend to move, more or less, from signs to portents, from representations to prophecies.

Because characters often see themselves in images, images are very powerful. The poem is a study of man's domination by images. The image of Arthur's beloved Faerie Queene dangerously works its spell on him during his combat with Pyrochles:

> But euer at *Pyrochles* when he smit,
>   Who *Guyons* shield cast euer him before,
>   Whereon the Faery Queenes pourtract was writ,
>   His hand relented, and the stroke forbore,
>   And his deare hart the picture gan adore,
>   Which oft the Paynim sau'd from deadly stowre.
>   [II.8.43.1-6]

This incident shows on another level the incorrigible iridescence of images that we noted before. Transformed by the particular realities of this situation, the image of the good, which arouses the necessary motivation of love, becomes, in spite of itself, an obstacle to the realization of the good. The promise of fulfillment which Arthur finds in the image of the Faerie Queene turns willy-nilly into the threat of destruction. The power of images for good or ill is inseparably linked with the potency and vulnerability of eyes. Spenser shares with other Renaissance poets a preoccupation with vision. With him, as with them, a glance is a person's most revealing gesture. Characters are distinguished and identified by their eyes. There are the "rude eyes [I.6.9.9]" of the fauns and satyrs who gaze awestruck at Una, the "sharpe staring eyes [II.9.52.6]" of Phantastes at the Castle of Alma, and there is the "vaunting eye [II.3.10.2]" that one meets at court. Because of their intimacy with a man's nature, eyes are the path both of a potentially destructive or creative assault upon one's nature and the potentially destructive or creative expression of that nature. Love exemplifies the creative glance; lust, the destructive. Lust, whether in its most active form as rape or its most passive form as prurience, is consuming. Hence the "fyrie lustfull eye [I.6.4.6]" of Sansloy when he is on the verge of trying to rape Una or the description of Acrasia with her lover Verdant in the Bower of Bliss, that haunt of voyeurs and exhibitionists: "And through his humid eyes did sucke his spright [II.12.73.7]." By contrast the glance of love transfigures, tends even to deify. When Britomart begins to fall in love with Artegall, his face appears in the mirror from behind his lifted ventail as "*Phoebus* face out of the east [III.2.24.6]," and hers, when he begins during his combat with her to fall in love with her, as the "ruddie morne [IV.6.19.6]." (The merging of the images beautifully testifies to the deep communion of spirit that is here set in motion and which their betrothal later declares. It shows again, if from a different angle, how Spenser uses images to see into people.) Involuntarily he sees her as divine, and he cannot deliver the final blow.

My point is that the eye is a microcosm. It holds the sum of man's possibilities. Under the stimulus of the image these

possibilities are activated. A description of Serena, who is
fleeing the scene of Disdain's capture of the Squire and
remembering her terrible experience with the Blatant Best,
illustrates the total involvement of a person's being in the
dialogue between eye and image:

> So fresh the image of her former dread,
> Yet dwelling in her eye, to her appeard,
> That euery foote did tremble, which did tread,
> And euery body two, and two she foure did read.
>
> [VI.8.31.6-9]

The eye is often an involuntary witness. It never has much
control over what it sees. Spenser takes full advantage of this
exposure. The assault on the eye is unceasing. No poet
delights more in making images. The whole poem is a kind of
Garden of Adonis issuing a riotous profusion of shapes,
which, because of the superb poetic control, seem to move at
a processional and decorous pace.

As images always emerge to solicit the eye the unexpected
becomes the norm. Florimell, fleeing from the forester,
bursts across our ken "All suddenly out of the thickest
brush,/Vpon a milk-white Palfrey all alone [III.1.15.1-2],"
and Arthur and Guyon impulsively set off in hot pursuit to
"win thereby/Most goodly meede, the fairest Dame aliue
[III.1.18.7-8]." Later in the chase Arthur again stands
convicted of mental infidelity to the Faerie Queene:

> Oft did he wish, that Lady faire mote bee
> His Faery Queene, for whom he did complaine:
> Or that his Faery Queene were such, as shee.
>
> [III.4.54.6-8]

The poet insists that he meant "To her no euill thought, nor
euill deed [III.4.50.3]" and he describes Florimell's "feare"
as "vaine[III.7.1.6]." (And later, Amoret, alone with Arthur,
is "as safe as in a Sanctuary [IV.9.19.6].") Nevertheless,
Arthur plainly departs here from the ideal of magnificence

that he is created to represent. In the letter to Raleigh Spenser sees magnificence as containing and perfecting all the other virtues, a fact that of course increases Arthur's importance as a potential source of unity. He not only figures in each of the six books (any unifying force here is nearly totally lost in the maze and multitude of episodes and characters), but he is also meant to be the working model of the perfection for which the good knights strive. The failure of this summational ideal in the figure of Arthur militates against it as a source of unity. But in the failure of the ideal there is the success of the real. Arthur is humanized by his lapse. Here he is neither a lecher nor magnificent. He is a man. The ambiguity of his motives adumbrates the inner struggle of the tempted good man, as, in his total response to the image of Florimell, both sides of his nature are brought into play. The impairment of one kind of unity yields another—the unity of a complete human being.

By summoning the whole man the image in a sense creates man. But, the question is now, what kind of man? Creation is more than evocation; it is also selection. In Book I, appropriately enough, where Red Crosse moves from the depths of sin to the height of glory, from the House of Pride and the dungeon of Orgoglio to the Mount of Heavenly Contemplation, man's possibilities are enumerated. Despair is called a "man of hell [I.9.28.5]." Red Crosse is called a "man of sin [I.9.46.1]" and a "man of earth [I.10.52.2]" and finally a "man of God [I.11.7.9]." From some such range of alternatives the image requires a man to choose who he will be.

It is the nature of the response to an image that separates man as beast from man as angel. Arthur, for instance, in spite of occasional trouble in sustaining it, makes the ideal response to the image of the Faerie Queene that he sees in his dream:

From that day forth I lou'd that face diuine;
From that day forth I cast in carefull mind,

To seeke her out with labour, and long tyne,
And neuer vow to rest, till her I find.

[I.9.15.5-8]

But Florimell's fisherman acquaintance behaves otherwise.
When he awakes to find her in his boat, he is quick to see
that she is "no vision, nor fantasticke sight [III.8.23.2] " and
he tries to rape her. In his response to beauty he presumes on
and debases the divine in himself which enables him to see
her as beautiful in the first place. The base man's sacrifice of
his better to his worse self is dramatized in Geryoneo's
idolatry:

On which that cursed Idole farre proclamed,
He hath set vp, and him his God hath named,
Offring to him in sinfull sacrifice
The flesh of men, to Gods owne likenesse framed.

[V.10.28.4-7]

One of Spenser's many discussions of the antique age
relates indirectly to the two very different responses of the
will that result in the creation of two very different kinds of
men:

Then beautie, which was made to represent
The great Creatours owne resemblance bright,
Vnto abuse of lawlesse lust was lent,
And made the baite of bestiall delight:
Then faire grew foule, and foule grew faire in sight,
And that which wont to vanquish God and man,
Was made the vassall of the victors might.

[IV.8.32.1-7]

Here the base man's will runs directly counter to God's. The
was made in the first line refers to a deliberate act of the will
on the part of God, while the *was made* in the last refers to a
similar act on the part of the evil imagination. The first

instance of the verb represents true creation; the second, perverted creation. The emphasis here on the dire consequences of the latter shows the fatefulness of the decision that man makes in his encounter with the image.

Spenser's confronting man with the need for decisions relates directly to the central human figure in the poem—the wayfarer. The call of the open road, summoning man to an active engagement with life, ever reminds that man's gifts from God must be used wholly. Any escape into passivity courts disaster. Surely there is a connection between the miserly Malbecco's withdrawl from life and his wife Hellenore's orgiastic excesses with the satyrs and between Cymochles' voyeurism in the Bower of Bliss and the ungovernable passions that lead to his violent death at the hands of Arthur. Spenser knew how man can be corrupted and consumed by his own unused energies. The painful truth is that any beneficent control over one's life comes from the unhesitating engagement of apparently overwhelming adversaries. Red Crosse coolly and determinedly finds his way out of the labyrinthine Wood of Error *after* he has fought and killed the monster. That he must kill her with his bare hands shows that an ideal always requires more than an intellectual commitment. It shows the terrible riskiness of that capability for commitment which is the condition, but, of course, not the guarantee of fully being human. As Arthur's fight with Pyrochles suggests, where his attraction to the Faerie Queene nearly leads to his undoing, one may easily be the victim of his potential—the victim even of his own proven virtuousness. Red Crosse suffers from self-pity and despair in the House of Holinesse. Guyon, after his successful passage through the Cave of Mammon, is prostrated by more than physical exhaustion. His self-righteousness has stealthily eroded his will. Every new potentiality, then, leads to a new vulnerability. Spenser is more than a Christian humanist; he is a Christian realist.

One of the many marvelous coexistences in the poem is this strong insistence on the necessity or risk within a climate of surmise. The speculative and meditative mood derives from more than the many questions that the poet asks. Like Chaucer, Spenser is intrigued by the different reactions of people to the same phenomenon, whether, to give just two examples, to the fallen Dragon in Book I or the advent of Cambina in her chariot in Book IV. Even more directly he admits his delight in the incalculable individuality of mental processes: "Wonder it is to see, in diuerse minds,/How diuersely loue doth his pageants play [III.5.1.1-2]." Such relaxed perception, which seems more aware, somehow even more vigilant, by being relaxed, is at work too when he sometimes confesses his own bafflement in the maze of life:

> In braue pursuit of honorable deed,
> There is I know not what great difference
> Betweene the vulgar and the noble seed.
>
> [II.4.1.1-3]

The poet's musing eye always comes to rest finally on the human form, erect, reclining, or supine. Spenser undertakes to answer the question that the psalmist asks God: "What is man, that thou art mindful of him?" Man is on trial. He must demonstrate on the plane of this life, in terms convincing to himself, that he has a claim to the divine order. Using images to lure the people of his poem toward self-exposure, Spenser is in effect saying to man what Una cries to Red Crosse when he is in the clutches of the monster Error: "Now now Sir knight, shew what ye bee [I.1.19.2]." Only after proving what he is can man envision what he may be. Red Crosse's vision on the Mount of Heavenly Contemplation is preceded by the anguish of his trials in the House of Holinesse which probe the core of his being. Man must show himself worthy to receive the heavenly recognition accorded him in the Christian plan of redemption. Explaining his boldness in the face of Daunger on the porch of the Temple of Venus, Scudamour says: "Vnworthy they of grace, whom one deniall/Excludes from fairest hope, withouten further triall

[IV.10.17.8-9]." The searching interrogation of man's nature justifies the iridescence of the image. To show what man is Spenser faces him with countless opportunities to err.

As I imply above, the vision of what man may be occurs in Book I on the Mount of Heavenly Contemplation, where Red Crosse sees the New Jerusalem that God has prepared for His chosen. He receives confirmation of what Una reveals when she rebukes him for falling into the clutches of Despayre: "In heauenly mercies hast thou not a part?/Why shouldst thou then despeire, that chosen art [I.9.53.4-5]?" It is incumbent on man in the next five books to prove that he is chosen for a part in "heauenly mercies." The calm, controlling sense of the order of things which pervades Book I, despite the violent vicissitudes of the life it presents, is exemplified by Una's friendly relationship with the lion or by Arthur's wearing a golden dragon on his helmet created by way of ornament. In Book II any firm basis for this intuition of control from without is removed. The dragon on the helmet takes on life without changing its position. It becomes that animated sword of Damocles, the "vgly feend [II.7.26.7]" that hovers at the heels of Guyon, claws extended, in the Cave of Mammon. In Books II-VI the "man of earth" is brought into violent contact with the "man of hell" and the former shows his potential to be a "man of God." At Mount Acidale the "man of earth" comes as close as he is able, without a plan of redemption, to becoming a "man of God." In Books II-VI, primarily by means of parallels with Book I, less importantly by means of Biblical echoes, Spenser keeps alive this vision of what man may be without destroying the validity of his experiment to show what man is.

One purpose of this study of man is to teach us our depths, to educate us, especially, to the profound treachery of our natures. Outside the Bower of Bliss sits the false Genius:

That is our Selfe, whom though we do not see,
Yet each doth in him selfe it well perceiue to bee.
[II.12.47.8-9]

The foe of life, that good enuyes to all,
That secretly doth vs procure to fall.
                                        [II.12.48.4-5]

Spenser exposes the artfulness of the forces of evil. The
instruction in the House of Holinesse that leads to a vision of
the eternal and Despayre's powerful argument for suicide
both really begin with the same premise: "If any strength we
haue, it is to ill [I.10.1.8]." Through a kind of diabolical
ventriloquism Phaedria's enticement of Cymochles to dally
on her island sounds like Christ's mild command to "consider
the lilies of the field, how they grow; they toil not, neither
do they spin":

Behold, O man, that toilsome paines doest take,
The flowres, the fields, and all that pleasant growes,
How they themselues doe think ensample make.
                                        [II.6.15.1-3]

The temptation to retreat into idleness and ease is couched in
the language intended in the Bible to bring man to a
courageous and active dependence upon God. The poem,
especially Book II, is a medley of importunate and intimida-
ting voices that would lure or frighten man away from the
ideal quest that moves him beyond himself.
    The good knights in the poem are besieged by conflicting
demands—the urge to rest and the need to persevere, the
desire to lust and the need to love. Plainly man must learn to
adjudicate the claims of rival powers upon his soul. He must
learn to make right distinctions, to discriminate between
reality and appearance, between art and nature, intuition and
impulse, valor and discretion; in short, between the voice of
conscience and the songs of the sirens. Man must formulate
some answer to Artegall's question of the giant who vainly
and presumptuously tries to weigh the universe:

Of things vnseene how canst thou deeme aright,
Then answered the righteous *Artegall*,
Sith thou misdeem'st so much of things in sight?

[V.2.39.1-3]

Man must not misjudge "so much of things in sight" if the
visible is to lead to the invisible, if image is to be replaced by
vision. The taxing mutability of the image is the earthly
apprenticeship of the human eye that must be served if it is
to see heaven.

Vision, as opposed to mere sight, comes through faith in a
reality beyond that of the empirical and the appetitive.
Through such a faith man sees beyond the physical. Love is
more discerning than lust, which is "blind . . . false colours to
descry [IV.2.11.5]," because it involves faith. The reliance
on the physical and immediate also involves faith. But the
higher and harder faith, by endeavoring to substitute an ideal
image for the real one, prevents the latter from becoming an
idol. When Mammon tempts Guyon with his wealth, saying,
"Loe here the worldes blis, loe here the end,/To which men
do ayme, rich to be made [II.7.32.7-8]," Guyon replies,
"Another blis before mine eyes I place,/Another happinesse,
another end [II.7.33.3-4]." Arthur's quest for the Faerie
Queene involves a similar transaction. His quest is a reliving
of his vision of her which keeps the divine image that she
reflects dominant amid the importunities of the immediate.
The poet's view of veiled dame Nature on Arlo Hill also
shows, if on a more mundane level, a choice between faiths.
Out of the two current opposite surmises—one, that she is of
"vncouth hew" [VII.7.6.2] and, two, that she is "beautious"
[VII.7.6.6], outshining the sun—he believes the latter: "That
well may seemen true: for, well I weene/ . . . Her garment
was so bright and wondrous sheene. . . . [VII.7.7.1,3]."

To see faith this way as a form of self-persuasion is part of
the practical thrust of Spenser's Christianity. Faith is

essential to the selection of that image which best evokes
one's total resources. (As Guyon's allusion to "another end"
in his reply to Mammon, or the fact that Arthur's quest
originates in an image, might suggest, the quest itself is a
metaphor for such an image.) The best image, the poem
asserts, in a hierarchy of images, all of which involve a
complete response, is the image of God. By requiring a faith
which is better described as courageous reasoning, it more
than motivates a complete response. It enables a vision of
that response. It more than activates a man's possibilities as
lesser images do, but it articulates them. It makes clearer to a
man his alternatives—painfully, but also, encouragingly
clearer. Greater access to the self can lead to more control
over it. To put it another way, the dialogue with this image is
a flow of visible and, therefore, challenging, contraries. But it
is precisely these contraries that best prepare the self to solve
a particular situation. Because of the problematic nature of
reality the optimum commands to the elf are often
ambiguous or even contradictory. Here we might consider
again the poet's statement, introducing Red Crosse's sojourn
in the House of Holinesse, "If any strength we haue, it is to
ill [I.10.1.8]," and the Hermit's advice to Serena and the
Squire:

> For in your selfe your onely helpe doth lie,
>   To heale your selues, and must proceed alone
> From your owne will, to cure your maladie.
>   [VI.6.7.1-3]

Both statements are true in effect. They are well-shaped to
meet different individual needs. In his pride and self-pity Red
Crosse needs to hear the first statement, as he will, in
different words, at the House of Holinesse. Mired in shame,
Serena and the Squire need to hear the second statement. Yet
neither statement is, in the context of the whole poem,
entirely true. Our self is not our only help. Nevertheless it is a
help, albeit a dangerous one. (A faith that endures a present

loss for a future gain and stays, in spite of the suffering that results from the full exercise of one's faculties, requires, after all, every resource of the will.) Because the two statements are parts of a whole, they only approach truth when read together.

Mixed commands are heard in the context of a single situation in the House of Busyrane. One inscription over the doors is *"Be bold* [III.11.54.3]*."* Another inscription is *"Be not too bold* [III.11.54.8]*."* Again, of these two contrasting signals neither one is wholly reliable. They must be read together if they are to summon the self which success in this situation requires. The tension of resolving the two commands creates the spirit that can follow both at once.

The existence of these contraries in the poem, and many more, of course (Mutabilitie's trial is, for the most part, a pageant of contraries.), suggests that the poem itself is a quest. The poem is in motion So many actions remain incomplete in the completed books. For instance, Archimago in Book I and the Blatant Beast in Book VI are captured only to break free. Nothing rests, nothing remains the same. Despite having successfully run his race in Book II, Guyon is intemperate in Book III in his pursuit of Florimell and in Book V when he must be forcibly restrained from killing the horse-thieving Braggadochio; while Red Crosse in Book III takes off his armor at Castle Joyeous [III.1.42.6-7] despite the fact that a similar lack of vigilance in Book I had led to disaster in the shape of Orgoglio. The harmonious moment is always disrupted. The dancing Graces disappear at the intrusion of Calidore, and Red Crosse's betrothal vows to Una are interrupted by the appearance of the false and slanderous messenger Archimago—and Red Crosse must separate soon from Una to return to court because of other vows. The open-endedness of nearly all the stories, together with the climate of surmise discussed earlier, builds into the poem a strong mood of expectancy, of waiting. The same note sounds in the recurring word, "afar." It is as if the poet's eye is scanning the horizon. The silence where one seeks in an image an omen of his fate ripples outward to cover the poem.

The poem seems not only alive, but lived, lived in and through—something completely used to tackle the problems of every day and, therefore, something suffered. The suffering, I think, is on record. After describing Faunus' spying on Diana and his subsequent Actaeon-like punishment and the curse on Arlo Hill, the poet begins the next canto this way:

> Ah! whither doost thou now thou greater Muse
> Me from these woods and pleasing forests bring?
> And my fraile spirit (that dooth oft refuse
> This too high flight, vnfit for her weake wing)
> Lift vp aloft . . .
>
> [VII.7.1.1-5]

The point of the juxtaposition, I think, is that Spenser, like Faunus, pays a certain price for vision. He seems in some ways, too, to participate in the ordeals of his knights. Immediately after Red Crosse rejoins Duessa, in spite of Fradubio's story, a reunion that Duessa assists with a timely swoon, the poet says:

> Nought is there vnder heau'ns wide hollownesse,
> That moues more deare compassion of mind,
> Then beautie brought t'vnworthy wretchednesse
> Through enuies snares or fortunes freakes vnkind.
>
> [I.3.1.1-4]

Spenser carefully specifies the kind of misfortune to beauty that moves him, and it does not apply to Duessa. She deserves any wretchedness that she suffers. But even as the poet shows that here, unlike Red Crosse, he can make important distinctions, he also admits his susceptibility to the damsel in distress, a role that Duessa can so skillfully act. He also shares with his knights the dangerous desire to rest: "Behold I see the hauen nigh at hand,/To which I meane my wearie course to bend [I.12.1.1-2]." (The language and the mood suggestively recall two lines in Despayre's speech to Red Crosse: "Sleepe after toyle, port after stormie seas,/Ease after warre, death after life does greatly please [I.9.40.8-9].") But another feeling breaking through in direct opposition to this one is that of robust perseverance. *The Faerie Queene* is full of mornings, and they always tend to restore courage and hope. Morning is the remembrance of a promise made to one's better self to excel that self. But the vigor with which Spenser arises is also due to his sense of urgency. His creation of man must take little longer than God's. Each day the world runs further "out of square [V.proem.1.7]."

The proem to Book I shows his commitment to his work:

> Lo I the man, whose Muse whilome did maske,
> As time her taught, in lowly Shepheards weeds,
> Am now enforst a far vnfitter taske.
>
> [I.proem.1.1-3]

Isolated against the immensity of his task yet undaunted by it, he is the man on the horizon for whom the world of the poem is waiting. He himself is the end of the poem's quest for the man that it teaches that life needs: one who can gracefully endure and coolly exploit paradox. His participation in the life of the poem shows that he can hold life's conflicting elements with poise, if not without pain. His capacity to spend himself lavishly in a climate of loss, to surmise in an age of crisis, to wonder in a time of increasing cynicism, all reflect in his real signature, his style, which exhibits the disciplined abandon of a dance. His protean ability to undergo radical changes, yet retain a basic identity, understanding flux without being overwhelmed by it, advances him as a model of living in a world that threatens to run out from under men's feet. He himself becomes the encouraging omen of man's destiny.

To conclude, the poem is a challenge. It must be remembered that the persuasive argument of Despayre, which contains two of the most memorable lines in Spenser (quoted above), finds its power almost entirely in a kind of catalogue of agonies attributable to mutability. Spenser replies to Despayre on Arlo Hill in the beautiful and brave form of the Titanesse Mutabilitie. As Kathleen Williams remarks, she is "one of us."[1 2] If we must reject her rude and shrill presumption, we dearly need her energy and ambitiousness. Spenser asserts that in change there in infinite opportunity. The allusion to Christ's transfiguration [VII.7.7.6-9] is to the point. His transfiguration that separates Him from the disciples chosen to learn His identity foreshadows no loss, but gain. The change in His appearance looks forward to a permanent and beneficent reality. Mutability does of course inevitably involve loss, but in the loss there can be gain. This is the promise of Arlo Hill where the heavenly and earthly orders momentarily touch. The proximity there of unity and mutability is an elaborate testament to the central dynamic of the poem as quest—namely the faith of finding a unity in mutability. As "the images of God in earthly clay [I.10.39.7]," men embody this unity and mutability. Both are necessary to victory in life and attainment of heaven. Because the desire for unity—ultimately for God—brings together opposites in a way that illuminates the hidden complexity of life, it is vital to the creation of a self virtuously capable for the moment and hence with a claim on heaven. This desire, then, must never be satisfied on earth lest it die. The existence of mutability is justified by its challenge and stimulus to this desire. Thus the mutability of the image—meaning by this both the copious production of images and their changes within themselves—is essential to the poet's triumph over indifference and despair. The poet submits his poem as evidence that the human spirit is "eterne in mutabilitie." By advancing this creative attitude toward life, which I see as the unity of the poem, the poet enters a community of commitment with all good wayfaring men.

STATE UNIVERSITY OF NEW YORK
AT BINGHAMTON

1. *The Structure of Allegory in The Faerie Queene* (Oxford, 1961), pp. 220-21. For a rebuttal of this scheme, and Hamilton's schemes in general, see Rudolf B. Gottfried, "Our New Poet: Archetypal Criticism and the Form of *The Faerie Queene*," PMLA 83 (October 1968), pp. 1362-77. The most satisfying schemes tend to show more restraint. Roche notes that the first half of the poem presents personal virtues—holiness, temperance, and chastity, and the second, social virtues—friendship, justice, and courtesy and that "a mirror relationship exists between individual books in each half: holiness: courtesy, temperance: justice, chastity: friendship." Thomas P. Roche, Jr., *The Kindly Flame* (Princeton, 1964), p. 200. More interesting and, I think, fairly convincing, is Berger's division of the poem into the "Hellenistic scheme for the divisions of the literary treatise:" *poesis* (Books I and II), *poema* (Books III and IV), and *poeta* (Books V and VI). Harry Berger, Jr., "A Secret Discipline: *The Faerie Queene*, Book VI" in *Form and Convention in the Poetry of Edmund Spenser*, ed. William Nelson (New York and London, 1961). pp. 35-6.

2. Richard Neuse, "Book VI as Conclusion to *The Faerie Queene*," ELH 35 (September 1968), p. 333.

3. Neuse, p. 352.

4. *Ibid.*, p. 345.

5. Northrop Frye, *Fables of Identity* (New York, 1963), p. 70.

6. Roche, p. 201. For the first part of this statement he indicates his indebtedness to Isabel E. Rathborne, *The Meaning of Spenser's Fairyland* (New York, 1937), p. 129.

7. Thomas Greene, *The Descent from Heaven* (New Haven and London, 1963), p. 331.

8. Joanne Field Holland, "The Cantos of Mutabilitie and the Form of *The Faerie Queene*." ELH 35 (March 1968), p. 29.

9. *The Allegory of Love* (New York, 1958), p. 358.

10. Holland's article also shows this in many other and interesting ways.

11. *A Preface to The Faerie Queene* (New York, 1963), p. 167.

12. *Spenser's World of Glass* (Berkeley and Los Angeles, 1966), p. 228.

Sherry L. Reames

Prince Arthur and
Spenser's Changing Design

The Faerie Queene we have is not the vast poem Spenser originally planned to write. His famous letter to Raleigh and Sonnet LXXX of the Amoretti both describe a work in twelve books, and even the title page of the 1596 edition confirms this plan: "*The Faerie Queene.* Disposed into twelue bookes, Fashioning XII. Morall vertues." The critical reader is faced at the outset, then, with questions about the nature of the six-book poem before him. There seem to be two distinct possibilities. *The Faerie Queene* may simply be an unfinished work, abandoned because of external circumstances at about the halfway point. If so its narrative will demand continuation, and one will not be able to talk with any certainty about its structure or its total meaning. Its parts will not comprise a single meaningful whole. If, on the other hand, Spenser did not abandon the poem but brought it to a deliberate close, *The Faerie Queene* may be essentially complete as it stands. The poet's plan, that is, may have altered enough so that the work's internal demands are fulfilled within six books and the Mutabilitie fragment. In that case the poem may contain the possibility of further extension, but it will not require such extension to complete either its meaning or its explicit form.[1]

Spenser's only published explanation of his total plan for *The Faerie Queene* is, of course, given in his letter to Raleigh, dated January 23, 1589 (1590, N.S.). According to this letter, there were to be twelve books about twelve knights, each representing one of the private moral virtues. The character of Prince Arthur was to tie all the rest together:

> So in the person of Prince Arthure I sette forth magnificence in particular, which vertue for that (according to Aristotle and the rest) it is the perfection of all the rest, and conteineth in it them all, therefore in the whole course I mention the deedes of Arthure applyable to that vertue, which I write of in that booke.

A second unifying device was to be the feast of Gloriana, which would bring all the major characters together and explain the origins of the various quests:

> The beginning therefore of my history, if it were to be told by an Historiographer [,] should be the twelfth booke, which is the last, where I deuise that the Faery Queene kept her Annuall feaste xii. dayes, vppon which xii. seuerall knights, are in these xii bookes seuerally handled and discoursed.

Gloriana's feast, of course, does not appear at all in the poem as we have it. In terms of Spenser's expressed intention, the resulting loss of unity and necessary background information would be a serious flaw in the poem—as serious, perhaps, as the loss of Chaucer's "General Prologue" to the *Canterbury Tales*. When one examines the poem itself, however, this verdict immediately is qualified. Book I begins, it is true, *in medias res;* and the opening description of the Red Crosse Knight, wearing battered armor on his first quest, would have been explained engagingly at the projected feast. All the really necessary explanations, however, are provided

gradually in Book I itself: Una is taking the knight to avenge
her parents [I.1.5.7-9]; the fame of Gloriana's court led her
to seek a champion there [I.7.46]; the Red Crosse Knight
was ideal for this task because of his purity and inexperience
[I.7.47.1-5]. Even the meaning of the armor is symbolically
defined. The origins of the quests in Books V and VI are
similarly explained and tied to Gloriana's court within the
narratives. Canto 1 of Book V in fact provides such an
explicit account that it is difficult to imagine Spenser's telling
it over again in a later scene.

With respect to the quests of Books II, III, and IV,
Spenser's projected explanations are not only unnecessary;
they conflict with the details actually given in the poem. Sir
Guyon's quest can really be said to begin with the discovery
of Mordant, Amavia, and the baby in the woods and with his
ensuing vow—not with the Palmer's bringing the baby to
court, as the letter would have it.[2] The champion of Book III
is Britomart, not Scudamour, and Britomart's quest has
nothing at all to do with Gloriana's feast. Scudamour himself,
moreover, cannot be considered seriously to have undertaken
Amoret's rescue at Gloriana's request. Amoret is his own
wife, stolen away from him at their wedding. Cambel and
Triamond, the nominal heroes of Book IV, are, once again,
unconnected with Gloriana's court—and they have no quest
at all.

It is difficult to believe, then, that Spenser would have
described anything like the projected feast of Gloriana had he
actually gone on to write Book XII. The explanatory
function of that feast is fulfilled more adequately by the
individual books themselves, which do not fit into the rigid
scheme of twelve assigned quests outlined in the letter. Even
the unifying function of the feast is superseded partially by
the links between the various books: each knight meets the
hero of the previous quest as he sets out on his own. (The
time intervening between their respective beginnings is
obviously more like a year than a day.) Their congratulations
and friendly help to one another tie them all together on a

human level, creating a kind of unity which is much less mechanical than having twelve parallel quests begin on twelve successive days.

One of the two devices with which Spenser planned to unify *The Faerie Queene*, the feast, then, probably could not have been worked into the poem satisfactorily. It has been set aside and partially replaced without noticeably impairing either the poem's meaning or its unity. The other and more important unifying factor was to be the figure of Prince Arthur—and his case is more complex. In Books I and II Arthur fulfills a necessary role in the action, rescuing the Red Crosse Knight from Orgoglio's dungeon and saving the unconscious Guyon from Cymochles and Pyrochles. In each case it is implied that Arthur surpasses the patron knight of the book in his own particular virtue. Without him neither knight could go on to complete his quest. Arthur's virtue, that is, here fulfills the description given of it in Spenser's letter: "it is the perfection of all the rest, and conteineth in it them all."

In the succeeding books, however, Arthur's relation to the other knights becomes more complementary than exemplary, and he is primarily involved in adventures peripheral to the main quests. In Book IV he kills Corflambo and rescues Placidas and Amyas. In Book V he kills Belge's oppressors and restores her to her kingdom. In Book VI he punishes Turpine and attempts to rescue Mirabella from Disdain and Scorn, only to be told that she must remain their prisoner. When he does come into contact with the patron knights of these books his role is that of a friend rather than a deliverer. He plays minor roles in the rescue of Amoret and the healing of Serena, aids Britomart and Scudamour in fighting off four attackers, and joins Artegall in subduing the foes of Mercilla. It is Britomart, not Arthur, who rescues Artegall from Radigund. And neither Britomart nor Calidore ever needs to be rescued by another knight.

Arthur's role in the poem thus is reduced considerably after the first two books. He is merely another knight, appearing a bit more frequently than the rest, who fights on the side of justice and virtue. The aura of mysterious power surrounding him in Books I and II is gradually lost. He is separated from his squire and worries about him, while the squire goes on to have adventures of his own. Arthur gallops wildly after Florimell, hoping that she will turn out to be Gloriana, and succeeds only in frightening her into further dangers. It is only by making an intellectual effort that one can see him as a major unifying force and center of meaning in the poem, despite his appearance in each book; and it is impossible to believe that Spenser consistently thought of him as the perfection of all the other virtues.

The ambiguities surrounding Arthur and his role are a major source of critical difficulty in *The Faerie Queene*— particularly for anyone seeking to read the poem as a self-contained whole. Not only is Arthur portrayed inconsistently; he also has a quest which is never completed. The poem of course abounds in minor loose ends which do not seriously trouble anyone. One is content to leave Sophy [II.9.6.9] and Sir Peridure [III.8.28.2] unidentified, to assume that Fradubio and Fraelissa will eventually be released from their enchantment, and to leave the shivering Serena to the honorable and loving care of Calepine. One can even insert the necessary stanzas at the proper place to describe the reuniting of Amoret and Scudamour. None of these unfinished stories is sufficient cause for questioning the essential completeness of the poem. Arthur, however, is a major loose end. He may not be the center of meaning in the poem, but he is an important character—as important as Britomart or the Red Crosse Knight—and considerable stress is placed on his search for Gloriana. In a sense it is inevitable to conclude that Spenser must have intended to continue Arthur's story, and the poem, beyond Book VI. A rereading of those passages in which Arthur's quest is mentioned, however, demonstrates that the problem is more complicated than one might expect.

A good deal is made in the early books of Arthur's romantic dream of Gloriana and his search for her. He tells the whole story to Una and the Red Crosse Knight, and they encourage his hopes:

> O happy Queene of Faeries, that hast found
> Mongst many, one that with his prowesse may
> Defend thine honour, and thy foes confound:
> True Loues are often sown, but seldom grow on ground.
>
> [I.9.16.6-9]

> And you, my Lord, the Patrone of my life,
> Of that great Queene may well gaine worthy grace:
> For onely worthy you through prowes priefe
> Yf liuing man mote worthy be, to be her liefe.
>
> [I.9.17.6-9]

In Book II Arthur recognizes the portrait on Guyon's shield and confesses his own desire to serve Gloriana. Guyon holds out rather a limited encouragement: surely he can hope to join the "knights of *Maydenhed*," and perhaps he will even be admitted to the circle of her favorites:

> And in her fauour high be reckoned,
> As *Arthegall*, and *Sophy* now beene honored.
>
> [II.9.6.8-9]

This is, of course, not quite what Arthur had in mind; but he wisely refrains from contradicting Guyon's idea of bliss. In the House of Alma the lady Prays-desire reminds him, as the Red Crosse Knight has already done, that in seeking Gloriana he is aiming very high indeed [II.9.38]. Arthur is not discouraged easily, however. As he mistakenly pursues Florimell he is clearly hoping to find a lady to love, as well as a queen to serve:

Oft did he wish, that Lady faire mote bee
His Faery Queene, for whom he did complaine:
Or that his Faery Queene were such, as shee . . .

[III.4.54.6-8]

At this point, if not before, it is clear that Spenser was getting onto very dangerous ground. For Arthur's quest to be completed, he had to reach Gloriana's court and attempt to win her love. Gloriana was not, however, the kind of fictional character whom Spenser could manipulate freely. Even if Arthur was not meant to have a specific counterpart in real life, Spenser could not allow him to win Gloriana unless Queene Elizabeth actually married. Yet the alternative outcome—to have Gloriana reject the prince who embodies all human virtue—would have been interpreted as a severe criticism of the queen's determined celibacy. Without the concurrence of historical events, therefore, Spenser could not allow Arthur even to approach the Faerie Queene.

Arthur's quest is, nevertheless, resolved by analogy. Perhaps because the Arthur-Gloriana story imposed such narrow restraints on him, Spenser chose also to represent the queen—with greater aesthetic distance—in the figures of Belphoebe and Britomart. In their stories are dramatized the two possible outcomes of Arthur's quest. Belphoebe remains a virgin, and her humble lover Timias serves and worships her from a respectful distance. Even when Belphoebe is depicted as cold or jealous, it is remembered that she is divinely born and Timias is only a squire; thus any implicit criticism of the queen is subdued. Similarly, the courtship of Britomart and Artegall would be more acceptable to Spenser's audience than a courtship between Arthur and Gloriana. Britomart is not a queen; and it is she and not Artegall who takes the initiative, searching for the man she saw in the mirror as Arthur searches for the lady of his dream.

When he wrote the opening stanzas of Book III Spenser may already have recognized that a royal marriage was not likely to resolve his dilemma. At least he is in no hurry to bring Arthur to Gloriana's court. After Guyon has sent the bound Acrasia to the court by messenger, he and Arthur set off in another direction. If Arthur were really intent on finding Gloriana, he obviously should have followed the messengers. Instead he and Guyon take an incredibly long way around:

Long so they trauelled through wastefull wayes,
　Where daungers dwelt, and perils most did wonne,
　To hunt for glorie and renowned praise;
　Full many Countries they did ouerronne,
　From the vprising to the setting Sunne . . .
　　　　　　　　　　　　　　　　　[III.1.3.1-5]

Later in Book III, after spending the night mourning that he could no longer follow the lady he hoped was Gloriana, Arthur meets Florimell's dwarf, who is coming from Gloriana's court. After learning Florimell's true identity, Arthur volunteers—without so much as a sigh or a backward glance—to go with the dwarf to find her. His only other concern at this point seems to be the fate of his squire. Of course one cannot expect completely consistent motivations in the kind of romance Spenser gives us in Books III and IV; nevertheless, it seems that Arthur is sidetracked rather easily.

In the last three books of the poem there is a noticeable change in the way Arthur's quest is presented. He becomes involved more and more frequently in adventures completely distinct from his own search, and he no longer tells anyone about his love or begs for information about Gloriana. In Book IV there is only one reference to his own quest, and that is rather vague:

Thus when the Prince had perfectly compylde
　These paires of friends in peace and setled rest,
　Him selfe, whose minde did trauell as with chylde,
　Of his old loue, conceau'd in secret brest,
　Resolued to pursue his former quest . . .
　　　　　　　　　　　　　　　　　[IV.9.17.1-5]

Book V's single reference is vaguer yet:

> Then to his first emprize his mind he lent,
> Full loath to Belge, and to all the rest:
> Of whom yet taking leaue, thenceforth he went
> And to his former iourney him addrest,
> On which long way he rode, ne euer day did rest.
>
> [V.11.35.5-9]

In Book VI, similarly, neither Gloriana's name nor a clearly defined quest is associated with Arthur. He becomes completely involved in the adventures of others and seems to have forgotten his own. He leaves Timias and Serena with the Hermit because he has "great affaires in mynd" [VI.5.41.1]; these great affairs turn out to be not the pursuit of Gloriana, but revenge on Turpine and Blandina. In Canto 7 he is briefly mentioned as a lover:

> The gentle Prince not farre away they spyde,
> Ryding a softly pace with portance sad,
> Deuizing of his loue more, then of daunger drad.
>
> [VI.7.6.7-9]

But a little later he is shown sleeping soundly, undisturbed by either present danger or the symptoms of love [VI.7.19]. When he rides out of sight entirely, in Canto 8, one is no longer sure where he is going:

> But Arthure with the rest, went onward still
> On his first quest, in which did him betide
> A great aduenture, which did him from them deuide.
>
> [VI.8.30.7-9]

It would be a mistake, then, to place too much emphasis on the incompleteness of Arthur's quest. The quest does not come to a sudden halt at the end of Book VI. Rather, Spenser allows it—deliberately, I believe—to wither away, and this process is discernible considerably before the end of the poem. The quest is unfinished because it could not be finished; therefore it does not comprise very good evidence that the poem itself is unfinished.

I have considered the problem of Arthur at length because it illustrates several important things about *The Faerie Queene*. The character of Arthur and the treatment of his quest undergo radical changes in the course of the poem, and particularly between the first three books (published in 1590) and the last three (published in 1596). One must conclude that Spenser's plan—at least with respect to Arthur—changed a good deal during the interval. Indeed, judging from the conflicts between his letter to Raleigh and Books I-III, his plan was only hazily worked out in 1590.[3] Before publication of the 1596 edition of all six books, however, Spenser did not rework the first three to iron out the inconsistencies which had arisen. The only major change he made was in the ending of Book III, postponing the reunion of Amoret and Scudamour so that their adventures could be expanded in Book IV.

As a consequence, the resulting poem resembles to some extent a novel which was serialized as it was written. Even in a completed novel of this kind there will frequently be "leads" or suggestions in the early chapters which the author has forgotten to pick up later—or decided against picking up, when the time came. One such suggestion is created in the first three books of *The Faerie Queene* by hints about an impending war against pagan invaders [I.12.18; III.3.27.6-9; etc.]. The decisive battle of such a war, with which Spenser may once have intended to replace Gloriana's feast in Book XII, would have provided a fitting climax to the poem. All the characters would be brought together in the great final event. Gloriana herself would at last appear, and Arthur might so distinguish himself as to win her love. Spenser seems, however, gradually to have abandoned this idea, like the ideas of Arthur's quest and Gloriana's feast. The hints cease after Book III, and with them another opportunity to

give the poem a continuous Aristotelian "plot." In the poem
as it stands one must look for a different kind of unifying
principle, one which grows out of the relationships among
the six books.

The six books of *The Faerie Queene* fall into several easily
discernible patterns. The first two books deal with private,
inner virtue—holiness and temperance. Holiness traditionally
has two aspects: the search of the individual soul for God and
the actions of the Christian toward his fellow man. Spenser's
emphasis in Book I, however, is definitely on the first of
these; the Red Crosse Knight's story is one of temptation,
weakness, and the steps toward purification of the soul.
Similarly, the legend of temperance depicts an inner condition. One need look only at the Pyrochles and Phedon
episodes to see that Guyon's primary interest lies not in
restoring social justice, but in teaching men how to rule their
passions—while, of course, continuing to rule his own. The
third virtue, that of chastity, could also be an inner state. As
exemplified by Britomart, however, chastity is an outward-
turning virtue, manifested first in the search for the right
kind of love (Book III) and then in the achieved relationship
between a man and a woman (Book IV). Friendship, the
nominal virtue of the fourth book, similarly concerns two
people—Amoret and Britomart, Cambell and Triamond,
Amyas and Placidas. With Books V and VI one moves into a
larger realm, into virtues that can no longer really be called
private. Justice is a public concern, and Artegall is above all a
public figure. His own feeling of compassion toward the
fallen Radigund is treated as a dangerous weakness; the
administration of justice has no room for private emotions.
Courtesy, the virtue of Book VI, is presented by Spenser as a
social virtue with connotations far beyond our modern
conception of the word. It includes good manners and tactful
speech—though, as the example of the speechless "saluage
man" demonstrates, these are not always necessary. The
essence of courtesy consists instead in succoring helpless

strangers—babies, weary travellers, the wounded Serena. The essence of discourtesy, as exemplified by the villains of the book, is cruelty.

The progression from private to public virtues constitutes, then, one pattern in *The Faerie Queene.* Another significant pattern is the pairing of books in the first and second halves of the poem. This pairing is not achieved by a rigid parallelism of incident, though there are of course parallels, but rather by subtler correspondences of atmosphere and perspective. Book I, for example, is a Christian book—and so, less obviously, is Book VI. If Book I illustrates one of the Christian commandments, love for God and his earthly representative, Truth, Book VI supplies the other, Christian charity or love for one's fellow man. In these books man is seen as weak and imperfect; his only hope rests in God's hands. The Red Crosse Knight cannot achieve his own salvation. Calidore arrives too late to prevent the murder of old Meliboe and the other shepherds. Archimago, Duessa, and the Blatant Beast are defeated, but the evils they represent cannot be destroyed or long confined. Neither Book I nor Book VI ends in an abiding victory; man's struggle in this world is endless.

Books II and V also belong together in conception and in atmosphere. Temperance and justice are Aristotelian virtues, the only truly classical concepts in the poem. The perspectives of these books are philosophical and, perhaps as a result, the allegories are rigorous. Guyon, as the representative of temperance, must steer a straight path between all excesses. He can no more become angry with Pyrochles than he can enjoy Phaedria's jokes. Most modern readers would object that he hardly seems human, except on those rare occasions when he succumbs to temptation—admiring the naked maidens in the Bower of Bliss or driving his body beyond endurance in Mammon's cave.

Guyon is not a Christian. He places his faith in reason rather than in grace; and his reaction to Amavia's death sets the tone of the entire book:

. . . Old syre
Behold the image of mortalitie,
And feeble nature cloth'd with fleshly tyre,
When raging passion with fierce tyrannie
Robs reason of her due regalitie,
And makes it seruant to her basest part:
The strong it weakens with infirmitie,
And with bold furie armes the weakest hart;
The strong through pleasure soonest falles, the weake
    through smart.
                                                    [II.1.57]

Book II is, then, a Stoic book. Spenser apparently intended
its hero to represent a man as perfectly governed by reason as
man can be. Guyon's strength differentiates him sharply from
the heroes of Books I and VI, and it also sets him above the
other characters in his own book—except for the Palmer, who
represents Reason itself. The classical perspective of Book II
is maintained except when Guyon faints outside Mammon's
cave. He is rescued at this point only because his view of the
world was wrong, because there is a force greater than human
reason:

And is there care in heauen? and is there loue
    In heauenly spirits to these creatures bace,
    That may compassion of their euils moue?
    There is: else much more wretched were the cace
    Of men, then beasts. But O th'exceeding grace
    Of highest God, that loues his creatures so,
    And all his workes with mercy doth embrace,
    That blessed Angels, he sends to and fro,
To serue to wicked man, to serue his wicked foe.
                                                    [II.8.1]

The perspective of Book II is momentarily transcended, and
the limitations of Guyon's philosophy are revealed.
    Artegall's relationship with Britomart renders him consid-
erably more human than Guyon; but within the context of

his own book he, too, is a rigidly allegorical figure. The justice which he represents is narrowly conceived, and his experiences serve rather to reinforce it than to change or develop it. Thus his encounter with Radigund demonstrates that human compassion is the enemy of justice rather than its necessary complement. At the court of Mercilla he does not learn mercy; instead, his own view of justice governs the proceedings. Arthur comes gradually to share his unbending position; and Mercilla herself, who alone feels compassion for Duessa, regards her emotion as a weakness [V.9.50]. The limitation of Artegall's perspective is suggested strikingly in the figure of Talus, who ruthlessly enforces Artegall's verdicts and whose very name recalls the kind of retribution transcended by Christianity. Nevertheless, Spenser does not criticize Artegall's attitude within Book V; indeed, that attitude seems to be vindicated when Duessa, whom more compassionate measures failed to control, is finally destroyed. It is only when one moves to Book VI, to the wider perspectives of a Calidore, that Artegall and Talus are placed in their proper light—most strikingly by Arthur's mercy to Turpine and by the humanity of the "saluage man."

Books III and IV occupy a sort of never-never land between the Christian and classical worlds. These books go together, of course, because all their major stories are linked; but they belong together also by virtue of a shared philosophy. The emphasis in both of them is more on living itself than on the moral implications of action. Knights meet each other in combat for the sheer joy and glory of showing their strength.[4] One need only imagine how a tournament would be treated in Book II to perceive the difference in moral atmosphere. The virtue of chastity itself is presented under multiple guises. It is represented by Britomart, Florimell, Amoret, Belphoebe—all different in their approaches to love, but all regarded as good women. There is a sense of freedom in this multiplicity, a recognition of the rich variety of human experience. The limits of virtue are broad enough to embrace many kinds of individuals—not, as in Books II and V, just one approach.

The freer moral perspective of Books III and IV extends even to their presentations of vice, particularly the vice of unchastity. The story of Malbecco and Hellenore might almost come from Chaucer. It is essentially a fabliau, a cynically humorous portrait of folly. The reader is expected to laugh and to draw his own conclusions; Spenser does not provide it with an explicit moral or pretend that Hellenore was punished. Similarly, the story told by the Squire of Dames is received with Satyrane's laughter; and when all the ladies at the tournament fail the test of Florimell's girdle, the poet makes no further comment. Instead of being an enemy, then, which chastity must defeat (as holiness must defeat pride or error, or justice must defeat injustice), unchastity simply takes its place within the wide range of human approaches to love. It is a more foolish approach than chastity, closer to the nature of beasts; and it is cynically implied to be the most common approach of all.

Books I, II, and III present three different perspectives on the world and on man, as well as three different private virtues. There is nothing in their arrangement to imply that Spenser could not have gone on indefinitely, adding new virtues and perspectives until he had examined all aspects of man's moral and philosophical approach to the world. The arrangement, that is, is open-ended. Moreover, the threads of continuity in these books—Arthur's quest, the hints about the impending war, and the unresolved pursuits of Book III—demand completion, probably in a much larger scheme. Books IV, V, and VI, however, introduce what seem to be major changes in the original plan. The threads implying an Aristotelian type of connecting plot are abandoned, and with them the necessity of extending the poem to a much greater length. The open-ended arrangement of books is replaced by two distinct patterns, the later books making explicit the progression from private to public virtues begun in the earlier ones and forming a mirror image of their perspectives. Most of the important stories are completed, or at least left sufficiently close to completion so that the reader is satisfied.

After Book VI the poem no longer reaches out toward an unwritten extension. It might be continued, probably by the addition of a second six-book "movement," but its own interior demands have been fulfilled. What I believe to have happened is that Spenser realized he might never complete the proposed twelve-book plan and designed Books IV, V, and VI accordingly. The best evidence for this theory lies naturally in Book VI, which must serve as a conclusion to the six-book poem.

Book VI is the most complex book in *The Faerie Queene.* Books I, II, and V presented the quests of individual knights, representing specific virtues, who were helped at strategic moments by Prince Arthur. Books III and IV had a number of interlocking stories, but all of them were clearly related to one another as variations on the themes of love and friendship or harmony. Book VI, however, cannot be said to have either a single theme or a single hero. The virtue of courtesy has extremely wide implications, ranging from good manners to charity to the poet's function to pursuit of the Blatant Beast. It seems, in fact, to take in all aspects of the individual's proper relation to society, and it includes rather than excludes virtues treated earlier—notably friendship and justice.

The characters of Book VI contribute to the range and fullness of the book. The reader is struck again and again by how familiar they seem. Their familiarity is explained in part by their nature as typical figures of romance,[5] but it comes also from the fact that most of them parallel earlier characters in *The Faerie Queene* itself. The baby whom Calepine rescues and for whom great deeds are forecast reminds one of the bloody-handed babe in Book II. Tristram's upbringing is similar to Arthur's. The "saluage man" who pities and helps Serena recalls the lion's and the satyrs' instinctive kindness to Una; acting as Arthur's instrument of vengeance, he helps to illuminate the nature of Talus. Serena, fleeing from danger into danger, reminds one of Florimell. Mirabella, the heartless and beautiful lady who

is being punished, has connections with Marinell and with the
female tyrants of Books II and V. And so on. The use of
parallels in itself is not unique to Book VI. Such critics as
Northrop Frye and C. S. Lewis have shown that these echoes
and contrasts and parodic images are an essential part of
Spenser's technique:[6] one character or incident interacts
with another, illuminating the true nature of each and
gradually building up major patterns of meaning. The
parallels in Book VI, however, seem to serve an additional
purpose. They are so numerous and so striking that the
reader is constantly taken back to earlier parts of the poem.
The effect is like that of an epitome, as if Book VI contains,
in miniature, the entire world of *The Faerie Queene.*

The settings of Book VI also draw together strands from
earlier parts of the poem. Much of *The Faerie Queene* takes
place in wilderness of one kind or another. One recalls the
wandering wood and the scorching plain of Book I, the
forests and seacoasts of Book III, the mountains of Book V.
Book VI, however, makes the wilderness explicit, consistent,
and thematic. Nearly all the characters in the book have
withdrawn from civilization for some reason—the "saluage
man," abandoned as a child; the hermit seeking solitude for
prayer; Mirabella, cast out at Cupid's command to do
penance; lovers seeking the privacy of the forest; the
shepherds, building their society on values different from
those of the court. Turpine, having violated the standards of
knighthood, is stripped by Arthur of his social status. The
cannibals and the bandits have their own parodic forms of
civilization.

It is paradoxical that the book of courtesy is set outside
the bounds of court and of the usual forms of knightly
contact, but it is essential that this be the case. Sir Calidore,
pursuing the Blatant Beast, is led gradually farther and
farther away from the court, where the Beast's ravages began.
As he proceeds with his quest, its whole nature changes. He
and the other heroes of the book encounter a savage who is
more civilized than some knights, a former knight who has
forsaken society to live as a hermit, and an old man who

explains that the lives of shepherds are better and happier than the lives of courtiers. It becomes clear that despite the definition of courtesy which begins Book VI the court is not the only source of that virtue. Indeed the narrative causes one to ask whether society's influence on the individual is at all beneficial. Calidore's abandonment of his assigned quest to live with the shepherds raises the complementary question of the individual's responsibility toward society. These questions are raised, and given partial answers, primarily in the story of Sir Calidore; but they are not Calidore's questions alone. The poet faces a similar dilemma as he seeks to please and instruct great persons at court while maintaining his own integrity. In *Colin Clouts Come Home Again* Spenser had shown how difficult it is to reconcile these two objectives. Colin reappears in Book VI, and his reappearance is like a signal to the reader. For the first time in *The Faerie Queene*, the poet himself becomes the focus of attention.

Spenser's explicit role in the first three books of the poem is quite minor. Speaking in his own voice at the beginnings or ends of some cantos, he makes short moral observations, or draws the reader's attention to the approaching end of a book, or praises the Queen. In the proems to these books he is concerned primarily with pointing out the resemblances between England and Faerie, Elizabeth and her virtuous counterparts in the poem. There are even some flattering implications that the real world is more brilliant than Faerie:

> And thou, O fairest Princesse vnder sky,
> In this faire mirrhour maist behold thy face,
> And thine owne realmes in lond of Faery,
> And in this antique Image thy great auncestry.

> The which O pardon me thus to enfold
> In couert vele, and wrap in shadowes light,
> That feeble eyes your glory may behold,
> Which else could not endure those beames bright,
> But would be dazzled with exceeding light.
>   [II.proem.4.6-9;5.1-5]

With the proem to Book IV, one observes the beginnings of a change in Spenser's attitude. This proem, defensive in tone, refers sharply to a powerful person who has apparently disparaged the moral value of imaginative writing in general and of Spenser's treatment of love in particular:

> The rugged forhead that with graue foresight
>   Welds kingdomes causes, and affaires of state,
>   My looser rimes (I wote) doth sharply wite,
>   For praising loue, as I haue done of late,
>   And magnifying louers deare debate;
>   By which fraile youth is oft to follie led,
>   Through false allurement of that pleasing baite,
>   That better were in vertues discipled,
> Then with vaine poemes weeds to haue their fancies fed.
>   [IV.proem.1]

There is also in this proem, I think, an implied criticism of Spenser's own time in contrast with an earlier, better age:

> Which who so list looke backe to former ages,
>   And call to count the things that then were donne,
>   Shall find, that all the workes of those wise sages,
>   And braue exploits which great Heroes wonne,
>   In loue were either ended or begunne . . .
>   [IV.proem.3.1-5]

As one proceeds through the last three books, this theme is stated unmistakably, and the degeneracy of Spenser's own age is seen to be at the root of his artistic dilemma. The present age is too corrupt to supply adequate models of virtue for his poem:

> Let none then blame me, if in discipline
>   Of vertue and of ciuill vses lore,
>   I doe not forme them to the common line
>   Of present dayes, which are corrupted sore,

> But to the antique vse, which was of yore,
> When good was onely for it selfe desyred,
> And all men sought their owne, and none no more . . .
>   [V.proem.3.1-7]

Yet, as he observes rather bitterly, the ideals which he draws
from "antique vse" will be misunderstood and condemned—
as the unnamed critic has already condemned Book III:

> Here well I weene, when as these rimes be red
>   With misregard, that some rash witted wight,
>   Whose looser thought will lightly be misled,
>   These gentle Ladies will misdeeme too light,
>   For thus conuersing with this noble Knight;
>   Sith now of dayes such temperance is rare
>   And hard to finde . . .
>   [IV.8.29.1-7]

The golden world of Faery thus comes to seem less and
less like an idealized image of Spenser's own world and
increasingly like an alternative to it. In the proem to Book VI
Faerie is described as a realm of pure delight from which the
poet draws encouragement and refreshment:

> The waies, through which my weary steps I guyde,
>   In this delightfull land of Faery,
>   Are so exceeding spacious and wyde,
>   And sprinckled with such sweet variety,
>   Of all that pleasant is to eare or eye,
>   That I nigh rauisht with rare thoughts delight,
>   My tedious trauell doe forget thereby;
>   And when I gin to feele decay of might,
> It strength to me supplies, and chears my dulled spright.
>   [VI.proem.1]

Within the narrative, however, Spenser does not maintain
Faerie as a world apart. At the end of Book V, the Blatant

Beast and the two hags burst from the poet's own imperfect
age into Artegall's experience; and Artegall's quest ends, not
in acclaim, but in a barrage of stones and insults. In Book VI,
likewise, the delights of Faerie are seen to be fragile and
tenuous. The real, imperfect world continually intrudes, and
its intrusions become more and more threatening.

The theme of danger, entering when it is least expected,
occupied Spenser's mind as early as the "Muiopotmas;" it
runs unobtrusively through the earlier books of *The Faerie
Queene.* The Red Crosse Knight gets into trouble whenever
he seeks refuge from the elements in a sheltering forest or
next to a refreshing spring. Guyon succumbs to temptation
just when he is feeling strongest. Florimell is seized by a new
peril whenever she stops to rest after escaping the last one. As
Berger has pointed out,[7] this theme becomes central in Book
VI. Whenever one feels safe and lets down one's guard,
disaster strikes. The hermit explains to Serena and Timias
that they can be cured of their wounds only be maintaining
constant vigilance:

> Abstaine from pleasure, and restraine your will,
> Subdue desire, and bridle loose delight,
> Vse scanted diet, and forbeare your fill,
> Shun secresie, and talke in open sight;
> So shall you soone repaire your present euill plight.
>   [VI.6.14.5-9]

The need for vigilance is not, as in Book I, a moral
imperative; one must abstain even from the innocent
pleasures of life. Something is obviously very much wrong
with a world in which constant vigilance is the price of one's
very survival. The Blatant Beast frequently attacks those who
don't deserve it. The human villains in the book prey only on
the unarmed, the innocent, and the helpless; and, as the
wounds inflicted by the beast become worse and worse, so do
the inhumanities of man to man. The book moves from
Crudor to Turpine to the cannibals to the bandits, who sell

their captives as slaves and slaughter them in senseless fury. There is, then, what Berger has called "a progressive flawing in the romance world" of Book VI.[8] The farther one goes away from the court and the more ideal and romantic one's surroundings become, the more cruel are the attacks of reality. The double movement reaches its peak in Cantos 9 and 10.

The pastoral idyll in Canto 9 presents a world completely removed from the temptations and dangers of the court, a little realm where men are innocent and good and where life is serene. It is a kind of ideal parody of society, with Pastorella as its queen and her gentle father as philosopher and king. Old Meliboe's explanation of its virtues, as against the vices of the court, sums up the eternal appeal of the pastoral life. Meliboe spends his days in simple, healthful activities and his nights in untroubled sleep. Free from envy and pride and ambition, he is at peace. He praises God for the blessings He has sent and shares those blessings freely with his guest. Here, then, is the Christian ideal of courtesy, raised to an entire way of life. One cannot condemn Calidore, after his encounters with cruelty and envy among knights, for remaining with the shepherds and the lovely Pastorella; and Spenser does not condemn him:

> For who had tasted once (as oft did he)
> The happy peace, which there doth ouerflow,
> And prou'd the perfect pleasures, which doe grow
> Amongst poore hyndes, in hils, in woods, in dales,
> Would neuer more delight in painted show
> Of such false blisse, as there is set for stales,
> T'entrap vnwary fooles in their eternall bales.
>
> [VI.10.3.3-9]

Indeed, it is obvious that this pastoral retreat appeals as strongly to Spenser as to Calidore. It is in such a setting of natural beauty and human serenity that the poet's visionary power reaches its height. On Mount Acidale the Graces dance for Colin Clout, and the eternal sources of physical and spiritual beauty are revealed:

> These three on men all gracious gifts bestow,
>   Which decke the body or adorne the mynde,
>   To make them louely or well fauoured show,
>   As comely carriage, entertainement kynde,
>   Sweete semblaunt, friendly offices that bynde,
>   And all the complements of curtesie . . .
> [VI.10.23.1-6]

Colin's vision thus dramatizes the gift of divine inspiration, for which the poet prayed at the beginning of Book VI:

> Reuele to me the sacred noursery
>   Of vertue, which with you doth there remaine,
>   Where it in siluer bowre does hidden ly
>   From view of men, and wicked worlds disdaine.
> [VI.proem.3.1-4]

The poet's vision is fragile, however. The Graces vanish as soon as Calidore tries to approach them, and Colin cannot call them back. Colin himself disappears from the poem as the pastoral ideal, equally fragile, crumbles before Calidore's eyes. The village is devastated by bandits and only two of its gentle inhabitants escape. The brutality and horror of the real world have, at least for the moment, vanquished the ideal.

The pastoral sequence in Book VI appears to mirror Spenser's own experience as well as that of Sir Calidore. Withdrawal into a more beautiful and well-ordered world is not possible for very long. Calidore must return to his duty, in the imperfect but still idealized world where duty is clearly defined and where the Blatant Beast can be caught. The poet, on the other hand, returns to a reality where the Beast will continue to rage, sparing not even this work from "his venomous despite [VI.12.41.2]." It is not surprising that

Book VI ends on a note of sorrow. Within the narrative the poet's power has been seen to be very precious and very limited. For a moment Colin Clout came into contact with the eternal manifestations of beauty and courtesy and grace; but then the bandits came. The powers of evil seem so overwhelming that one is tempted to abandon Colin's vision as irrelevant to the real world. On the autobiographical level the poet does not seem to have fared much better. He has created a golden world to serve as an inspiration for his own society, but that society is so corrupt and so intolerant of criticism that one questions its receptiveness to such an inspiration. The explicit statement offered by Book VI, then, appears to be that there can be no reconciliation between the poet and his society. Even the temporary solution of *Colin Clouts Come Home Again* has been denied. The shepherd can no longer find a peaceful retreat in which to tend his sheep and make his songs.

Spenser thus seems to have reached a kind of impasse at the end of Book VI. It would be a mistake, however, to infer that he abandoned *The Faerie Queene* in a fit of despair. Despite the tragedy and horror of its events, Book VI remains a Christian book. Its tone is established most clearly in Meliboe's advice to Calidore:

> In vaine . . . doe men
> The heauens of their fortunes fault accuse,
> Sith they know best, what is the best for them:
> For they to each such fortune doe diffuse,
> As they doe know each can most aptly vse.
> For not that, which men couet most, is best,
> Nor that thing worst, which men do most refuse;
> But fittest is, that all contented rest
> With that they hold: each hath his fortune in his brest.
> [VI.9.29]

The message is one of resignation and Christian hope in the midst of trials. From such a perspective Meliboe's own fate

loses much of its sting, and so does the predicament of the
poet. Society's immediate response becomes less important
than the poet's own faith and his determination "most aptly
[to] vse" the abilities given him. It is possible, I believe, to
see this kind of determination at work in the second half of
The Faerie Queene. The beauty and careful artistry of Book
VI witness that Spenser had lost neither his powers nor his
faith in the instrinsic value of his work; and the very form of
this last book mirrors and reaffirms his intentions in the
larger poem. Book VI moves into, then out of, the idealized
world of romance; *The Faerie Queene* moves from the weak
and imperfect Christian knight into a central core of romance
and then back to the imperfect state of contemporary
society. The poem is, then, something like an arch, with both
ends grounded in reality. The central golden world is not a
thing apart. As if in response to the unnamed critic's
challenge, Spenser makes new efforts in Books IV-VI to
clarify its moral purpose. By drawing explicit comparisons
between Faerie and his own society, he demonstrates to his
readers the relevance of the ideal, its use as a measure of their
own world and of themselves. When, toward the end of the
poem, he permits reality to rush in upon the ideal and
destroy it, he is not denying its value; instead, the violence
seems to be a last effort to shock readers into recognizing
their profound need for such an ideal.

The reappearance of the Blatant Beast at the end of Book
VI, then, is not an admission of defeat. Spenser realizes that
some of his readers will still misunderstand and attack him,
but he is confident of the value and intergrity of his work. In
fact, he has won a kind of victory by refusing to turn aside
from his purpose:

> Like as a ship, that through the Ocean wyde
>   Directs her course vnto one certaine cost,
>   Is met of many a counter winde and tyde,
>   With which her winged speed is let and crost,
>   And she her selfe in stormie surges tost;

> Yet making many a borde, and many a bay,
> Still winneth way, ne hath her compasse lost:
> Right so it fares with me in this long way,
> Whose course is often stayd, yet neuer is astray.
>
> [VI.12.1]

The poem Spenser actually wrote thus reaches a logical culmination in Book VI. There is a sense of finality in the way this book recapitulates earlier parts of *The Faerie Queene*, completes the symmetry of the work, and reaffirms the poet's purpose in the face of attacks. Above all there is a finality in the perspective of Book VI. Human imperfection and suffering are shown to be universal and profound. Courtesy, by introducing kindness and beauty into everyday relationships, can help to make the human condition more bearable; but neither the knightly hero nor the poet can really set the world right. Man's cure is beyond human power.

It is hard to imagine how Spenser could have planned to write six more books of the poem. There are, of course, other virtues besides those already treated, but the theme of human virtue itself appears to have been exhausted the Mutabilitie Cantos, which provide our only insight into Spenser's further plans, seem rather to complete the movement implicit in Book VI than to provide a new beginning. In these cantos, as at the end of Chaucer's *Troilus*, man's perspective is transcended. The world of human action is left behind as the poem rises to a cosmological plane where gods debate and the cycles of nature move in solemn procession. The problems of evil and human frailty, overwhelming in the terms of Book VI, are seen from the new distance as small parts of a cosmic pattern. The universe is fallen, and Mutabilitie rules over all created things. The limitations of man's perspective prevent his seeing either the limits of Mutabilitie's power or the permanence within change itself. He can only reach out—as Book VI reaches out—toward a reality beyond his vision. Within the solemn framework of the Mutabilitie Cantos this reality at last becomes manifest, as Nature appears in a radiance like that of the transfigured Christ and makes the promise which is the ultimate ground of man's hope:

> But time shall come that all shall changed bee,
> And from thenceforth, none no more change shall see.
> [VII.7.59.4-5]

The prayer which follows, bringing Spenser's known writings to a close, seems the only possible response.

TUSKEGEE INSTITUTE

1. The formulation of these alternatives began with a paragraph in Northrop Frye's article, "The Structure of Imagery in *The Faerie Queene*," in *Fables of Identity: Studies in Poetic Mythology* (New York, 1963), p. 69.

2. The vague references to a quest beginning before this discovery [II.1.32.6-9 and II.2.43] should perhaps be taken as half-hearted attempts to revise a book already written. There is nothing in Guyon's response to Amavia's story to indicate that he has ever heard of Acrasia before—much less already undertaken to destroy her.

3. He had not even noticed that twelve quests plus Gloriana's feast would require more than twelve equal books.

4. Graham Hough, *A Preface to the Faerie Queene* (New York, 1962), p. 168.

5. Harry Berger, Jr., "A Secret Discipline: *The Faerie Queene*, Book VI," in *Form and Convention in the Poetry of Edmund Spenser*, ed. William Nelson (New York and London, 1961), p. 50.

6. Frye, pp. 79-86; *The Allegory of Love* (New York, 1958), pp. 324-333, 339-345.

7. Berger, p. 40.

8. *Ibid.*, p. 39.

Works Cited

Arnheim, Rudolf. *Art and Visual Perception*. Berkeley, 1954.

Arthos, John. *On the Poetry of Spenser and the Form of Romances*. London, 1951.

Bennett, Josephine Waters. *The Evolution of The Faerie Queene*. New York, 1960.

Berger, Harry Jr. *The Allegorical Temper: Vision and Reality in Book II of Spenser's Faerie Queene*. New Haven, 1957.

————. "A Secret Discipline: *The Faerie Queene*, Book VI, in *Form and Convention in the Poetry of Edmund Spenser*, ed. William Nelson, New York and London, 1961.

Burke, Kenneth. *Counter-Statement*. New York, 1931.

Cheney, Donald. *Spenser's Image of Nature*. New Haven, 1966.

Coleridge, Samuel Taylor. *Biographia Literaria*, Ch. 18.

Frye, Northrop. *Fables of Identity*. New York, 1963.

Gottfried, Rudolf B. "Our New Poet: Archetypal Criticism and the Form of *The Faerie Queene*," *PMLA, LXXXIII* (October, 1968), 1362-77.

Greene, Thomas. *The Descent from Heaven: A Study in Epic Continuity*. New Haven and London, 1963.

Guth, Hans P. "Unity and Multiplicity in Spenser's *Faerie Queene*," *Anglia, LXXIV* (1956),1.

Hamilton, A. C. *The Structure of Allegory in The Faerie Queene*. Oxford, 1961.

Holland, Joanne Field. "The Cantos of Mutabilitie and the Form of *The Faerie Queene, ELH, XXXV* (March, 1968), 21-31.

Holland, Norman. "Literary Value: A Psychoanalytic Approach," *Literature & Psychology, XIV* (1964), 43-55.

Hough, Graham. *A Preface to The Faerie Queene.* New York, 1963.

James, Henry. *The Art of the Novel.* New York, 1934.

Katz, David. *Gestalt Psychology.* 1950.

Koffka, Kurt. "Problems in the Psychology of Art," *Art: A Bryn Mawr Symposium.* Bryn Mawr, 1940.

Kubie, Lawrence. *Neurotic Distortion of the Creative Process.* Lawrence, Kansas, 1958.

Lewis, C. S. *The Allegory of Love: A Study in Medieval Tradition.* New York, 1958.

Lord, Catherine. "Unity with Impunity," *Journal of Aesthetics & Art Criticism, XXVI* (1967), 103-106.

Mann, Thomas. *Doctor Faustus: The Life of the German Composer Adrian Leverkuhn, as told to a Friend.* trans. H. T. Lowe-Porter. New York, 1965.

Meyer, Leonard. *Emotion and Meaning in Music.* Chicago, 1956.

Nelson, William, ed. *Form and Convention in the Poetry of Edmund Spenser.* New York and London, 1961.

———. *The Poetry of Edmund Spenser: A Study.* New York, 1963.

Neuse, Richard. "Book VI As Conclusion to *The Faerie Queene,"ELH, XXXV* (September, 1968), 329-353.

Parker, M. Pauline. *The Allegory of the Faerie Queene.* Oxford, 1960.

Peckham, Morse. *Man's Rage for Chaos.* New York, 1967.

Roche, Thomas P. *The Kindly Flame: A Study of the Third and Fourth Books of Spenser's Faerie Queene.* Princeton, 1964.

Rosenblatt, Louise M. "Toward a Transactional Theory of Reading," *Journal of Reading Behavior*, I (1969), 31-50.

Smith, Barbara. *Poetic Closure: A Study of How Poems End.* Chicago, 1968.

Straus, Erwin W. "Aesthiology and Hallucinations," *Existence: A New Dimension in Psychiatry and Psychology*, ed. Rollo May, Ernest Angel, Henri F. Ellenberger. New York, 1958.

Williams, Kathleen. *Spenser's World of Glass: A Reading of The Faerie Queene.* Berkeley and Los Angeles, 1966.

Date Due

NOV. 5 1990

Demco 38-297